An American National Standard

IEEE Standard for A Versatile Backplane Bus: VMEbus

Published by
The Institute of Electrical and Electronics Engineers, Inc

Distributed in cooperation with
Wiley-Interscience, a division of John Wiley & Sons, Inc

ANSI/IEEE
Std 1014-1987

An American National Standard

IEEE Standard for A Versatile Backplane Bus: VMEbus

Sponsor

Technical Committee on Microprocessors and Microcomputers of the IEEE Computer Society

Approved March 12, 1987

IEEE Standards Board

Approved September 11, 1987

American National Standards Institute

ISBN 0-471-61601-X

Library of Congress Catalog Number 87-46413

The Institute of Electrical and Electronics Engineers, Inc
345 East 47th Street, New York, NY 10017, USA

March 28, 1988 *SH11544*

Abstract

This IEEE 1014 standard specifies a high-performance backplane bus for use in microcomputer systems that employ single or multiple microprocessors. It is based on the VMEbus specification, released by the VME Manufacturers' Group in August of 1982. The bus includes four subbuses: data transfer bus, priority interrupt bus, arbitration bus, and utility bus. The data transfer bus supports 8-, 16-, and 32-bit transfers over a non-multiplexed 32-bit data and address highway. The transfer protocols are asynchronous and fully handshaken. The priority interrupt bus provides real-time interrupt services to the system. The allocation of bus mastership is performed by the arbitration bus, which allows to implement round robin and prioritized arbitration algorithms. The utility bus provides the system with power-up and power-down synchronization. The mechanical specifications of boards, backplanes, subracks, and enclosures are based on IEC 297 specification, also known as the Euroboard form factor.

IEEE Standards documents are developed within the Technical Committees of the IEEE Societies and the Standards Coordinating Committees of the IEEE Standards Board. Members of the committees serve voluntarily and without compensation. They are not necessarily members of the Institute. The standards developed within IEEE represent a consensus of the broad expertise on the subject within the Institute as well as those activities outside of IEEE which have expressed an interest in participating in the development of the standard.

Use of an IEEE Standard is wholly voluntary. The existence of an IEEE Standard does not imply that there are no other ways to produce, test, measure, purchase, market, or provide other goods and services related to the scope of the IEEE Standard. Furthermore, the viewpoint expressed at the time a standard is approved and issued is subject to change brought about through developments in the state of the art and comments received from users of the standard. Every IEEE Standard is subjected to review at least once every five years for revision or reaffirmation. When a document is more than five years old, and has not been reaffirmed, it is reasonable to conclude that its contents, although still of some value, do not wholly reflect the present state of the art. Users are cautioned to check to determine that they have the latest edition of any IEEE Standard.

Comments for revision of IEEE Standards are welcome from any interested party, regardless of membership affiliation with IEEE. Suggestions for changes in documents should be in the form of a proposed change of text, together with appropriate supporting comments.

Interpretations: Occasionally questions may arise regarding the meaning of portions of standards as they relate to specific applications. When the need for interpretations is brought to the attention of IEEE, the Institute will initiate action to prepare appropriate responses. Since IEEE Standards represent a consensus of all concerned interests, it is important to ensure that any interpretation has also received the concurrence of a balance of interests. For this reason IEEE and the members of its technical committees are not able to provide an instant response to interpretation requests except in those cases where the matter has previously received formal consideration.

Comments on standards and requests for interpretations should be addressed to:

Secretary, IEEE Standards Board
345 East 47th Street
New York, NY 10017
USA

Foreword

(This Foreword is not a part of ANSI/IEEE Std 1014-1987, IEEE Standard for A Versatile Backplane Bus: VMEbus.)

The architectural concepts of the VMEbus are based on the VERSAbus, which was developed in the late 1970's by Motorola. Motorola's European Microsystems group in Munich, West Germany proposed the development of a VERSAbus-like product line based on the Eurocard mechanical standard. To demonstrate the concept, Max Loesel and Sven Rau developed three prototype boards: a 68000 CPU board, a dynamic memory board, and a static memory board. They named the new bus VERSAbus-E. It was the VERSAbus-E, renamed VMEbus, that Motorola, Mostek, and Signetics have agreed to jointly develop and support.

John Black of Motorola, Craig MacKenna of Mostek, and Cecil Kaplinsky of Signetics developed the first draft of the VMEbus specification. In October of 1981, at the *System 81* show in Munich, West Germany, Motorola, Mostek, and Signetics announced their joint support of the VMEbus, and placed Revision A of the specification in the public domain.

In August of 1982, Revision B of the VMEbus specification was published by the newly formed VMEbus Manufacturers' Group. This new revision refined the electrical specifications for the signal line drivers and receivers, and also brought the mechanical specifications more in line with the developing IEC 297-3 standard, the formal specifications of the Eurocard mechanical formats.

In the later part of 1982, the French delegation to the International Electrotechnical Commission (IEC) proposed Revision B of the VMEbus as an international standard. The IEC SC47B subcommittee nominated Mira Pauker of Philips, France, as the chairperson of an editorial committee, formally starting international standardization of the VMEbus.

In March of 1983, the IEEE Microprocessor Standards Committee (MSC) requested authorization to establish a working group to standardize the VMEbus. This request was approved by the IEEE Standards Board, and the P1014 Working Group was established. Wayne Fischer was appointed first chairman of the working group. John Black served as chairman of the P1014 Technical Subcommittee.

The IEC and the IEEE distributed copies of Revision B for comment, and both received requests for change. Additional requests for change were received from the members of the VMEbus Manufacturers' Group. These comments made it clear that it was time to go onward past Revision B. In December of 1983, a meeting was held that included John Black, Mira Pauker, Wayne Fischer, and Craig MacKenna. It was agreed that a Revision C should be created, and that it should take into consideration all the comments received by the three organizations. John Black and Shlomo Pri-Tal of Motorola incorporated the changes from all sources into a common document. The Manufacturers' Group called it Revision C.1, the IEEE called it P1014 draft 1.2, and the IEC called it the IEC 821 BUS. Subsequent ballots in the IEEE P1014 Working Group and in the MSC resulted in more comments, and required that the IEEE P1014 draft be updated. This work resulted in draft IEEE P1014.

The process that led to the development of ANSI/IEEE Std 1014 embodies the philosophy that the "...*IEEE will cooperate with standardizing groups throughout the world in the preparation of standards*..." as expressed in the IEEE Standards Manual.

The development of the VMEbus was a team effort, which involved experts from the United States, Britain, West Germany, France, and many other countries. It is truly an internationally developed standard. However, the contribution of several individuals is worthy of special recognition:

John Black and Craig MacKenna were the key individuals in the creation of the VMEbus specification. Their efforts, expertise, and perseverance have guided the development of the VMEbus to its present form.

Max Loesel and Sven Rau are recognized for proposing and demonstrating the feasibility of a Eurocard-based 32-bit backplane bus.

Eike Waltz contributed extensively to the mechanical specifications.

Wayne Fischer, the first Chairman, guided the IEEE P1014 Working Group during its first three years.

Mira Pauker, Arlan Harris, and Shlomo Pri-Tal contributed to the development of Revision C of the specification.

Also worthy of recognition are Paul Borrill who contributed to the electrical specifications, Ken Smith who contributed to the mechanical specifications, and T. J. Chaney who was instrumental in preparing Appendix D.

And finally, special thanks to Tom Leonard who assisted Shlomo Pri-Tal as Vice Chairman of the P1014 Working Group.

The IEEE P1014 Technical Subcommittee had the following membership:

John Black, *Chairman* **Craig MacKenna,** *Secretary*

Thomas Harkaway
Arlan Harris
Shlomo Pri-Tal
Doug Kraft
Thomas Leonard

The IEEE P1014 Working Group had the following membership:

Shlomo Pri-Tal, *Chairman* **Thomas Leonard,** *Vice Chairman*

Philip E. Abbate
Stephen Ades
Robert L. Ayers
Don Baril
Richard F. Barry
Drew Berding
I. M. Bisset
John Black
Neil Borkowicz
Paul Borrill
Steven Brandon
Duncan Campbell
Raymond W. Chateau
K. R. Clohessy
Richard M. DeBock
Steve Deiss
Glen Diestelhorst
Gary Dool
Ian R. Duncan
Tim J. Elsmore
Ken Finster
Wayne Fischer
Gene Freehauf
Ken Goertzen
Jim Green
Thomas Harkaway
Arlan Harris
Bill Holloway
Tom Hunter
Jurgen Jakel
Hugh Johnson
Cecil Kaplinsky
Hans Karlsson
Doug Kraft
Patrick E. Lannan
D. C. Liddell
Craig MacKenna
Rick Main
Andy McMillan
Lance McNally
Frank Melanson
Jeffrey R. Millar
Joseph Ng
L. Parker
Mira Pauker
Robert Phillips
Robert Pogson
Sven Rau
Jack Regula
Kim Rubin
Norman Schneidewind
George Schreck
Ron Schreck
Craig Scott
Bill Shields
Ken Smith
Basil Smith
Larry Sollman
Bob Squirrell
Michael Thompson
Michael UnTerweger
Gregory S. Urban
S. P. Verma
Eike Waltz
David Weller
John Wemekamp
Bryant West
C. J. White
William D. Winget
Ron Wolfe

The following members of the Microprocessor Standards Committee voted in the ballot that approved the IEEE P1014 for sponsor ballot by the Technical Committee on Microprocessor and Microcomputer (TCMM):

Bob Davis, *Chairman* **Clyde Camp,** *Secretary*

Matt Biewer
Richard Boberg
Paul Borrill
Steve Cooper
Wayne Fischer
Gordon Force
Martin Freeman
David Gustavson
Tom Harkaway
David James
Laurel Kaleda
Richard Karpinski
Doug Kraft
Patrick Laprocina
Gerry Laws
Tom Leonard
Gary Lyons
Craig MacKenna
Deene Ogden
Shlomo Pri-Tal
Michael Smolin
Robert Stewart
Eike Waltz
George White
Fritz Whitting

The members of the Executive Committee of the Technical Committee on Microprocessors and Microcomputers were as follows:

Martin Freeman, *Chairman*

Bob Davis
Jim Flournoy
Bob Stewart
Glen Langdon
Michael Smolin

The following members of the Technical Committee on Microprocessors and Microcomputers were on the balloting body that approved this document for submission to the IEEE Standards Board:

Andrew Allison
J. Ashenden
Geoff Baldwin
Matt Biewer
John Black
Richard Boberg
Paul Borrill
Bradley Brown
Clyde Camp
John D. Charlton
William Cody
Steve Cooper
Tim Davey
Bob Davis
Randy Davis
Shirish P. Deodhar
Steve Diamond
Wayne Fischer
Jim Flournoy
Gordon Force
Martin Freeman
S. Ganesan
D. Gustavson
Thomas Harkaway
Richard James
David James
Laurel Kaleda
Richard Karpinski
Doug Kraft
Glen Langdon
Gerry Laws
Tom Leonard
Gary Lyons
Rae McLellan
Jim Mooney
Gary Nelson
Deene Ogden
Shlomo Pri-Tal
Richard Rawson
Mike Smolin
Michael Teener
Eike Waltz
Carl Warren
George White
Fritz Whittington
Thomas Wicklund
Andrew Wilson
Anthony Winter

When the IEEE Standards Board approved this standard on June 11, 1987, it had the following membership:

Donald C. Fleckenstein, *Chairman*

Marco W. Migliaro, *Vice Chairman* **Andrew G. Salem,** *Secretary*

James H. Beall
Dennis Bodson
Marshall L. Cain
James M. Daly
Stephen R. Dillon
Eugene P. Fogarty
Jay Forster
Kenneth D. Hendrix
Irvin N. Howell
Leslie R. Kerr
Jack Kinn
Irving Kolodny
Joseph L. Koepfinger*
Edward Lohse
John May
Lawrence V. McCall
L. Bruce McClung
Donald T. Michael*
L. John Rankine
John P. Riganati
Gary S. Robinson
Frank L. Rose
Robert E. Rountree
Sava I. Sherr*
William R. Tackaberry
William B. Wilkens
Helen M. Wood

*Member emeritus

Contents

SECTION PAGE

FIGURES

FIGURES PAGE

TABLES PAGE

TABLES PAGE

APPENDIXES

APPENDIX FIGURES

APPENDIX TABLES PAGE

1. Introduction

1.1 Objectives. This standard defines an interfacing system used to interconnect data processing, data storage, and peripheral control devices in a tightly coupled hardware configuration. The system has the following objectives:

(1) To allow communication between devices on the bus without disturbing the internal activities of other devices interfaced to the bus.

(2) To specify the electrical and mechanical system characteristics required to design devices that will reliably and unambiguously communicate with other devices interfaced to the bus.

(3) To specify protocols that precisely define the interaction between the bus and devices interfaced to it.

(4) To provide terminology and definitions that describe system protocols.

(5) To allow a broad range of design latitude so that the designer can optimize cost or performance, or both, without affecting the system compatibility.

(6) To provide a system where performance is primarily device limited, rather than system interface limited.

1.2 Interface System Elements

1.2.1 Basic Definitions. The structure of the system can be described from its mechanical structure and its functional structure. The mechanical specification describes the physical dimensions of subracks, backplanes, front panels, plug-in boards, etc. The functional specification describes the manner in which the bus operates, the functional modules that are involved in each transaction, and the rules that govern their behavior. This section provides informal definitions for some basic terms used to describe the physical and the mechanical structure.

1.2.1.1 Terms Used to Describe the Mechanical Structure

backplane. A printed-circuit board (pcb) with 96-pin connectors and signal paths that bus (connect corresponding) connector pins. Some systems have a single pcb, J1 backplane. It provides the signal paths needed for basic operation. Other systems also have an optional second pcb, J2 backplane. It provides the additional 96-pin connectors and signal paths needed for wider data and address transfers. Still others have a single pcb, J1/J2 backplane, which provides the signal conductors and connectors of the J1 and J2 backplanes.

board. A printed-circuit board (pcb), its collection of electronic components, and either one or two 96-pin connectors that can be plugged into backplane connectors.

slot. A position where a printed-circuit board (pcb) can be inserted into the backplane. When the system has a J1 and a J2 backplane (or a combination J1/J2 backplane) each slot provides a pair of 96-pin connectors. When the system has only a J1 backplane, then each slot provides a single 96-pin connector.

subrack. A rigid framework that provides mechanical support for printed-circuit boards (pcb) inserted into the backplane, ensuring that the connectors mate properly and that adjacent pcb do not contact each other. It also guides the cooling airflow through the system and ensures that inserted pcb do not disengage themselves from the backplane due to vibration or shock.

1.2.1.2 Terms Used to Describe the Functional Structure. Figure 1 shows a simplified block diagram of the functional structure, including the signal lines, backplane interface logic, and functional modules.

arbiter. A functional module that accepts bus requests from requester modules and grants control of the data transfer bus (DTB) to one requester at a time.

arbritration bus. One of the four buses provided by the backplane. This bus allows an arbiter module and several requester modules to coordinate use of the DTB.

backplane interface logic. Special logic that takes into account the characteristics of the backplane; its signal line impedance, propagation time, termination values, etc. The specification prescribes certain rules for the design of this logic based on the maximum length of the backplane and its maximum number of printed-circuit board (pcb) slots.

bus timer. A functional module that measures the time each data transfer takes on the DTB and terminates the DTB cycle when the transfer time is not within reason. Without this module, when the master attempts to transfer data to or from a nonexistent slave location it could wait forever. The bus timer prevents this delay by terminating the cycle.

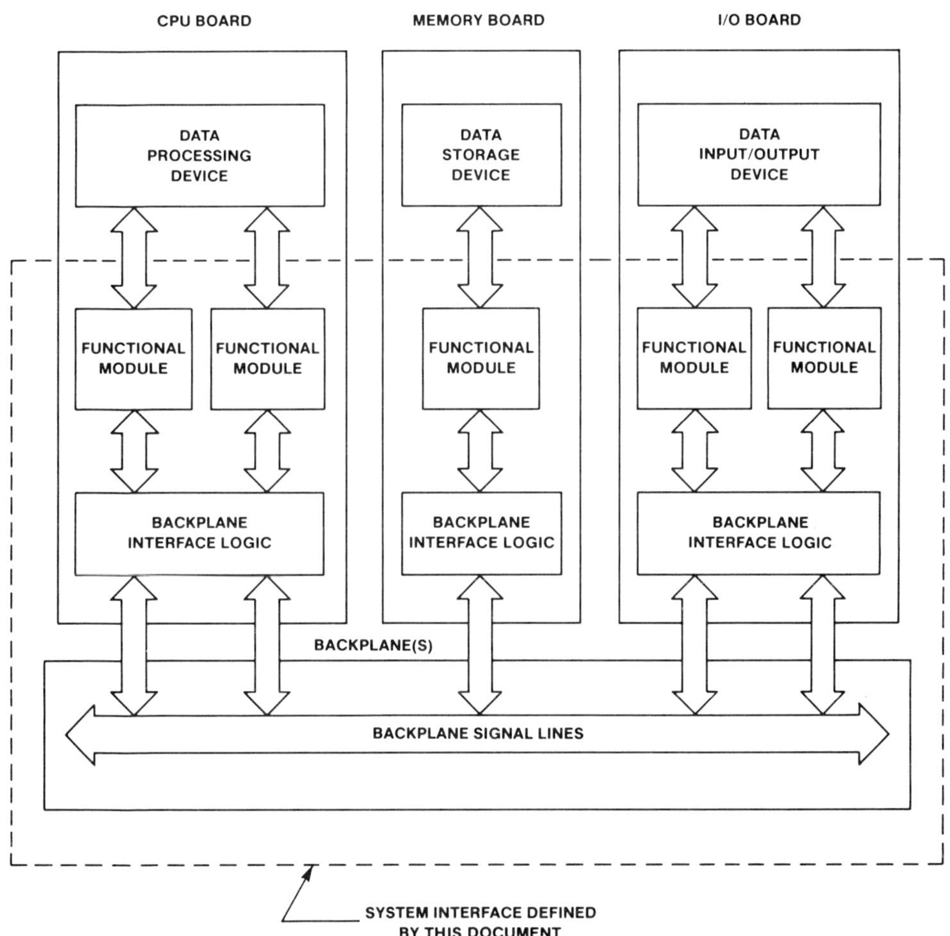

Fig 1
System Elements Defined by the Standard

daisy-chain. A special type of signal line that is used to propagate a signal level from printed-circuit board (pcb) to pcb, starting with the first slot and ending with the last slot. There are four bus grant daisy-chains and one interrupt-acknowledge daisy-chain on the backplane.

data transfer bus (DTB). One of the four buses provided by the backplane. The data transfer bus allows masters to direct the transfer of binary data among themselves and slaves.

data-transfer-bus cycle. A sequence of level transitions on the signal lines of the DTB that result in the transfer of an address or an address and data between a master and a slave. The data-transfer-bus cycle is divided into two portions (1) the address broadcast and (2) zero or more data transfers.

functional module. A collection of electronic circuitry that resides on one printed-circuit board (pcb) and works together to accomplish a task.

IACK daisy-chain driver. A functional module that activates the interrupt-acknowledge daisy-chain whenever an interrupt handler acknowledges an interrupt request. This daisy-chain ensures that only one interrupter responds with its status/ID when more than one has generated an interrupt request.

interrupter. A functional module that generates an interrupt request on the priority interrupt bus, and then provides status/ID information when the interrupt handler requests it.

interrupt handler. A functional module that detects interrupt requests generated by interrupters and responds to those requests by asking for status/ID information.

location monitor. A functional module that monitors data transfers over the data transfer bus (DTB) to detect accesses to the locations it has been assigned to watch. When an access to one of these assigned locations occurs, the location monitor generates an on-board signal.

master. A functional module that initiates data transfer bus (DTB) cycles to transfer data between itself and a slave module.

power monitor. A functional module that monitors the status of the primary power source to the system, and signals when that power has strayed outside the limits required for reliable system operation. Since most systems are powered by an ac source, the power monitor is typically designed to detect drop-out or brown-out conditions on ac lines.

priority interrupt bus. One of the four buses provided by the backplane. The priority interrupt bus allows interrupter modules to send interrupt requests to interrupt-handler modules.

requester. A functional module that resides on the same printed-circuit board (pcb) as an interrupt handler or a master and requests use of the data transfer bus (DTB) whenever its interrupt handler or master needs it.

serial clock driver. A functional module that provides a periodic timing signal that synchronizes the operation of IEEE P1132* serial bus. Timing specifications for the SERIAL CLOCK DRIVER of the IEEE P1132 are given in Appendix C. Two backplane signal lines are reserved for use by a serial bus. However, the protocols of the serial bus are completely independent of this standard, and the inclusion of a serial bus is not a required feature of this standard.

*At the time of publication of this standard, IEEE P1132 is in preparation. When IEEE P1132 is approved and published it will become a part of this standard.

slave. A functional module that detects data transfer bus (DTB) cycles initiated by a master and, when those cycles specify its participation, transfers data between itself and the master.

system clock driver. A functional module that provides a 16 MHz timing signal on the utility bus.

system controller board. A board that resides in slot 1 of the backplane and has a system clock driver, an arbiter, an iack daisy-chain driver, and a bus timer. Some also have a serial clock driver, a power monitor, or both.

utility bus. This bus includes signals that provide periodic timing and coordinate the power-up and power-down of the systems. It is one of the four buses provided by the backplane.

1.2.1.3 Types of Cycles

read cycle. A data transfer bus (DTB) cycle that is used to transfer 1, 2, 3, or 4 bytes from a slave to a master. The cycle begins when the master broadcasts an address and an address modifier. Each slave captures the address and the address modifier, and verifies if it will respond to the cycle. If it is intended to respond, it retrieves the data from its internal storage, places it on the data bus and acknowledges the transfer. The master then terminates the cycle.

write cycle. A data transfer bus (DTB) cycle that is used to transfer 1, 2, 3, or 4 bytes from a master to a slave. The cycle begins when the master broadcasts an address and an address modifier and places data on the data transfer bus (DTB). Each slave captures the address and the address modifier and verifies if it will respond to the cycle. If it is intended to respond, it stores the data and then acknowledges the transfer. The master then terminates the cycle.

block read cycle. A data transfer bus (DTB) cycle that is used to transfer a block of bytes ranging in number from 1 to 256 bytes from a to a master. This transfer is executed by using a string of 1-, 2-, or 4-byte data transfers. Once the block transfer is initiated, the master does not release the DTB until all of the bytes have been transferred. This operation differs from a string of read cycles insofar as the master broadcasts only one address and one address modifier (at the beginning of the cycle). The slave then increments this address on each transfer so that the data for the next transfer is retrieved from the next higher location.

block write cycle. A data transfer bus (DTB) cycle used to transfer a block of bytes ranging in number from 1 to 256 bytes from a master to a slave. It uses a string of 1-, 2-, or 4-byte data transfers. Once the block transfer is initiated, the master does not release the DTB until all of the bytes have been transferred. It differs from a string of write cycles insofar as the master broadcasts only one address and one address modifier (at the beginning of the cycle). The slave then increments this address on each transfer so that the data from the next transfer is stored in the next higher location.

read-modify-write cycle. A data transfer bus (DTB) cycle that is used to both read from, and write to, a slave location without permitting any other master to access that location. This cycle is most useful in multiprocessing systems where certain memory locations are used to provide semaphore functions.

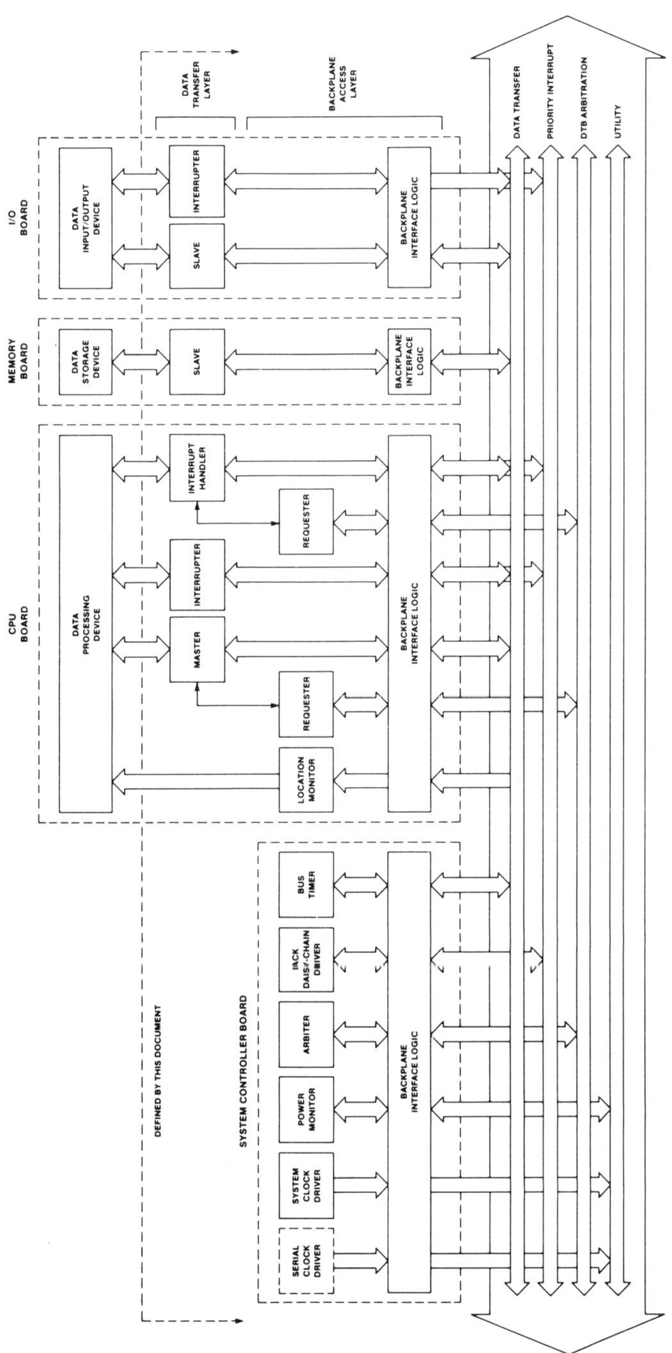

Fig 2
Functional Modules and Buses Defined by the Standard

address-only cycle. A data transfer bus (DTB) cycle that consists of an address broadcast, but does not have a data transfer. Slaves do not acknowledge address-only cycles and masters terminate the cycle without waiting for an acknowledgment.

interrupt acknowledge cycle. A data transfer bus (DTB) cycle, initiated by an interrupt handler,that reads a status/ID from an interrupter. An interrupt handler generates this cycle whenever it detects an interrupt request from an interrupter and it has control of the DTB.

1.2.2 Basic Structure. The interface system consists of backplane interface logic, four groups of signal lines referred to as buses, and a collection of functional modules, which can be configured as required. The functional modules communicate with each other using the backplane signal lines.

The functional modules are used as vehicles for discussion of the bus protocol, and need not be considered a constraint to logic design. For example, the designer might choose to design logic that interacts with the bus in the manner described, but uses different on-board signals, or monitors additional backplane signals. Boards can be designed to include various combinations of the defined functional modules.

The functional structure is divided into four categories. Each consists of a bus and its associated functional modules that work together to perform specific duties. Figure 2 shows the functional modules and buses. Each category is briefly summarized in 1.2.2.1 through 1.2.2.4.

1.2.2.1 Data Transfer Bus. Devices transfer the data over the data transfer bus (DTB), which contains data and address pathways and associated control signals. The functional modules, masters, slaves, interrupters, and interrupt handlers use the DTB to transfer data among each other. Two other modules, a bus timer and an iack daisy-chain driver, also assist them in this process.

1.2.2.2 DTB Arbitration Bus. Since systems can be configured with more than one master or interrupt handler, a means is provided to transfer control of the DTB among them in an orderly manner, and to guarantee that only one controls the DTB at any given time. The arbitration bus modules, requesters and arbiter, coordinate the control transfer.

1.2.2.3 Priority Interrupt Bus. The priority interrupt capability provides a means by which devices can request service from an interrupt handler. These interrupt requests can be prioritized into a maximum of seven levels. Interrupters and interrupt handlers use the priority-interrupt-bus signal lines.

1.2.2.4 Utility Bus. Periodic clocks, initialization, and failure detection are provided by the utility bus. It includes two clock lines, a system reset line, a system fail line, an ac fail line, and a serial data line.

1.3 Specification Diagrams. Several types of diagrams are used to help define or describe bus operations.

(1) Timing diagrams show the timing relationships between signal transitions. The times involved have minimum or maximum limits, or both. Some of the times specify the behavior of the backplane interface logic, while others specify the interlocked behavior of the functional modules.

(2) Sequence diagrams are similar to timing diagrams but only show the interlocked relationships of functional modules. They show a sequence of events, rather than specify the times involved. For example, a sequence diagram indicates that module A cannot generate signal transition B until it detects module C's generation of signal transition D.

(3) Flow diagrams show a stream of events as they occur during a bus operation. The events are stated in words and result from interaction of two or more functional modules. They describe bus operations in a sequential manner and, at the same time, show how the functional modules interact.

1.4 Terminology. To avoid confusion, and to make very clear the requirements for compliance the following keywords indicate the type of informatiion specified by each category

(1) Rule
(2) Recommendation
(3) Suggestion
(4) Permission
(5) Observation

These keywords are used as follows:

Rule. Rules form the basic framework of this standard are sometimes expressed in text form and sometimes in the form of figures, tables, or drawings. All rules shall be followed to ensure compatibility. Rules are characterized by an imperative style. The words *shall* and *shall not* are reserved for stating rules, and are not used for any other purpose.

NOTE: When the rule number is listed the first number corresponds to the section area and the second number uniquely identifies the rule within the section.

Recommendation. Wherever a recommendation is suggested, designers are cautioned to take the advice given. Doing otherwise might result in some awkward problems or poor performance. While the bus has been designed to support high performance systems, it is possible to design a system that complies with all the rules, but has abysmal performance. In many cases, a designer needs a certain level of experience to design printed-circuit boards (pcb) that deliver top performance. Recommendations are based on this type of experience, and are provided to designers to speed their traversal of the learning curve.

NOTE: When the recommendation number is listed the first number corresponds to the section area and the second number uniquely identifies the recommendation within that section.

Suggestion. A suggestion contains advice that is helpful but not vital. The user is encouraged to consider the advice before discarding it. Some design decisions are difficult until experience has been gained. Suggestions are included to help the designer who has not yet gained this experience. Suggestions are concerned with designing printed-circuit boards (pcb) that can be easily reconfigured for operation with other pcb,and with designing the pcb that ease system debugging, etc.

NOTE: When the suggestion number is listed the first number corresponds to the section area and the second number uniquely identifies the suggestion within that section.

Permission. In some cases a rule does not specifically prohibit a certain design approach, but the user might wonder whether that approach will violate the rule, or whether it will lead to some subtle problem. Permissions reassure the user that a certain approach is acceptable, and will not cause problems. The word may is reserved for stating permissions, and is not used for any other purpose.

NOTE: When the permission number is listed the first number corresponds to the section area and the second number to the sequence of the permission within that section.

Observation. Observations do not offer any specific advice. They usually follow naturally from what has just been discussed. They spell out the implications of certain rules and bring attention to situations that might otherwise be overlooked. They also give the rationale behind certain rules, so that the user understands why the rule must be followed.

NOTE: When the observation number is listed the first number corresponds to the section area and the second number to the sequence of the observation within that section.

Any text not labeled with one of these keywords describes the system structure or operation. It is written in either a descriptive or a narrative style.

1.4.1 Signal Line State. Bus protocols are described in terms of levels and transitions on bus lines. A signal line is always assumed to be in one of two levels, or in transition between these levels. Whenever the term ***high*** is used, it refers to a high TTL voltage level. The term *low* refers to a low TTL voltage level. A signal line is *in transition* when its voltage is moving between these levels. (For voltage thresholds see Section 6).

There are two possible transitions that can appear on a signal line, and these are referred to as *edges*. A rising edge is the time during which a signal makes its transition from a low level to a high level. The falling edge is the time during which a signal makes its transition from a high level to a low level.

Some bus specifications prescribe maximum or minimum rise and fall times for these edges. There is one problem. Printed-circuit board (pcb) designers have very little control over these times. If the backplane is heavily loaded, the rise and fall times will be long. If it is lightly loaded, these times might be short. Even when designers know what the maximum and minimum loading will be, they still need to spend time in the laboratory, experimenting to confirm which drivers provide the needed rise and fall times. Rise and fall times are the result of a complex set of interactions involving the signal line impedances of the backplane, its terminations, the source impedance of the drivers, and the capacitive loading of the signal line. To trade off all of these factors it is necessary for the pcb designer to study transmission-line theory, and certain specific parameters of drivers and receivers that are not normally found in most manufacturers' data sheets.

Recognizing all of this, this standard does not specify rise and fall times. Instead, it specifies the electrical characteristics for drivers and receivers, and suggests how to design the backplane. It also instructs designers how the worst case bus loading will affect the propagation delay of these drivers so that they can ensure that the required timing is met before building a pcb. When designers follow these guidelines, their pcb will operate reliably with other pcb under worst-case conditions.

1.4.2 Use of the Asterisk. To help define usage, signal mnemonics have an asterisk suffix where required.

(1) An asterisk following the name of signals that are level significant denotes that the signal is true or valid when the signal is low.

(2) An asterisk following the name of signals that are edge significant denotes that the actions initiated by that signal occur on a high to low transition.

Observation 1.1 The asterisk is not applicable to the asynchronously running clock lines SYSCLK and SERCLK. There is no fixed phase relationship between these clock lines and other signals.

1.5 Protocol. There are two layers of protocol. The lowest layer, referred to as the backplane access layer, is composed of the backplane interface logic, the utility bus modules, and the arbitration bus modules. The data second layer is the transfer layer, which is composed of the data transfer bus modules and priority interrupt bus modules. Figure 2 shows this layering.

> **Observation 1.2** The signal lines used by the data transfer layer modules form a special class because they are driven by different modules at different times. They are driven with line drivers that can be turned on and off at each pcb, based upon signals generated in the backplane access layer. It is very important that their turn-on and turn-off times be carefully controlled to prevent two drivers from attempting to drive the same signal line to different levels. Special timing diagram notation is used in this standard to specify their turn-on and turn-off times. It is shown in Fig 3.

Fig 3
Signal Timing Notation

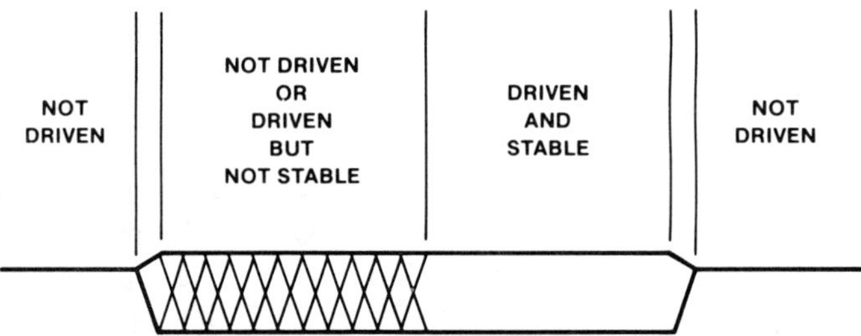

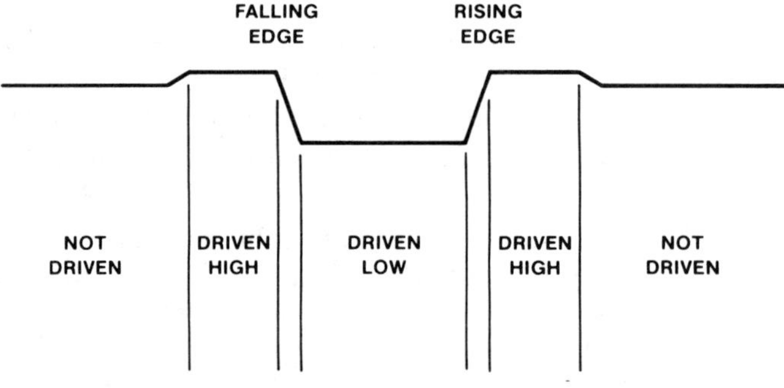

There are two basic kinds of protocol on the bus (1) closed-loop protocols and (2) open-loop protocols. Closed-loop protocols use interlocked bus signals while open-loop protocols use broadcast bus signals.

1.5.1 Interlocked Bus Signal. An interlocked bus signal is sent from a specific module to another specific module. The signal is acknowledged by the receiving module. An interlocked relationship exists between the two modules until the signal is acknowledged. For example, an INTERRUPTER can send an interrupt request that is answered later with an interrupt acknowledge signal (a time limit is not prescribed). The interrupter does not remove the interrupt request until the interrupt handler acknowledges it.

Interlocked bus signals coordinate internal functions of the system, as opposed to interacting with external stimuli. Each interlocked signal has a source module and a destination module within the system.

The address strobe and data strobes are especially important interlocking signals. They are interlocked with the data transfer acknowledge and bus error signals, and coordinate the transfer of addressing information and data that are the basis for all information flow between modules in the data transfer layer.

1.5.2 Broadcast Bus Signal. A module generates a broadcast signal in response to an event. There is no protocol for acknowledging a broadcast signal. Instead, the broadcast is maintained for a minimum specified time that is sufficient to ensure that all appropriate modules detect the signal. Broadcast signals might be activated at any time, irrespective of any other activity taking place on the bus. They are each sent over a dedicated signal line. Some examples are the system reset and ac failure lines. These signal lines are not sent to any specific module, but announce special conditions to all modules.

1.6 System Examples and Explanations. A protocol specification describes, in detail, the behavior of the various functional modules. It discusses the manner in which a module responds to a signal without disclosing the origin of the signal. Because of this procedure, a protocol specification does not give the reader a complete picture. To assist the user, this standard provides examples of typical bus operations. Each example shows one possible sequence of events; other sequences are also possible. However, in providing these examples, there is the danger that users will assume that the sequence shown in the example is the only legal one. To help users avoid this misconception, all examples are given in a narrative style. This is in contrast to the imperative style used when rules for compliance with the standard are given.

2. Data Transfer Bus

2.1 Introduction. This standard includes a high-speed asynchronous parallel data transfer bus (DTB). Figure 4 shows a typical system, including all of the DTB functional module. Masters use the DTB to select storage locations provided by slaves, and to transfer data to or from those locations. Some masters and slaves use all of the DTB lines, while others use only a subset.

Location monitors monitor data transfers between masters and slaves. When an access is done to one of the byte locations that it monitors, a location monitor generates an on-board signal. For example, it might signal its on-board processor by means of an interrupt request. In such a configuration, when processor board A writes into a location of the global memory that is monitored by processor B location monitor, processor B will be interrupted.

After a master initiates a data transfer cycle, it waits for the responding slave to respond before finishing the cycle. The asynchronous definition of the bus allows a slave to take all the time it needs to respond. When a slave fails to respond because of some malfunction, or when the master accidentally addresses a location where there is no slave, the bus timer intervenes, allowing the cycle to be terminated.

2.2 Data-Transfer-Bus Lines. The data-transfer-bus lines are grouped into three categories

Addressing Lines	Data Lines	Control Lines
A01-A31	D00-D31	AS*
AM0-AM5		DS0*
DS0*		DS1*
DS1*		BERR*
LWORD*		DTACK*
		WRITE*

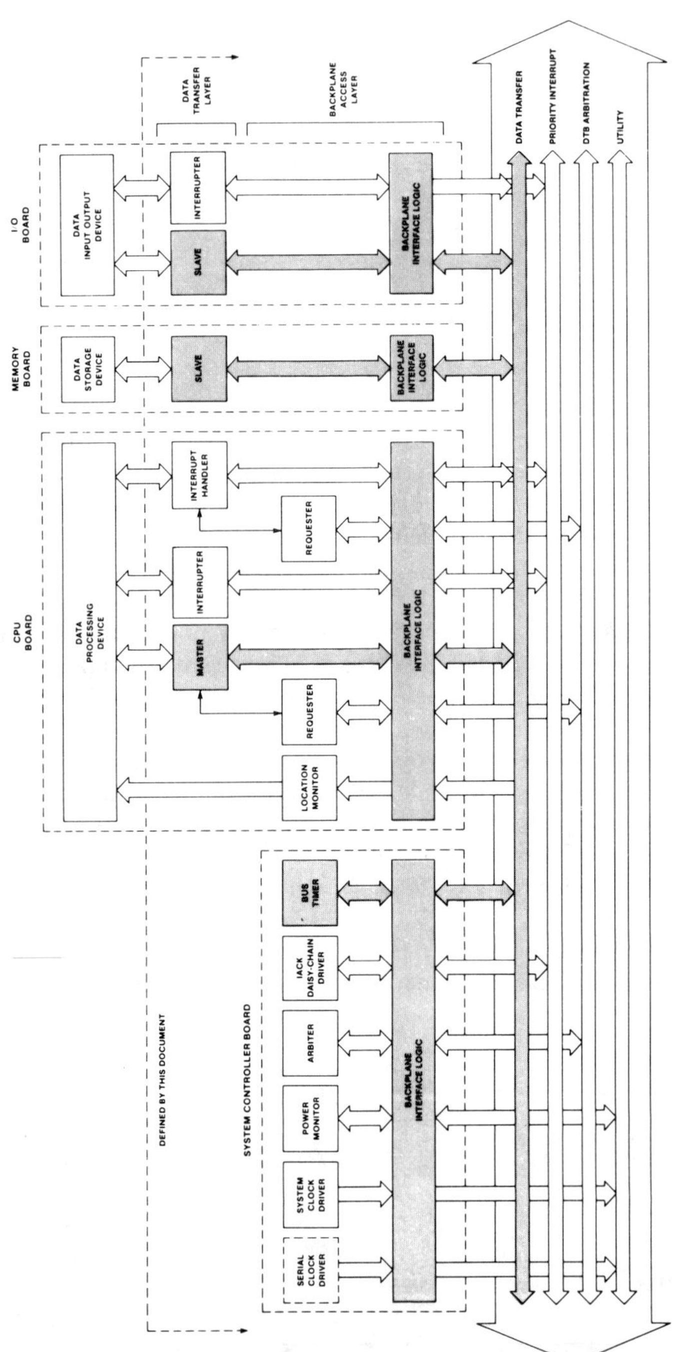

Fig 4
Data Transfer Bus Functional Block Diagram

Observation 2.1 The two data strobes DS0* and DS1* serve a dual function.

(1) Their levels are used to select which byte(s) are accessed.

(2) Their edges are also used as timing signals to coordinate the transfer of data between the master and the slave.

2.2.1 Addressing Lines. The smallest addressable unit of storage is the byte location. Each byte location is assigned a unique binary address. Each byte location can be assigned to one of four categories, according to the least significant two bits of its address (see Table 1).

Table 1
The Four Categories of Byte Locations

Category	Byte Address
BYTE(0)	XXXXXX.....XXXXXX00
BYTE(1)	XXXXXX.....XXXXXX01
BYTE(2)	XXXXXX.....XXXXXX10
BYTE(3)	XXXXXX.....XXXXXX11

A set of byte locations whose addresses differ only in the two least significant bits, is referred to as 4-byte group or a BYTE(0-3) group. Some, or all, of the bytes in a 4-byte group can be accessed simultaneously by a single DTB cycle.

Masters use address lines A02-A31 to select which 4-byte group will be accessed. Four additional lines, DS1*, DS0*, A01, and LWORD*, are then used to select which byte location(s) within the 4-byte group are accessed during the data transfer. Using these four lines, a master can access 1-, 2-, 3-, or 4-byte locations simultaneously, as shown in Table 2.

Observation 2.2 When driving both data strobes low, one data strobe might go low slightly after the other. In this case the signal levels indicated in Table 2 are the final levels.

Observation 2.3 Given the 4-signal line levels shown in Table 2, there are 16 possible combinations of levels. Of these 16, there are two illegal combinations that are not used (see Rule 2.1).

Rule 2.1 Masters shall not generate DTB cycles where the final levels of DS0*, DS1*, A01, and LWORD* are either of the following illegal combinations:

DS1*	DS0*	A01	LWORD*
high	low	high	low
low	high	high	low

Permission 2.1 When a master accesses byte locations BYTE(1-2) (see Table 2), it may generate either of the two combinations described in Rule 2.1 briefly as transition states (that is, while one data strobe has fallen, but the other has not).

Observation 2.4 Whenever a master drives LWORD* low and A01 high it drives both data strobes low (Any other combination is illegal). Board designers can take advantage of this to simplify the logic on slaves.

Permission 2.2 To simplify the required logic, slaves that respond to a cycle that accesses byte location BYTE(1-2) (see Table 2) may be designed without logic to distinguish between these cycles and the two illegal cycles described in Rule 2.1.

2.2.2 Address-Modifier Lines. There are six address-modifier lines. They allow the master to pass additional binary information to the slave during DTB cycles. Table 3 lists all of the 64 possible address-modifier (AM) codes and classifies each into one of three categories:

(1) Defined, including:

(a) Short addressing AM codes indicate that address lines A02-A15 are being used to select a BYTE(0-3) group

(b) Standard addressing AM codes indicate that address lines A02-A23 are being used to select a BYTE(0-3) group

(c) Extended addressing AM codes indicate that address lines A02-A31 are being used to select a BYTE(0-3) group

(2) Reserved

(3) User-defined

Table 2
Use of DS0*, DS1*, A01, and LWORD* To Select Byte Locations

Byte Locations Selected	DS1*	DS0*	A01	LWORD*
Single-byte access				
BYTE(0)	low	high	low	high
BYTE(1)	high	low	low	high
BYTE(2)	low	high	high	high
BYTE(3)	high	low	high	high
Double-byte access				
BYTE(0-1)	low	low	low	high
BYTE(1-2)	low	low	high	low
BYTE(2-3)	low	low	high	high
Triple-byte access				
BYTE(0-2)	low	high	low	low
BYTE(1-3)	high	low	low	low
Quad-byte access				
BYTE(0-3)	low	low	low	low

Rule 2.2 Except for the user-defined codes, the codes defined in Table 3 shall not be used for purposes other than those specified.

Rule 2.3 Slaves shall not respond to reserved address-modifier codes.

Observation 2.5 Reserved address-modifier codes are for future enhancements. When slave boards respond to these codes, incompatibilities might result at some future date, when usage of these codes is defined.

Permission 2.3 User-defined codes may be used for any purpose that board vendors or board users deem appropriate (page switching, memory protection, master or task identification, privileged access to resources, etc).

Table 3
Address Modifier Codes

HEX Code	Address Modifier 5	4	3	2	1	0	Function
3F	H	H	H	H	H	H	Standard supervisory block transfer
3E	H	H	H	H	H	L	Standard supervisory program access
3D	H	H	H	H	L	H	Standard supervisory data access
3C	H	H	H	H	L	L	Reserved
3B	H	H	H	L	H	H	Standard nonprivileged block transfer
3A	H	H	H	L	H	L	Standard nonprivileged program access
39	H	H	H	L	L	H	Standard nonprivileged data access
38	H	H	H	L	L	L	Reserved
37	H	H	L	H	H	H	Reserved
36	H	H	L	H	H	L	Reserved
35	H	H	L	H	L	H	Reserved
34	H	H	L	H	L	L	Reserved
33	H	H	L	L	H	H	Reserved
32	H	H	L	L	H	L	Reserved
31	H	H	L	L	L	H	Reserved
30	H	H	L	L	L	L	Reserved
2F	H	L	H	H	H	H	Reserved
2E	H	L	H	H	H	L	Reserved
2D	H	L	H	H	L	H	Short supervisory access
2C	H	L	H	H	L	L	Reserved
2B	H	L	H	L	H	H	Reserved
2A	H	L	H	L	H	L	Reserved
29	H	L	H	L	L	H	Short nonprivileged access
28	H	L	H	L	L	L	Reserved
27	H	L	L	H	H	H	Reserved
26	H	L	L	H	H	L	Reserved
25	H	L	L	H	L	H	Reserved
24	H	L	L	H	L	L	Reserved
23	H	L	L	L	H	H	Reserved
22	H	L	L	L	H	L	Reserved
21	H	L	L	L	L	H	Reserved
20	H	L	L	L	L	L	Reserved
1F	L	H	H	H	H	H	User-defined
1E	L	H	H	H	H	L	User-defined
1D	L	H	H	H	L	H	User-defined
1C	L	H	H	H	L	L	User-defined
1B	L	H	H	L	H	H	User-defined
1A	L	H	H	L	H	L	User-defined
19	L	H	H	L	L	H	User-defined
18	L	H	H	L	L	L	User-defined
17	L	H	L	H	H	H	User-defined
16	L	H	L	H	H	L	User-defined
15	L	H	L	H	L	H	User-defined
14	L	H	L	H	L	L	User-defined

Table 3 (*Continued*)
Address Modifier Codes

HEX Code	Address Modifier 5	4	3	2	1	0	Function
13	L	H	L	L	H	H	User-defined
12	L	H	L	L	H	L	User-defined
11	L	H	L	L	L	H	User-defined
10	L	H	L	L	L	L	User-defined
0F	L	L	H	H	H	H	Extended supervisory block transfer
0E	L	L	H	H	H	L	Extended supervisory program access
0D	L	L	H	H	L	H	Extended supervisory data access
0C	L	L	H	H	L	L	Reserved
0B	L	L	H	L	H	H	Extended nonprivileged block transfer
0A	L	L	H	L	H	L	Extended nonprivileged program access
09	L	L	H	L	L	H	Extended nonprivileged data access
08	L	L	H	L	L	L	Reserved
07	L	L	L	H	H	H	Reserved
06	L	L	L	H	H	L	Reserved
05	L	L	L	H	L	H	Reserved
04	L	L	L	H	L	L	Reserved
03	L	L	L	L	H	H	Reserved
02	L	L	L	L	H	L	Reserved
01	L	L	L	L	L	H	Reserved
00	L	L	L	L	L	L	Reserved

L = low-signal level
H = high-signal level

Recommendation 2.1 To allow users to tailor the use of the user-defined address-modifier codes to their own needs and decode them in a flexible way on slave boards. Users can then configure the board to give any decoding required by their system.

Observation 2.6 Socketed programmable devices provide a flexible way for decoding the address-modifier codes.

Suggestion 2.1 Where slaves are manufactured with a programmed device (for example, a PROM or a FPLA) installed in the socket, program the device so that the slave responds to the following AM codes:
A16 slaves with D08(O), D08(EO), D16, or D32 capability: 29, 2D
A24 slaves with D08(O), D08(EO), D16, or D32 capability: 39, 3A, 3D, and 3E
A32 slaves with D08(O), D08(EO), D16, or D32 capability: 09, 0A, 0D, and 0E
A24 slaves with BLT capability: 3B, 3F
A32 slaves with BLT capability: 0B, 0F

(The mnemonics A16, A24, and A32 are defined in Table 9. The D08(O), D08(EO), D16, D32, and BLT are defined in Tables 10 and 11.

2.2.3 Data Lines. Systems can be built with a backplane configuration that provides either 16 data lines (D00-D15) or 32 data lines (D00-D31). Backplane configurations that provide 16 data lines allow a master to access only 2-byte locations simultaneously, while those with 32 data lines allow it to access up to 4-byte locations simultaneously. When the master has selected 1-, 2-, 3-, or 4-byte locations, using the method described in 2.2.1, it can transfer binary data between itself and those locations over the data bus. Table 4 shows how the data lines are used to access byte locations.

Table 4
Use of the Data Lines to Access Byte Locations

Byte Locations Accessed	D24-D31	D16-D23	D08-D15	D00-D07
BYTE(0)			BYTE(0)	
BYTE(1)				BYTE(1)
BYTE(2)			BYTE(2)	
BYTE(3)				BYTE(3)
BYTE(0-1)			BYTE(0)	BYTE(1)
BYTE(1-2)		BYTE(1)	BYTE(2)	
BYTE(2-3)			BYTE(2)	BYTE(3)
BYTE(0-2)	BYTE(0)	BYTE(1)	BYTE(2)	
BYTE(1-3)		BYTE(1)	BYTE(2)	BYTE(3)
BYTE(0-3)	BYTE(0)	BYTE(1)	BYTE(2)	BYTE(3)

2.2.4 Data-Transfer-Bus Control Lines. The following signal lines are used to control the movement of data over the data transfer lines:

AS*	Address Strobe
DS0*	Data Strobe Zero
DS1*	Data Strobe One
BERR*	Bus Error
DTACK*	Data Transfer Acknowledge
WRITE*	Read/Write

2.2.4.1 AS*. A falling edge on AS* informs all slaves that the address is stable and can be captured.

2.2.4.2 DS0* and DS1*. In addition to their function in selecting byte locations for data transfer, as described in 2.2.1, the data strobes also serve additional functions. On write cycles, the first falling edge of a data strobe indicates that the master has placed valid data on the data bus. On read cycles, the first rising edge tells the slave that it can remove its data from the data bus.

Observation 2.7 As specified in 2.6, masters are not permitted to drive either of the data strobes low before driving AS* low. However, due to the fact that AS* might be more heavily loaded on the backplane than the data strobes, slaves and location monitors might detect a falling edge on a data strobe, before they detect the falling edge on AS*.

Permission 2.5 Slaves that do not have block transfer capability (as defined in 2.3.7), and location monitors may be designed to capture the address when they detect a falling edge on a data strobe instead of on the falling edge of AS*.

Observation 2.8 Slaves and location monitors that capture the address on the falling edge of the data strobe(s) need not monitor AS*.

Observation 2.9 To take full advantage of address pipelining as described in 2.4.2, or to perform block read and write cycles, a slave should capture the address on the falling edge of AS*.

2.2.4.3 DTACK*. The slave drives DTACK* low to indicate that it has successfully received the data on a write cycle. On a read cycle, the slave drives it low to indicate that it has placed data on the data bus.

2.2.4.4 BERR*. BERR* is driven low by the slave or by the bus timer to indicate to the master that the data transfer was unsuccessful. For example, when a master tries to write to a location that contains read-only memory, the responding slave can drive BERR* low. When the master tries to access a location that is not provided by any slave, the bus timer drives BERR* low after a specified period.

Suggestion 2.2. Design slaves to respond with a falling edge on BERR* when they detect an uncorrectable error in the data they retrieve from their internal storage during a read cycle.

2.2.4.5 WRITE*. WRITE* is a level-significant signal line that is strobed by the falling edge of the first data strobe. It is used by the master to indicate the direction of data transfer operations. When WRITE* is driven low, the data transfer direction is from the master to the slave. When WRITE* is driven high, the data transfer direction is from the slave to the master.

2.3 DTB Modules — Basic Description. In addition to the address-only cycle, the DTB protocol defines 33 different cycle types that are used to transfer data. Each of these 34 cycle types can be used in any of three addressing modes:

(1) Short (16 bit)
(2) Standard (24 bit)
(3) Extended (32 bit).

The capabilities of masters, slaves, and location monitors are described by a list of mnemonics that show what cycle types they can generate, accept, or monitor respectively. These mnemonics are described in 2.3.5 through 2.3.10.

Block diagrams for the four types of DTB functional modules, that is, master, slave, location monitor, and bus timer, are provided in 2.3.1 and 2.3.4.

Rule 2.7 Output signal lines shown with solid lines in Figs 5, 6, 7, and 8 shall be driven by the module, unless it would always drive them high.

Observation 2.11 When an output signal line is not driven, then terminators on the backplane ensure that it is high.

Rule 2.8 Input signal lines shown with solid lines in Figs 5, 6, 7, and 8 shall be monitored and responded to in the appropriate fashion.

Observation 2.12 Rules and permissions for driving and monitoring signal lines shown with dotted lines in Figs 5, 6, and 8 are given in Tables 5, 6, and 8.

2.3.1 Master. The block diagram of the master is shown in Fig 5. The dotted lines show signals whose use varies among the various types of masters. Table 5 specifies the requirements of the various types of masters to drive and monitor these lines. Further rules describing how the various types of masters drive the address lines are given in Table 20, the data lines in Table 21, and the LWORD*, DS0*, and DS1* and A01 lines in Table 20.

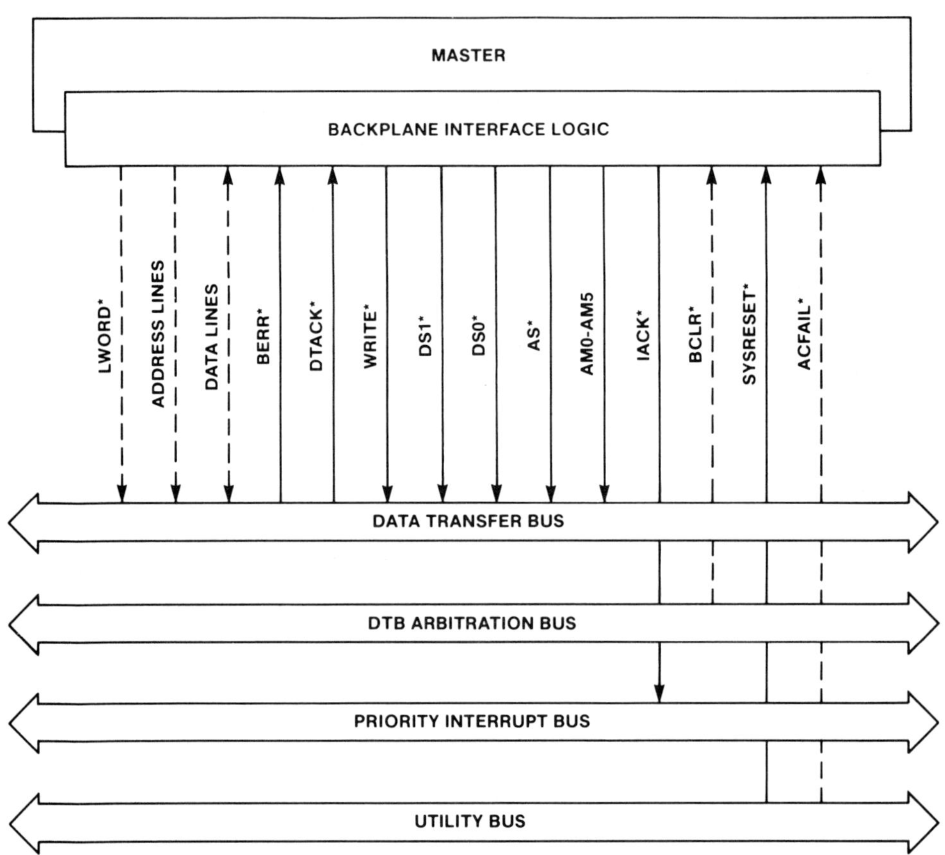

Fig 5
Block Diagram: Master

Table 5
Masters: Rules and Permissions for Monitoring and Driving the Dotted Lines

Type of Master	Rules and Permissions
D08(EO) and D16	Shall monitor and drive D00-D15 May or may not drive LWORD* May or may not drive or monitor D16-D31
D32	Shall drive LWORD* Shall monitor and drive D00-D31
A16	Shall drive A01-A15 May or may not drive A16-A31
A24	Shall drive A01-A23 May or may not drive A24-A31
A32	Shall drive A01-A31
ALL	May or may not monitor BCLR*, or ACFAIL* (see Sections 3 and 5)

NOTES: (1) The mnemonics D08(EO), D16, and D32 are defined in Table 10.
(2) The mnemonics A16, A24, and A32 are defined in Table 9.

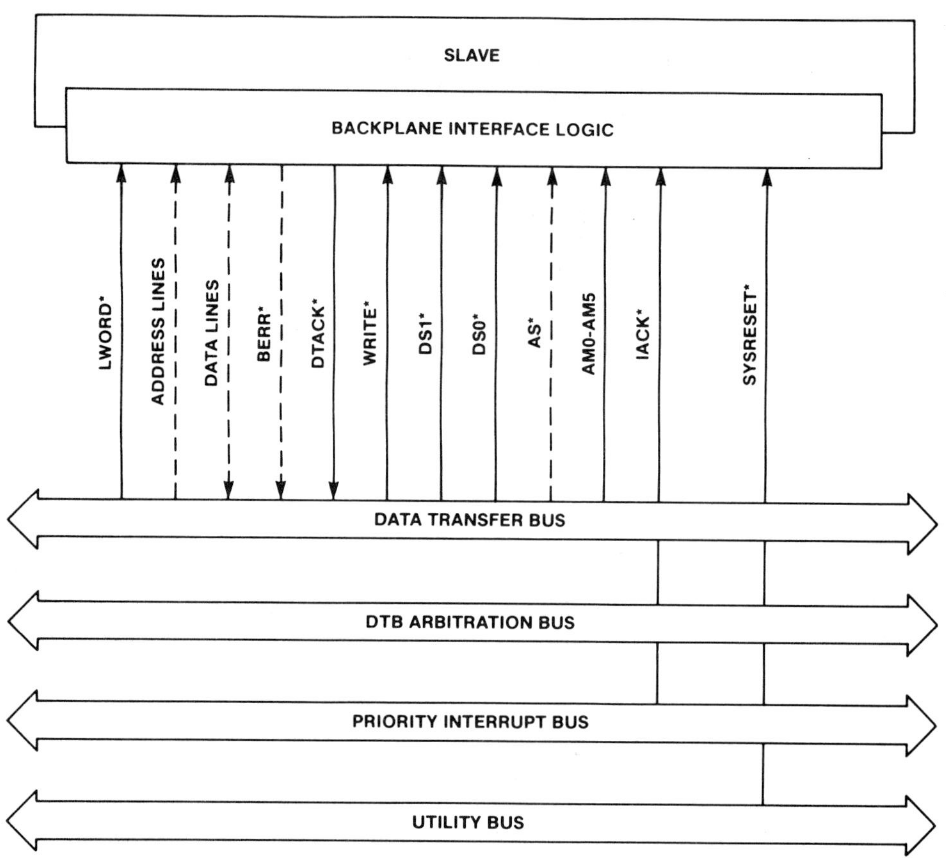

Fig 6
Block Diagram: Slave

2.3.2 Slave. The block diagram of the slave is shown in Fig 6. The dotted lines show signals whose use varies among the various types of slaves. Table 6 specifies the requirements of the various types of slaves to drive and monitor these lines. Further information describing how the various types of slaves drive the data lines is given in Table 21.

Table 6
Slaves; Rules and Permissions for Monitoring and Driving the Dotted Lines

Type of Slave	Rules and Permissions
D08(O)	Shall monitor and drive D00-D07 May or may not monitor or drive D08-D31 May or may not monitor AS*
D08(EO) and D16	Shall monitor and drive D00-D15 May or may not monitor or drive D16-D31 May or may not monitor AS*
D32	Shall monitor and drive D00-D31 May or may not monitor AS*
BLT	Shall monitor AS*
A16	Shall monitor A01-A15 May or may not monitor A16-A31
A24	Shall monitor A01-A23 May or may not monitor A24-A31
A32	Shall monitor A01-A31
ALL	May or may not drive BERR*

NOTES: (1) The mnemonics D08(O), D08(EO), D16, and D32 are defined in Table 10.
(2) The mnemonic BLT is defined in Table 11.
(3) The mnemonics A16, A24, and A32 are defined in Table 9.

2.3.3 Bus Timer. The block diagram of the bus timer is shown in Fig 7. Bus timers can be designed to drive BERR* low after various periods of time. Table 7 shows how the mnemonic BTO( ) is used to describe the various types of bus timers.

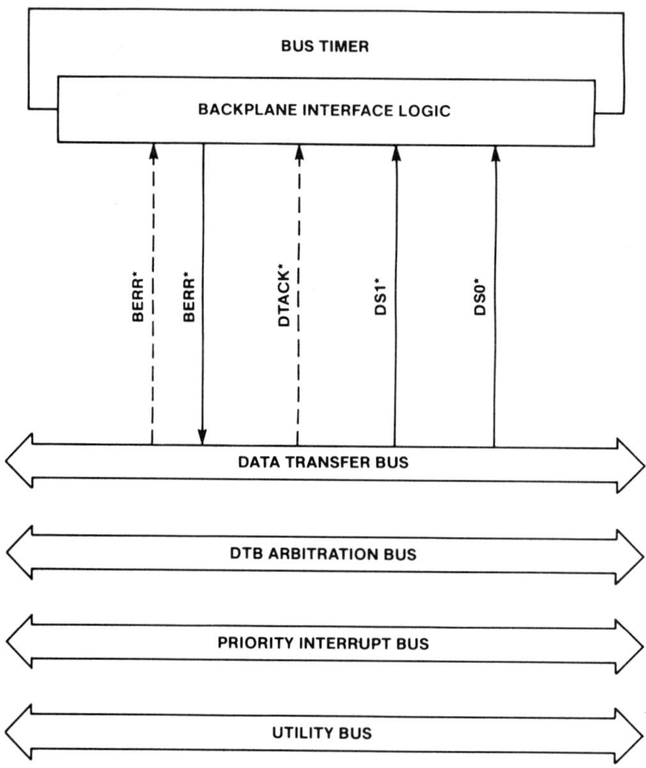

Fig 7
Block Diagram: Bus Timer

Table 7
Use of the BTO( ) Mnemonic to Specify the Time-Out Period of Bus Timers

The Following Mnemonic	When Applied to a	Means that It
BTO(x)	Bus Timer	Drives BERR* low when the first data strobe stays low for longer than x us.

Observation 2.13 The dotted DTACK* and BERR* lines shown in Fig 7 allow designers to implement a bus timer in one of two ways

(1) To drive BERR* low when the first data strobe stays low for longer than the bus time-out period, regardless of the levels on the DTACK* and BERR* lines

(2) To drive BERR* low when the first data strobe stays low for longer than the bus time-out period, but only when both DTACK* and BERR* are high at the point of time-out.

2.3.4 Location Monitor. The block diagram of the location monitor is shown in Fig 8. The dotted lines show signals whose use varies among the various types of location monitors. Table 8 specifies the requirements of the various types of location monitors to monitor these lines.

Fig 8
Block Diagram: Location Monitor

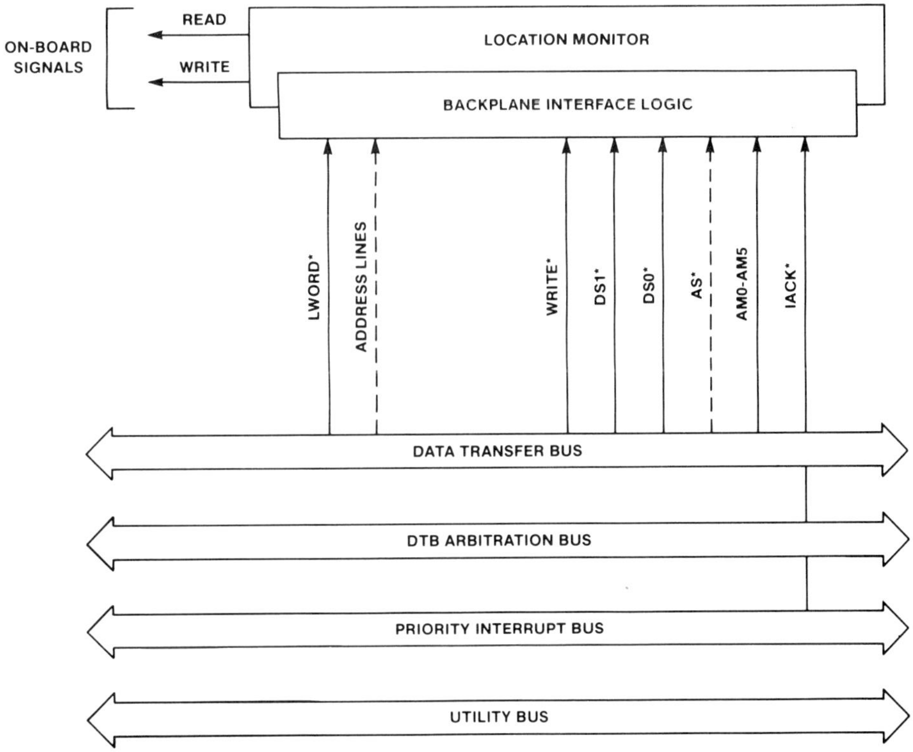

Table 8
Location Monitors: Rules and Permissions for Monitoring the Dotted Lines

Type of Location Monitor	Rules and Permissions
A16	Shall monitor A01-A15 May or may not monitor A16-A31
A24	Shall monitor A01-A23 May or may not monitor A24-A31
A32	Shall monitor A01-A31
ALL	May or may not monitor AS*

NOTE: The mnemonics A16, A24, and A32 are defined in Table 9.

2.3.5 Addressing Modes. Masters broadcast an address over the DTB at the beginning of each cycle. This address might be a 16-bit, a 24-bit, or a 32-bit address, depending upon the capabilities of the master broadcasting it. Sixteen-bit addresses are referred to as short addresses, 24-bit addresses are referred to as standard addresses, and 32-bit addresses are referred to as extended addresses. Table 9 shows the various mnemonics used to describe these capabilities, and how each is used to describe masters, slaves, and location monitors.

Table 9
Mnemonics that Specify Addressing Capabilities

The Following Mnemonic	When Applied to a	Means that It
A16	Master	Can generate cycles with short (16-bit) addresses
	Slave	Can accept cycles with short (16-bit) addresses
	Location Monitor	Can monitor cycles with short (16-bit) addresses
A24	Master	Can generate cycles with standard (24-bit) addresses
	Slave	Can accept cycles with standard (24-bit) addresses
	Location Monitor	Can monitor cycles with standard (24-bit) addresses
A32	Master	Can generate cycles with extended (32-bit) addresses
	Slave	Can accept cycles with extended (32-bit) addresses
	Location Monitor	Can monitor cycles with extended (32-bit) addresses

The master broadcasts an address modifier (AM) code along with each address to inform slaves whether the address is short, standard, or extended.

Short addressing is intended primarily for addressing I/O devices. It allows A16 slaves to be designed with less logic, since they do not have to decode as many address lines. While I/O boards can be designed to decode standard addresses and extended addresses, short addressing usually makes this unnecessary.

Standard and extended addressing modes are intended primarily for addressing memory, although there is no rule against designing I/O boards that respond to these addressing modes. Standard and extended addressing modes allow much larger addressing ranges.

Rule 2.9 Slave boards shall decode all of the address modifier lines.

Observation 2.14 Decoding all the address modifier lines allows a slave to differentiate short addresses, standard addresses, and extended addresses.

Observation 2.15 In addition to the three modes of addressing described here, there is a fourth mode that is used on interrupt acknowledge cycles (see Section 4). These interrupt acknowledge cycles can be distinguished from data transfer cycles by the fact that the IACK* signal line is low instead of high.

Rule 2.10 Whenever a master broadcasts an address over the address bus, it shall ensure that IACK* is high.

Permission 2.7 The master may either drive IACK* high during the address broadcast or it may leave IACK* undriven (The bus terminators will then hold it high).

Rule 2.11 Slaves shall not respond to DTB cycles when IACK* is low.

Observation 2.86 Many systems include a mixture of A16, A24, and A32 slaves.

Rule 2.61 A32 masters shall include the A24 and A16 capabilities.

Rule 2.62 A24 masters shall include the A16 capability.

Suggestion 2.6 Do not assume that the above rules are known to the readers of product specifications. Rather specify A32 master products as "A32, A24, and A16". Similarly, specify an A24 master product as "A24 and A16".

2.3.6 Basic Data Transfer Capabilities. There are four basic data transfer capabilities associated with the DTB: D08(O) (Odd byte only), D08(EO) (Even and Odd byte), D16, and D32. These capabilities allow flexibility when interfacing different types of processors and peripherals to the bus.

Eight-bit processors can be interfaced to the bus as D08(EO) masters. Sixteen-bit processors can be interfaced to the bus as D16 masters. The D16 slave is useful for interfacing 16-bit memory devices or 16-bit I/O devices to the DTB.

Many existing peripheral chips have registers that are only 8 bits wide. While these chips often have several of these registers, they cannot provide the contents of two registers simultaneously when a D16 master attempts to access two adjacent locations with a double-byte read cycle. These 8-bit peripheral IC can be interfaced to the DTB as D08(O) slaves, which provide only BYTE(1) and BYTE(3) locations, and respond only to single-odd-byte accesses (This simplifies the D08(O) slave's interface logic, since single-odd-byte accesses always take place over D00-D07).

Rule 2.63 D32 masters, D32 slaves, and D32 location monitors shall include the D08(EO) and the D16 capabilities.

Rule 2.64 D16 masters, D16 slaves, and D16 location monitors shall include the D08(EO) capability.

Suggestion 2.7 Do not assume that the above rules are known to the readers of product specifications. Rather specify products that have the D32 capability as "D32, D16, and D08(EO)". Similarly, specify D16 products as "D16 and D08(EO)".

Rule 2.4 D16 slaves shall not respond by driving DTACK* low during cycles that request access to byte locations BYTE(1-2), BYTE(0-2), BYTE(1-3), or BYTE(0-3).

Rule 2.5 D08(EO) slaves shall not respond by driving DTACK* low during cycles that request access to byte locations BYTE(0-1), BYTE(1-2), BYTE(2-3), BYTE(0- 2), BYTE(1-3), or BYTE(0-3).

Rule 2.65 D08(O) slaves shall not respond with a falling edge on DTACK* during cycles that request access to byte locations BYTE(0), BYTE(2), BYTE(0-1), BYTE(1-2), BYTE(2-3), BYTE(0-2), BYTE(1-3), or BYTE(0-3).

Suggestion 2.8 Design slaves to respond with a falling edge on BERR* in the following situations:

(1) When a D08(O), D08(EO), or D16 slave is requested to do a quad-byte cycle

(2) When a D08(O) or D08(EO) slave is requested to do a double-byte cycle

(3) When a D08(O), D08(EO), or D16 slave is requested to do an unaligned transfer (That is, a triple-byte transfer or a double-byte BYTE(1-2) transfer)

Table 10 shows the various mnemonics used to describe the basic-data-transfer capabilities, and the function of each to describe masters, slaves, and location monitors.

Table 10
Mnemonics that Specify Basic-Data-Transfer Capabilities

The Following Mnemonic	When Applied to a	Means that It
D08(O)	Slave	Can accept the following cycles: Single-byte read cycles: BYTE(1) READ BYTE(3) READ Single-byte write cycles: BYTE(1) WRITE BYTE(3) WRITE
D08(EO)	Master Slave Location Monitor	Can generate the following cycles: Can accept the following cycles: Can monitor the following cycles: Single-byte read cycles: BYTE(0) READ BYTE(1) READ BYTE(2) READ BYTE(3) READ Single-byte write cycles: BYTE(0) WRITE BYTE(1) WRITE BYTE(2) WRITE BYTE(3) WRITE
D16	Master Slave Location Monitor	Can generate the following cycles: Can accept the following cycles: Can monitor the following cycles: Double-byte read cycles: BYTE(0-1) READ BYTE(2-3) READ Double-byte write cycles: BYTE(0-1) WRITE BYTE(2-3) WRITE
D32	Master Slave Location Monitor	Can generate the following cycles: Can accept the following cycles: Can monitor the following cycles: Quad-byte read cycle: BYTE(0-3) READ Quad-byte write cycle: BYTE(0-3) WRITE

Observation 2.16 It might seem logical to define *even-byte-only* slaves that respond to the even-byte memory locations adjacent to the D08(O) slaves. But, this cannot be done because there is only one DTACK* line. When a master selects both an even-byte and an odd-byte location simultaneously, by doing a double-byte transfer, both slaves drive DTACK* at the same time, and the master doesn't know whether both boards have acknowledged the access.

Observation 2.17 Since D08(O) slaves respond only to odd-byte addresses, they cannot provide contiguous memory. The D08(O) slaves are useful only for I/O, status, or control registers, while D08(EO), D16, and D32 slaves are also useful for memory.

2.3.7 Block-Transfer Capabilities. Masters often access several memory locations in ascending order. When this is the case, block transfer cycles are very useful. They allow the master to provide a single address, and then access data in that location and those at higher addresses, without providing additional addresses.

When a master initiates a block transfer cycle, the responding slave latches the address into an on-board address counter. The master, upon completing the first data transfer, (that is, driving the data strobes high) does not allow the address strobe to go high. Instead, it repeatedly drives the data strobe(s) low in response to data transfer acknowledgments from the slave, and transfers data to or from sequential memory locations in ascending order. To access the next location(s), the slave increments an on-board counter that generates the address for each transition of the data strobe(s).

Observation 2.18 Block transfer cycles of indefinite length complicate the design of memory boards. Specifically, all block transfer slaves (the one that responds and those that do not) need to latch the initial address and then increment the address counter on each bus transfer. All slaves then have to decode the incremented address to determine whether the transfer has crossed a board boundary into their address range. While this is certainly possible, such address decoding typically limits access times of the slave. To simplify the design of these slaves and to permit faster access times, Rule 2.12 was formulated.

Rule 2.12 Block transfer cycles shall not cross any 256-byte boundary.

Observation 2.19 Rule 2.12 limits the maximum length of block transfers to 256 bytes. However, knowing that only A01 through A07 will change during the course of the block transfer simplifies the design of block transfer slaves. The upper address lines only have to be decoded once, at the beginning of the block transfer cycle, allowing faster access times on all subsequent data transfers.

Observation 2.20 In some cases it might be necessary to transfer a large block of data that crosses one or more 256-byte boundaries. In such a case, when the hardware on the board that does the block transfer is designed to recognize the arrival at a 256-byte boundary, it can momentarily drive AS* high and then initiate another block transfer without the intervention of system software.

The block read cycle is very similar to a string of read cycles. Likewise, the block write cycle is very similar to a string of write cycles. The difference is that only the initial address is broadcast by the master and the address strobe is held low during all of the data transfers.

Observation 2.21 Control of the DTB cannot be transferred during block transfer cycles because AS* is held low through all of the data transfers, and control of the DTB can only be transferred while AS* is high.

Rule 2.66 Slaves that include block transfer capability shall monitor AS*, and shall capture the addressing information when they detect a falling edge on AS*.

Observation 2.86 During single-byte block transfers, data is transferred 8 bits at a time over D00-D07 or D08-D15. One example is as follows:

	D08-D15	D00-D07
First data transfer		BYTE(1)
	BYTE(2)	
		BYTE(3)
	BYTE(0)	
		BYTE(1)
	BYTE(2)	
Last data transfer		BYTE(3)

Table 11
Mnemonics That Specify Block Transfer Capabilities

The Following Mnemonic	When Applied to a	Means that It
BLT	D08(EO) MASTER D08(EO) SLAVE D08(EO) LOC MON	Can generate the following cycles: Can accept the following cycles: Can monitor the following cycles: Block read cycles: SINGLE-BYTE BLOCK READ Block write cycles: SINGLE-BYTE BLOCK WRITE
	D16 MASTER D16 SLAVE D16 LOC MON	Can generate the following cycles: Can accept the following cycles: Can monitor the following cycles: Block read cycles: DOUBLE-BYTE BLOCK READ Block write cycles: DOUBLE-BYTE BLOCK WRITE
	D32 MASTER D32 SLAVE D32 LOC MON	Can generate the following cycles: Can accept the following cycles: Can monitor the following cycles: Block read cycles: QUAD-BYTE BLOCK READ Block write cycles: QUAD-BYTE BLOCK WRITE

Observation 2.87 During double-byte block transfers, data is transferred 16 bits at a time over D00-D15. One example is as follows:

	D08-D15	D00-D07
First data transfer	BYTE(2)	BYTE(3)
	BYTE(0)	BYTE(1)
	BYTE(2)	BYTE(3)
	BYTE(0)	BYTE(1)
	BYTE(2)	BYTE(3)
Last data transfer	BYTE(0)	BYTE(1)

Table 11 lists the mnemonic used to describe block transfer capabilities and how it is used to describe the various types of masters, slaves, and location monitors.

2.3.8 Read-Modify-Write Capability. In multiprocessor systems that share resources, such as memory and I/O, a method is needed to allocate these resources. One very important goal of this allocation algorithm is to ensure that a resource being used by one task cannot be used by another at the same time. The problem is best described by the following example:

Two processors in a multiprocessing system share a common resource (for example, a printer). Only one processor can use the resource at a time. The resource is allocated by a byte in memory, that is, when the byte is set, the resource is busy; when it is cleared, the resource is available. To gain use of the resource, processor A reads the byte and tests it to determine whether it is cleared. When the byte is cleared, processor A sets the byte to lock out processor B. This operation takes two data transfers; a read to test the byte, and a write to set the byte. However, difficulty might arise when the bus is given to processor B between these two transfers. Processor B might then also find the byte cleared and assume the resource is available. Both processors will then set the byte in the next available cycle and attempt to use the resource.

Table 12
Mnemonic That Specifies Read-Modify-Write Capabilities

The Following Mnemonic	When Applied to a	Means that It
RMW	D08(O) SLAVE	Can accept the following cycles:
		Single-odd-byte RMW cycles: BYTE(1) READ-MODIFY-WRITE BYTE(3) READ-MODIFY-WRITE
	D08(EO) MASTER D08(EO) SLAVE D08(EO) LOC MON	Can generate the following cycles: Can accept the following cycles: Can monitor the following cycles:
		Single-byte RMW cycles: BYTE(0) READ-MODIFY-WRITE BYTE(1) READ-MODIFY-WRITE BYTE(2) READ-MODIFY-WRITE BYTE(3) READ-MODIFY-WRITE
	D16 MASTER D16 SLAVE D16 LOC MON	Can generate the following cycles: Can accept the following cycles: Can monitor the following cycles:
		Double-byte RMW cycles: BYTE(0-1) READ-MODIFY-WRITE BYTE(2-3) READ-MODIFY-WRITE
	D32 MASTER D32 SLAVE D32 LOC MON	Can generate the following cycles: Can accept the following cycles: Can monitor the following cycles:
		Quad-byte RMW cycles: BYTE(0-3) READ-MODIFY-WRITE

This conflict is avoided by defining a read-modify-write cycle that prevents transferring control of the DTB between the read portion and the write portion of the cycle. This cycle is very similar to a read cycle immediately followed by a write cycle. The difference is that the address strobe is held low during both transfers. This ensures that, unlike a read cycle followed by a write cycle, control of the DTB cannot be transferred during a read-modify-write cycle, as this is only possible while the address strobe is high.

Table 12 lists the mnemonic used to describe read-modify-write capabilities and how it is used to describe the various types of masters, slaves, and location monitors.

2.3.9 Unaligned Transfer Capability. Some 32-bit microprocessors store and retrieve data in an unaligned fashion. For example, a 32-bit value might be stored in four different ways, as shown in Fig 9.

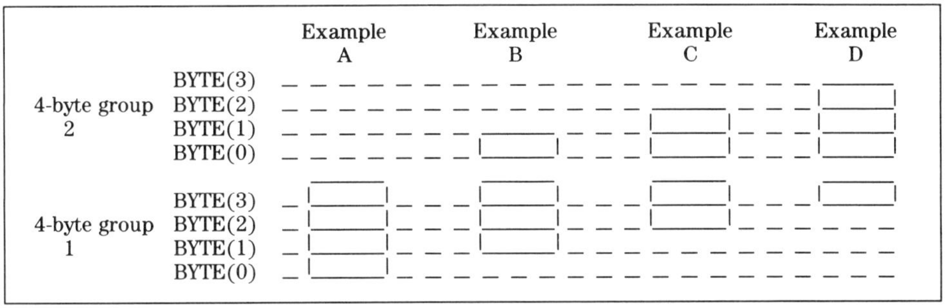

Example A
Example B
Example C
Example D

4-byte group 2
BYTE(3)
BYTE(2)
BYTE(1)
BYTE(0)

4-byte group 1
BYTE(3)
BYTE(2)
BYTE(1)
BYTE(0)

Fig 9
Four Ways That 32 Bits of Data Might Be Stored In Memory

The master can transfer the 32 bits of data using several different sequences of DTB cycles. For example, it can transfer the data one byte at a time, using four single-byte data transfers. However, a master can accomplish the transfer much quicker by using one of the cycle sequences shown in Table 13.

> **Observation 2.22** The sequences shown in Table 13 is typical of a master that accesses the byte locations in ascending order. The DTB protocols do not require this.

As shown in Table 13, each of these 32-bit transfers can be accomplished with a combination of single-byte and double-byte transfers. However, examples B and D require three bus cycles when this procedure is followed. Because of this, the DTB protocol also includes two triple-byte transfer cycles. When used in combination with a single-byte cycle, these triple-byte cycles allow data to be stored as shown in examples B and D using only two bus cycles.

Some 32-bit microprocessors also store and retrieve data 16 bits at a time, in an unaligned fashion, as shown in Fig 10.

Table 13
Transferring 32 Bits of Data Using Multiple-Byte Transfer Cycles

Example	Cycle Sequences Used to Accomplish the Transfer	Data Bus Lines Used	Byte Locations Accessed (See Fig 9)
A	Quad-byte transfer	D00-D31	Grp 1, BYTE(0-3)
B	Single-byte transfer	D00-D07	Grp 1, BYTE(1)
	Double-byte transfer	D00-D15	Grp 1, BYTE(2-3)
	Single-byte transfer	D08-D15	Grp 2, BYTE(0)
	or		
	Triple-byte transfer	D00-D23	Grp 1, BYTE(1-3)
	Single-byte transfer	D08-D15	Grp 2, BYTE(0)
C	Double-byte transfer	D00-D15	Grp 1, BYTE(2-3)
	Double-byte transfer	D00-D15	Grp 2, BYTE(0-1)
D	Single-byte transfer	D00-D07	Grp 1, BYTE(3)
	Double-byte transfer	D00-D15	Grp 2, BYTE(0-1)
	Single-byte transfer	D08-D15	Grp 2, BYTE(2)
	or		
	Single-byte transfer	D00-D07	Grp 1, BYTE(3)
	Triple-byte transfer	D08-D31	Grp 2, BYTE(0-2)

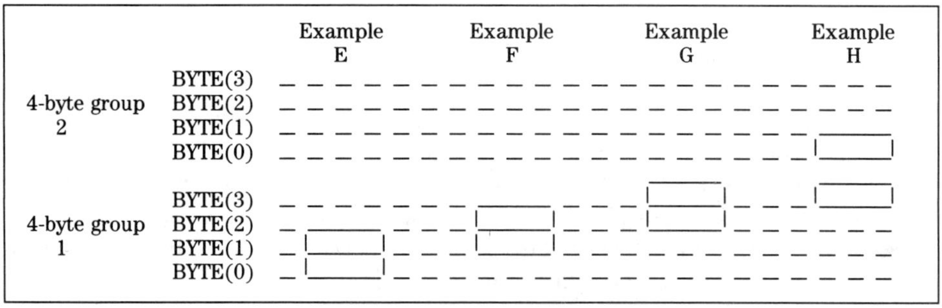

Fig 10
Four Ways That 16 Bits of Data Might Be Stored in Memory

The master can transfer the 16 bits of data using several different sequences of DTB cycles as listed in Table 14.

Observation 2.23 The sequences listed in Table 14 is typical of a master that accesses the byte locations in ascending order. The DTB protocols do not require this.

As shown in Table 14, the 16-bit transfer in example F can be accomplished with two single-byte transfers. However, this requires two bus cycles. Because of this, the DTB protocol also includes a double-byte transfer cycle that allows data to be stored as shown in example F using only one bus cycle.

Table 14
Transferring 16 Bits of Data Using Multiple-Byte Transfer Cycles

Example	Cycle Sequences Used to Accomplish the Transfer	Data Bus Lines Used	Byte Locations Accessed (See Fig 10)
E	Double-byte transfer	D00-D15	Grp 1, BYTE(0-1)
F	Single-byte transfer	D00-D07	Grp 1, BYTE(1)
	Single-byte transfer	D08-D15	Grp 1, BYTE(2)
	or		
	Double-byte transfer	D08-D23	Grp 1, BYTE(1-2)
G	Double-byte transfer	D00-D15	Grp 1, BYTE(2-3)
H	Single-byte transfer	D00-D07	Grp 1, BYTE(3)
	Single-byte transfer	D08-D15	Grp 2, BYTE(0)

Observation 2.24 Since unaligned transfers make use of all 32 data lines, only D32 masters and D32 slaves can do unaligned transfers.

Rule 2.67 D32 slaves and location monitors shall include UAT capability.

> **Rule 2.6** D08(O), D08(EO), and D16 slaves shall not respond by driving DTACK* low during a cycle that accesses byte locations BYTE(1-2), BYTE(0-2), or BYTE(1-3).

Table 15 lists how the unaligned transfer (UAT) mnemonic is used to describe masters.

Table 15
Mnemonic That Specifies Unaligned Transfer Capability

The Following Mnemonic	When Applied to a	Means that It
UAT	D32 MASTER	Can generate the following cycles: Triple-byte read cycles: BYTE(0-2) READ BYTE(1-3) READ Triple-byte write cycles: BYTE(0-2) WRITE BYTE(1-3) WRITE Double-byte read cycle: BYTE(1-2) READ Double-byte write cycle: BYTE(1-2) WRITE

2.3.10 Address-Only Capability. The address-only cycle is the only cycle on the DTB that is not used to transfer data. It begins as a typical DTB cycle, with the address, address modifier code, IACK* and LWORD* lines becoming valid and AS* falling after a setup time. However, the data strobes are never driven low. After holding the various lines strobed by AS* stable for a prescribed minimum period, the master terminates the cycle without waiting for DTACK* or BERR* to go low (The address-only cycle is also the only type of DTB cycle that does not require a response to complete). Table 16 shows how the mnemonic ADO is used to describe masters.

Table 16
Mnemonic That Specifies Address Only Capability

The Following Mnemonic	When Applied to a	Means that It
ADO	MASTER	Can generate address-only cycles.

Observation 2.25 Address-only cycles can be used to enhance board performance by allowing a CPU board that is already in control of the bus to broadcast an address before it has determined whether or not that address selects a slave on the bus. Broadcasting the address in this fashion allows slaves to decode the address concurrently with the CPU board.

Rule 2.68 All slaves shall be designed to accommodate ADO cycles without loss of data or erroneous separation.

2.3.11 Interaction Between DTB Functional Modules. Data transfers take place between masters and slaves. The master is the module controlling the transfer. The slave that recognizes the address as its own is the responding slave, and all other slaves are nonresponding slaves.

After initiating a data transfer cycle, the master waits for a response from the responding slave. When the master detects that response, it drives its data strobes and address strobe high, terminating the cycle. The slave responds by releasing its response line.

Observation 2.26 Although the timing for the address and the data are largely independent, there are two exceptions:

(1) The master waits until it has driven AS* low before driving either DS0* or DS1* low

(2) The slave acknowledges both the AS*, and DS0* and DS1* with either DTACK* or BERR*.

Rule 2.13 If a slave responds to a data transfer cycle, then it shall either drive DTACK* low or it shall drive BERR* low, but it shall not drive both low.

Observation 2.27 Because of possible bus skew due to different loading of AS* and of DS0* and DS1*, the falling edge of DS0*, DS1*, or both, might be detected by the slave slightly before the falling edge on AS*.

Observation 2.28 The WRITE* line is high to identify a read cycle, and low to identify a write cycle before the first data strobe is driven low, and remains stable until both data strobes are high.

Rule 2.14 Before driving the data bus, the master shall ensure that the previous responding slave has stopped driving the data bus. It does so by verifying that DTACK* and BERR* are both high before it drives either the DS0* or DS1*, or both, low on any cycle, and before it drives any of D00-D31 during a write cycle.

Rule 2.15 At the end of a read cycle the responding slave shall release the data bus before allowing DTACK* to go high.

Rule 2.16 During read cycles, the responding slave shall maintain valid data on the data bus until it detects the first data strobe high.

Suggestion 2.3 For optimum performance, design masters so that they drive DS0* and DS1* high as soon as possible after DTACK* or BERR* goes low. Also, design slaves so that they release the data bus and DTACK* as soon as possible after detecting that DS0* and DS1* are high. This allows the maximum data transfer rate on the bus.

Observation 2.29 Addressing information on the bus might change soon after a module drives DTACK* or BERR* low, and before the master drives DS0* and DS1* or AS* high.

A third type of module, the location monitor , monitors the data transfer and generates either, or both, of two on-board signals whenever a byte location that it monitors is accessed. When the access is a write cycle, then the on-board WRITE signal is generated. When the access is a read cycle, then the on-board READ signal is generated. When a read-modify-write cycle is performed, then both on-board signals are generated.

When the cycle takes too long, a fourth module, a bus timer, intervenes by driving BERR* low, completing the data-transfer handshake, and allowing the bus to resume operation.

Rule 2.17 There is a strict interlock between the rising and falling edges of the DS0*/DS1* and DTACK*/BERR*. Before driving either DS0* or DS1* low, a master shall ensure that both DTACK* and BERR* are high. Once it has driven either DS0* or DS1* low, it shall not drive them high and finish a transfer without first detecting DTACK* or BERR* low.

Observation 2.30 A board containing a processor, which directs data transfers between itself and other boards, contains a master module. When the same board also contains memory accessible from the bus, it also contains a slave module. An intelligent peripheral controller might receive commands through a slave interface from a general purpose processor board. It then might act as a master to access global memory to execute the command it has been given.

2.4 Typical Operation. Masters initiate data transfers over the DTB. The addressed slave then acknowledges the transfer. After receiving the data-transfer acknowledge, the master terminates the data transfer cycle. The asynchronous nature of the DTB allows the slave to control the time taken for the transfer.

Before initiating any data transfers, a master has to be granted exclusive control of the DTB. This ensures that multiple masters will not try to use the DTB at the same time. The master gains control of the DTB using the modules and

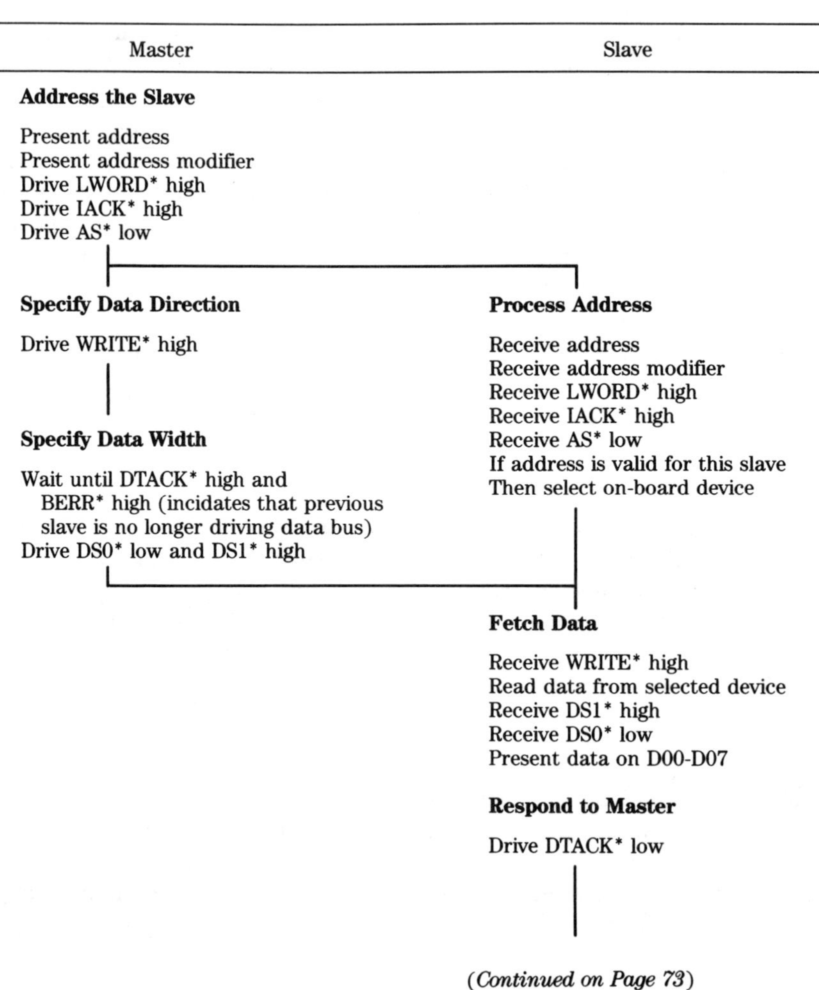

(*Continued on Page 73*)

Fig 11
An Example of a Single-Byte Read Cycle

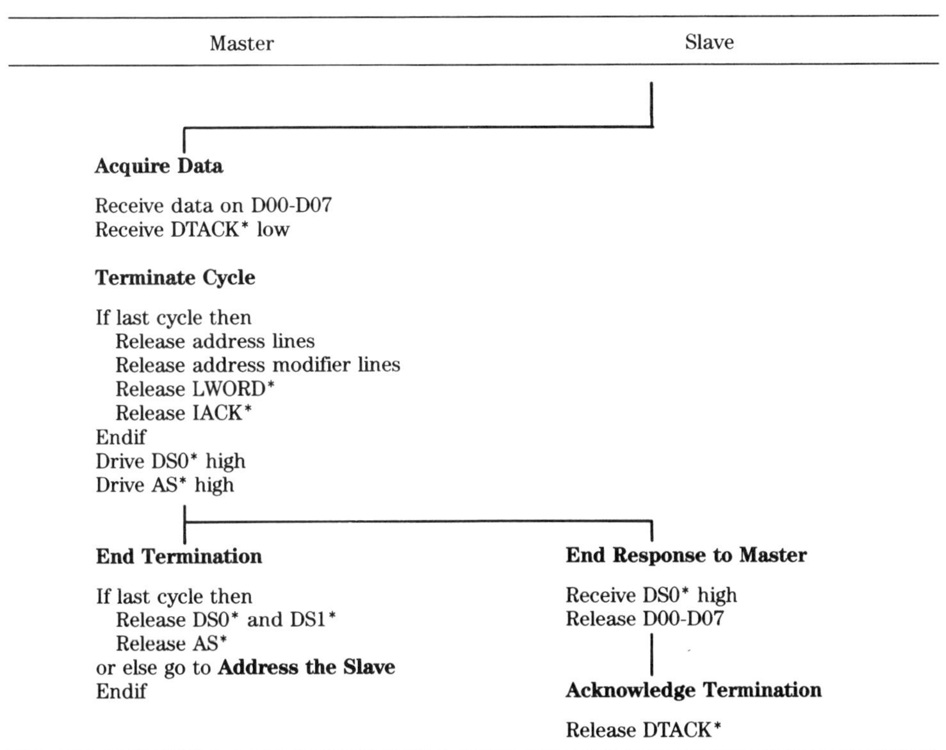

Fig 11 (*Continued*)
An Example of a Single-Byte Read Cycle

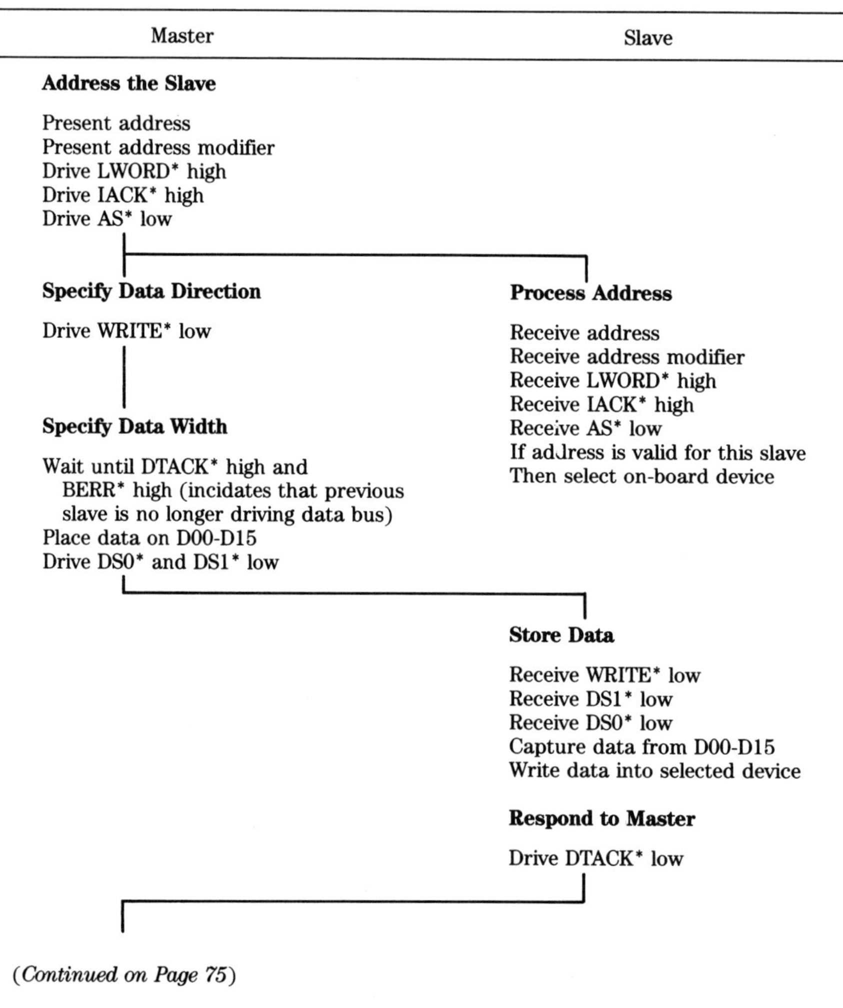

(*Continued on Page 75*)

Fig 12
An Example of a Double-Byte Write Cycle

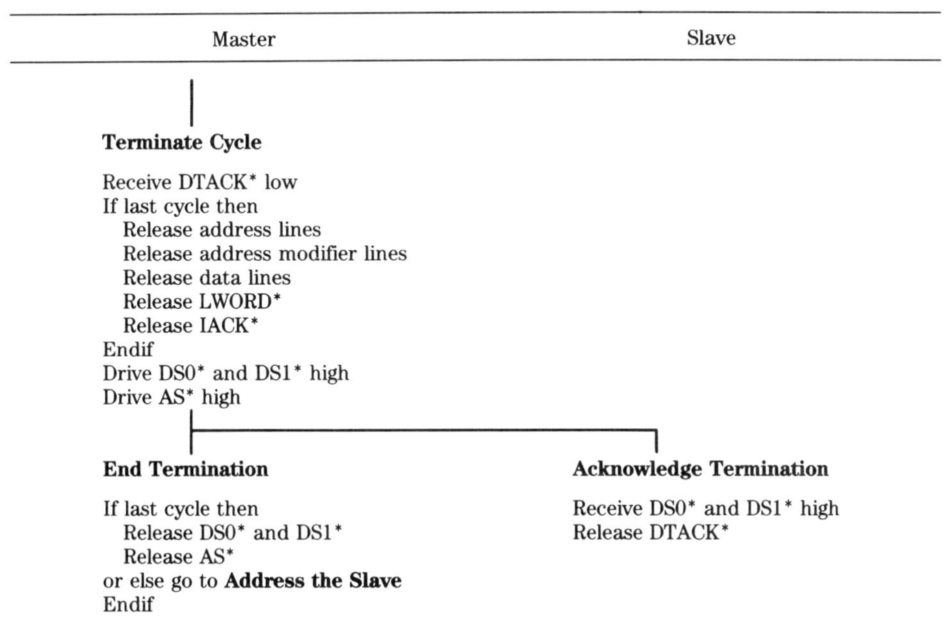

Fig 12 (*Continued*)
An Example of a Double-Byte Write Cycle

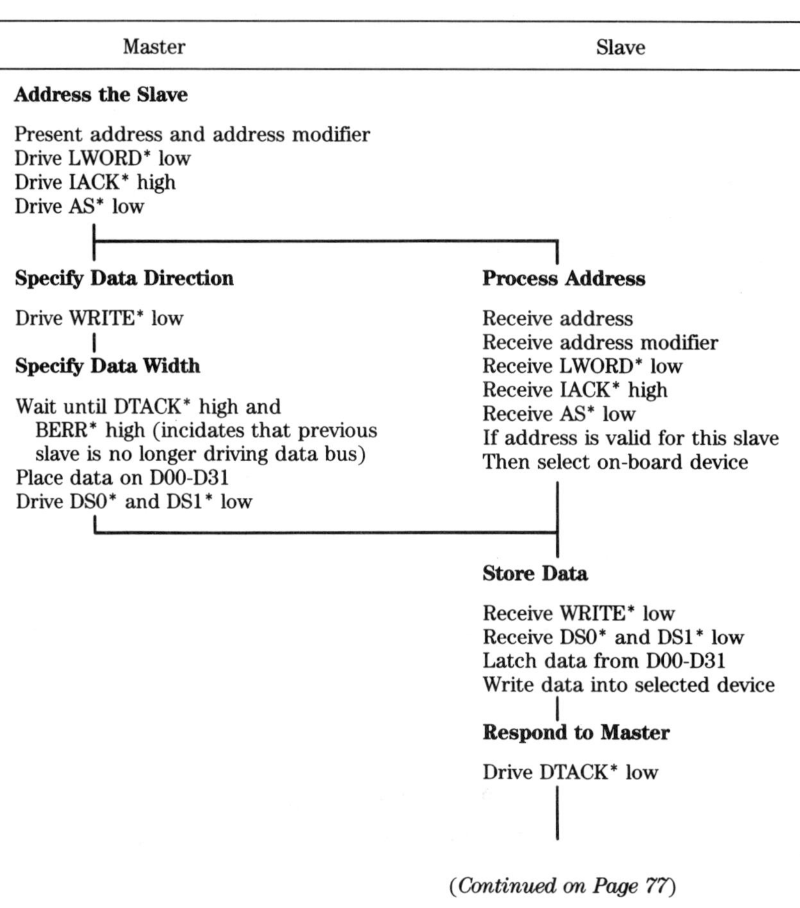

(*Continued on Page 77*)

Fig 13
An Example of a Quad-Byte Write Cycle

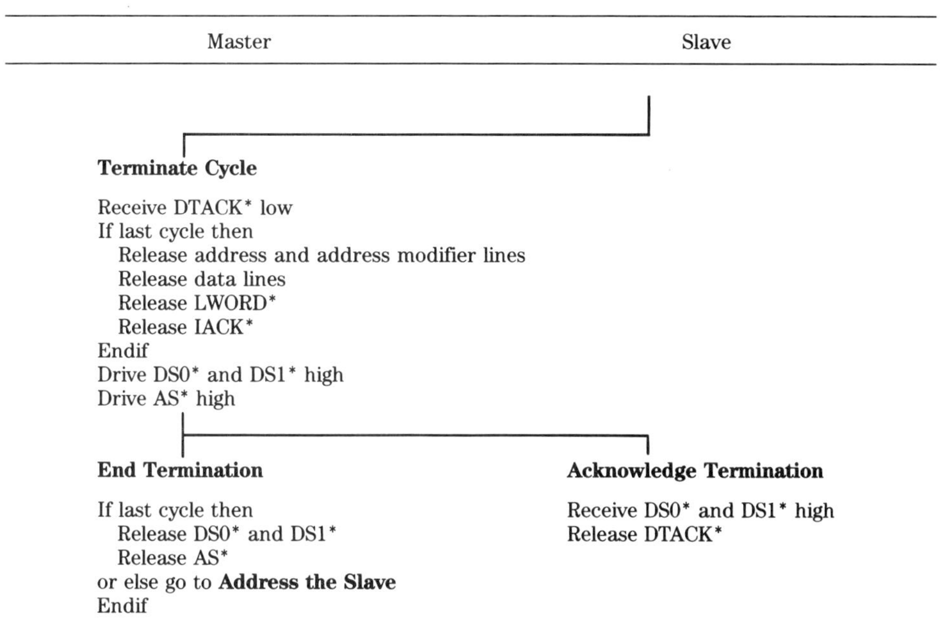

Fig 13 (*Continued*)
An Example of a Quad-Byte Write Cycle

signal lines of the arbitration bus (This is explained in more detail in 2.5). The following discussion presumes that the master has already been granted and assumed control of the DTB.

2.4.1 Typical Data-Transfer Cycles. Figure 11 shows a typical single-byte read cycle. To start the transfer, the master drives the addressing lines with the desired address and address modifier code. Since this example is a BYTE(1) read cycle, the master drives LWORD* high and A01 low. Since it is not doing an interrupt acknowledge cycle, it does not drive IACK* low. The master then waits for a specified setup time before driving AS* low, to allow the address lines and the address modifier lines to stabilize before the slaves sample them.

Each slave determines whether it should respond by examining the levels on the address lines, the address modifier lines, and IACK*. While this is happening, the master drives WRITE* high to indicate a read operation. The master then verifies that DTACK* and BERR* are high to ensure that the slave from the previous cycle is no longer driving the data bus. When this is the case, the master then drives DS0* low, while keeping DS1* high.

The responding slave then determines which 4-byte group and which byte of that group is to be accessed, and starts the transfer. After it has retrieved the data from its internal storage and placed it on data lines D00-D07, the slave signals the master by driving DTACK* low. The slave then holds DTACK* low and maintains the data valid for as long as the master holds DS0* low.

When the master receives DTACK* driven low, it captures the data on D00-D07, releases the address lines, and drives DS0* and AS* high. The slave responds by releasing D00-D07 and releasing DTACK* high.

> **Observation 2.31** The master in Fig 11 releases all of the DTB lines at the end of the data transfer. This is not required unless the master's requester released BBSY* during the data transfer as described in 2.5.

The flow for double-byte and quad-byte data transfer cycles are very similar to the single-byte cycle. Flow diagrams for these cycles are shown in Figs 12 and 13.

2.4.2 Address Pipelining. Since separate strobes for the address and the data are defined, masters can broadcast the address for the next cycle while the data transfer for the previous cycle is still in progress. This is called *address pipelining.*

Permission 2.8 When the master detects that the responding slave has driven DTACK* or BERR* low, it may change the address, and, after driving AS* high for a minimum time, drive AS* low again.

For example, when a slave drives DTACK* low on a read cycle, the master is allowed to place a new address on the address bus while it is reading the data from the bus. This amounts to an overlapping of one cycle with the next one, and permits greater speeds on the bus.

Rule 2.18 All slaves shall be designed to accommodate address pipelining without loss of data or erroneous operation.

The following example offers two designs that comply with the requirements to accommodate address pipelining:

Observation 2.32 The responding slave might recognize its address and respond very quickly on the DTACK* or BERR* lines. Since the master is permitted to remove the address after the responding slave drives DTACK* or BERR* low, nonresponding slaves might not be able to decode the addressing information before the master removes it from the bus.

Observation 2.33 Because a master might broadcast a new address while a previous cycle is finishing, the designer of slave boards needs to ensure that the second assertion of AS* does not invalidate the first address when it is still needed by on-board logic to maintain the data on the bus.

Suggestion 2.4 Design the slaves to monitor the AS*, and to capture the addressing information on the falling edge of AS*.

Observation 2.34 A master might drive AS* low for a new cycle before it drives either DS0* or DS1* high from the previous cycle. Because of this, there might be a period when the AS* for the new cycle, and at least one of DS0* or DS1* from the previous cycle coincide during the cycle overlap.

Suggestion 2.5 Design the slaves to initiate data transfers to and from the bus when one or both of DS0* and DS1* are low, and DTACK* and BERR* are both high, instead of a simultaneous low level on AS* and one or both of DS0* and DS1*.

Permission 2.9 Masters may be designed without the ability for address pipelining. (for example, they may wait until the responding slave releases DTACK* or BERR* before driving AS* low for the next cycle).

2.5 Data-Transfer-Bus Acquisition

Rule 2.19 A master shall obtain permission to use the DTB, as described in Section 3, before transferring any data on the DTB.

Several masters might want to use the DTB at the same time. The process that determines which master can use the DTB is called arbitration and is discussed in Section 3. Because arbitration is closely tied to the operation of the DTB, it is briefly described here.

Figure 14 provides two examples that show possible sequences when a master (called Master A) finishes using the DTB and allows arbitration to take place.

In Fig 14, Example (a), Master A, partway into its last transfer, indicates that it no longer needs the DTB. It does this by having its requester release the bus busy (BBSY*) signal line. Since Master A gives this early notice that the DTB will soon be available, the arbitration takes place during the last data transfer. The arbitration is completed and Master B is granted permission to use the DTB

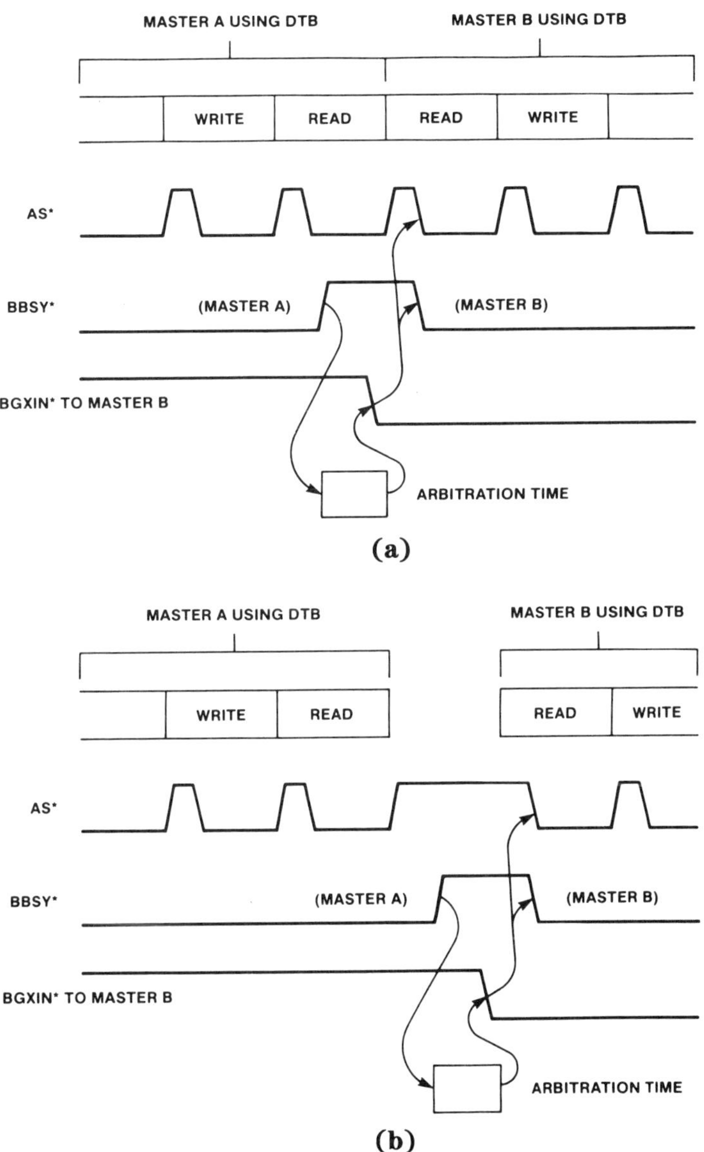

Fig 14
Data Transfer Bus Master Exchange Sequence
Example (a) Arbitration During the Last Data Transfer
Example (b) Arbitration After the Last Data Transfer

before Master A has terminated its cycle, but it waits until Master A releases AS* (This ensures that Master B will not start driving the DTB before Master A has finished with its last data transfer).

In Fig 14, Example (b), Master A waits until after its last transfer (that is, after AS* is released) before releasing BBSY*. In this case the DTB is idle while the arbitration is taking place. Master B is then granted the bus and, since AS* is already high, it begins using the DTB immediately.

Rule 2.20 Once a master's requester releases BBSY* to high, the master shall not drive AS* from high to low (that is, it shall not begin a new cycle) until its requester receives a new bus grant.

2.6 DTB Timing Rules and Observations. This section describes the timing rules and observations that govern the behavior of masters and slaves. This timing information is in the form of figures and tables.

(1) Table 17 lists a timing table and timing diagrams that specify master, slave, and location monitor operation.

(2) Table 18 defines the various mnemonics that are used in this section.

(3) Tables 19 through 21 specify the use of the DTB signals.

(4) Tables 22 through 27 specify the timing parameters of the DTB (The reference numbers used in Tables 24 through 27 correspond to the timing parameter numbers in Tables 22 and 23).

(5) Figures 15 through 18 specify the timing rules and observations during the address broadcast portion of the cycle.

(6) Figures 19 through 24 specify the timing rules and observations for masters, slaves, and location monitors during the data transfer portion of the cycle.

(7) Figures 25 through 27 specify the timing rules and observations for masters and slaves between DTB cycles.

(8) Figure 28 is the timing diagram for master, slave, and bus timer during a timed-out cycle.

(9) Figure 29 shows the timing during the mastership transfer of the DTB.

To meet the timing specifications, board designers need to take into account the worst case propagation delays of bus drivers and receivers used on their boards. The propagation delay of the drivers depends on their output loads, but manufacturer's specifications do not always give enough information to calculate the propagation delays under various loads. To help the board designer, some suggestions are offered in Section 6.

The observations specify the timing of incoming lines signal transitions. These times can be relied upon when the rules for the backplane loading, specified in Section 6, are not violated. The rules for the bus terminators in Section 6 guarantee that the timing parameters for signal lines that are released after they have been driven, are met.

Typically, for each timing rule there is a corresponding observation. However, the time that is guaranteed in the observation might differ from the time specified by the rule. For example, a careful inspection of the timing diagrams shows that the master is required to provide 35 ns of address and data setup time, but the slave is only guaranteed 10 ns. This is because the address and data bus drivers are not always able to drive the backplane's signal lines completely from low to high through the threshold region until the transition propagates to the end of the backplane and is reflected back. The falling edges of the address and data strobes, however, typically cross the 0.8 V threshold without waiting for a

Table 17
Timing Diagrams that Define Master, Slave, and Location-Monitor Operation
(See Table 22 for Timing Values)

Mnemonic	Type of Cycles	Address Broadcast Timing Diagram	Data Transfer Timing Diagram
ADO	Address-Only	Fig 15	N/A
D08(EO)	Single-even-byte transfer		
	BYTE(0) READ	Figs 15 and 16	Fig 19
	BYTE(2) READ	Figs 15 and 16	Fig 19
	BYTE(0) WRITE	Figs 15 and 16	Fig 20
	BYTE(2) WRITE	Figs 15 and 16	Fig 20
D08(EO) or DO8(O)	Single-odd-byte transfers		
	BYTE(1) READ	Figs 15 and 16	Fig 19
	BYTE(3) READ	Figs 15 and 16	Fig 19
	BYTE(1) WRITE	Figs 15 and 16	Fig 21
	BYTE(3) WRITE	Figs 15 and 16	Fig 21
D16	Double-byte transfers		
	BYTE(0-1) READ	Figs 15 and 16	Fig 20
	BYTE(2-3) READ	Figs 15 and 16	Fig 20
	BYTE(0-1) WRITE	Figs 15 and 16	Fig 22
	BYTE(2-3) WRITE	Figs 15 and 16	Fig 22
D32	Quad-byte transfers		
	BYTE(0-3) READ	Figs 15 and 16	Fig 20
	BYTE(0-3) WRITE	Figs 15 and 16	Fig 22

(*Continued on Page 85*)

reflection. The resulting setup time at the slave is the master's setup time less two bus propagation times.

A special notation was used to describe the data strobe timing. The two data strobes (DS0* and DS1*) do not always make their transitions simultaneously. For purposes of the timing diagrams, DSA* represents the first data strobe to make its transition (whether that is DS0* or DS1*). DSB* represents the second data strobe to make its transition (whether that is DS1* or DS0*). The broken line shown while the data strobes are stable is to indicate that the first data strobe to make a falling transition might not be the first to make its rising transition, that is, DSA* can represent DS0* on its falling edge and DS1* on its rising edge.

Table 17 *(Continued)*
Timing Diagrams that Define Master, Slave, and Location-Monitor Operation (See Table 22 for Timing Values)

Mnemonic	Type of Cycles	Address Broadcast Timing Diagram	Data Transfer Timing Diagram
D08(EO): BLT	Single-byte block transfers		
	SINGLE-BYTE BLOCK READ	Figs 15 and 17	Fig 19
	SINGLE-BYTE BLOCK WRITE	Figs 15 and 17	Fig 21
D16: BLT	Double-byte block transfers		
	DOUBLE-BYTE BLOCK READ	Figs 15 and 17	Fig 20
	DOUBLE-BYTE BLOCK WRITE	Figs 15 and 17	Fig 22
D32: BLT	Quad-byte block transfers		
	QUAD-BYTE BLOCK READ	Figs 15 and 17	Fig 20
	QUAD-BYTE BLOCK WRITE	Figs 15 and 17	Fig 22
D08(EO): RMW	Single-byte RMW transfers		
	BYTE(0) READ-MODIFY-WRITE	Figs 15 and 18	Fig 23
	BYTE(1) READ-MODIFY-WRITE	Figs 15 and 18	Fig 23
	BYTE(2) READ-MODIFY-WRITE	Figs 15 and 18	Fig 23
	BYTE(3) READ-MODIFY-WRITE	Figs 15 and 18	Fig 23
D16: RMW	Double-byte RMW transfers		
	BYTE(0-1) READ-MODIFY-WRITE	Figs 15 and 18	Fig 24
	BYTE(2-3) READ-MODIFY-WRITE	Figs 15 and 18	Fig 24
D32: RMW	Quad-Byte RMW transfers		
	BYTE(0-3) READ-MODIFY-WRITE	Figs 15 and 18	Fig 24
D32: UAT	Unaligned transfers		
	BYTE(0-2) READ	Figs 15 and 16	Fig 19
	BYTE(1-3) READ	Figs 15 and 16	Fig 19
	BYTE(1-2) READ	Figs 15 and 16	Fig 20
	BYTE(0-2) WRITE	Figs 15 and 16	Fig 21
	BYTE(1-3) WRITE	Figs 15 and 16	Fig 21
	BYTE(1-2) WRITE	Figs 15 and 16	Fig 22

Tables 19, 20, and 21 show how the various signal lines of the DTB are used to broadcast addresses and to transfer data. These tables are referenced by the various timing diagrams that follow. To keep these tables compact, mnemonics are used to describe when and how the various lines are driven. These mnemonics are defined in Table 18.

Table 18
Definitions of Mnemonics Used in Tables 19, 20, and 21

Mnemonic	Description	Comments
DVBM	Driven valid by master	**Rule 2.21** The master shall drive DVBM lines to a valid level.
DLBM	Driven low by master	**Rule 2.22** The master shall drive DLBM lines to a low level.
DHBM	Driven high by master	**Rule 2.23** The master shall drive DHBM lines to a high level.
dhbm?	Driven high by master?	**Permission 2.10** The master may drive dhbm? lines high. **Rule 2.24** The master shall not drive dhbm? lines low
dxbm?	Driven by master?	**Permission 2.11** The master may drive dxbm? lines, or it may leave these lines undriven. (When dxbm? lines are driven, they carry no valid information.)
DVBS	Driven valid by slave	**Rule 2.25** The responding slave shall drive DVBS lines to a valid level.
dxbs?	Driven by slave?	**Permission 2.12** The responding slave may drive dxbs? lines, or it may leave these lines undriven. (When dxbs? lines are driven, they carry no valid information.)
DVBB	Driven valid by both slave and master	**Rule 2.26** During the read portion of a read-modify-write cycle, the responding slave shall drive DVBB lines with valid data. During the write portion of a read-modify-write cycle, the master shall drive DVBB lines with valid data.
dxbb?	Driven by both slave and master?	**Permission 2.13** During the read portion of a read-modify-write cycle, the responding slave may drive dxbb? lines, or it may leave them undriven. During the write portion of a read-modify-write cycle, the master may drive dxbb? lines, or it may leave them undriven. (When dxbb? lines are driven they carry no valid information.)

Table 19
Use of the Address Lines to Select a 4-Byte Group

Mnemonic	Addressing Mode	A02-A15 See NOTE	A16-A23	A24-A31	IACK*
A16	SHORT	DVBM	dxbm?	dxbm?	dhbm?
A24	STANDARD	DVBM	DVBM	dxbm?	dhbm?
A32	EXTENDED	DVBM	DVBM	DVBM	dhbm?

NOTE: A01 is used in conjunction with LWORD*, DS0 and DS1 to select which of the four bytes within the 4-byte group is accessed (see Table 20).

Table 20
Use of DS1*, DS0*, A01, and LWORD* During the Various Cycles

Mnemonic	Type of Cycles	DS1*	DS0*	A01	LWORD*
ADO	ADDRESS-ONLY	dhbm?	dhbm?	dxbm?	dxbm?
D08(EO)	Single-even-byte transfers				
	BYTE(0) READ or WRITE	DLBM	dhbm?	DLBM	dhbm?
	BYTE(2) READ or WRITE	DLBM	dhbm?	DHBM	dhbm?
D08(EO) or D08(O)	Single-odd-byte transfers				
	BYTE(1) READ or WRITE	dhbm?	DLBM	DLBM	dhbm?
	BYTE(3) READ or WRITE	dhbm?	DLBM	DHBM	dhbm?
D16	Double-byte transfers				
	BYTE(0-1) READ or WRITE	DLBM	DLBM	DLBM	dhbm?
	BYTE(2-3) READ or WRITE	DLBM	DLBM	DHBM	dhbm?
D32	Quad-byte transfers				
	BYTE(0-3) READ or WRITE	DLBM	DLBM	DLBM	DLBM
D08(EO) :BLT	Single-byte block transfers				
	SINGLE-BYTE BLOCK READ or WRITE	——— NOTE (1) ———			dhbm?
D16:BLT	Double-byte block transfers				
	DOUBLE-BYTE BLOCK READ or WRITE	DLBM	DLBM	NOTE (2)	dhbm?
D32:BLT	Quad-byte block transfers				
	QUAD-BYTE BLOCK READ or WRITE	DLBM	DLBM	DLBM	DLBM
D08(EO) :RMW	Single-byte RMW transfers				
	BYTE(0) READ-MODIFY-WRITE	DLBM	dhbm?	DLBM	dhbm?
	BYTE(1) READ-MODIFY-WRITE	dhbm?	DLBM	DLBM	dhbm?
	BYTE(2) READ-MODIFY-WRITE	DLBM	dhbm?	DHBM	dhbm?
	BYTE(3) READ-MODIFY-WRITE	dhbm?	DLBM	DHBM	dhbm?
D16:RMW	Double-byte RMW transfers				
	BYTE(0-1) READ-MODIFY-WRITE	DLBM	DLBM	DLBM	dhbm?
	BYTE(2-3) READ-MODIFY-WRITE	DLBM	DLBM	DHBM	dhbm?
D32:RMW	Quad-byte RMW transfers				
	BYTE(0-3) READ-MODIFY-WRITE	DLBM	DLBM	DLBM	DLBM

Table 20 (*Continued*)
Use of DS1*, DS0*, A01, and LWORD* During the Various Cycles

Mnemonic	Type of Cycles	DS1*	DS0*	A01	LWORD*
D32:UAT	Unaligned transfers				
	BYTE(0-2) READ or WRITE	DLBM	dhbm?	DLBM	DLBM
	BYTE(1-3) READ or WRITE	dhbm?	DLBM	DLBM	DLBM
	BYTE(1-2) READ or WRITE	DLBM	DLBM	DHBM	DLBM

NOTES: (1) During single-byte block transfers, the two data strobes are alternately driven low. Either data strobe might be driven low on the first transfer. If the first accessed byte location is BYTE(0) or BYTE(2), then the master drives DS1* low first. If the first accessed byte location is BYTE(1) or BYTE(3), then it drives DS0* low first. A01 is valid only on the first data transfer (that is, until the slave drives DTACK* or BERR* low the first time) and might be either high or low depending upon which byte the single byte block transfer begins with. If the first byte location is BYTE(0) or BYTE(1), then the master drives A01 to low. If the first byte location is BYTE(2) or BYTE(3), then the master drives A01 to high.

An example of the use of DS0*, DS1*, A01, and LWORD* during a single-byte block transfer cycle that starts with BYTE(2) is given below.

		DS1*	DS0*	A01	LWORD*
First data transfer	BYTE(2)	DLBM	DHBM	DHBM	dhbm?
↓	BYTE(3)	DHBM	DLBM	dxbm?	dxbm?
	BYTE(0)	DLBM	DHBM	dxbm?	dxbm?
	BYTE(1)	DHBM	DLBM	dxbm?	dxbm?
Last data transfer	BYTE(2)	DLBM	DHBM	dxbm?	dxbm?

(2) During a double-byte block transfer, A01 is valid only on the first data transfer (that is, until the slave drives DTACK* or BERR* low the first time) and is driven either high or low depending upon what double-byte group the double-byte block transfer begins with. If the first double-byte group is BYTE(0-1), then the master drives A01 low. If the first double-byte group is BYTE(2-3), then the master drives A01 high.

Table 21
Use of the Data Lines to Transfer Data

Mnemonic	Type of Cycles	D24-D31	D16-D23	D08-D15	D00-D07
ADO	ADDRESS-ONLY	dxbm?	dxbm?	dxbm?	dxbm?
D08(EO)	Single-even-byte transfers				
	BYTE(0) READ	dxbs?	dxbs?	DVBS	dxbs?
	BYTE(2) READ	dxbs?	dxbs?	DVBS	dxbs?
	BYTE(0) WRITE	dxbm?	dxbm?	DVBM	dxbm?
	BYTE(2) WRITE	dxbm?	dxbm?	DVBM	dxbm?
D08(EO) or D08(O)	Single-odd-byte transfers				
	BYTE(1) READ	dxbs?	dxbs?	dxbs?	DVBS
	BYTE(3) READ	dxbs?	dxbs?	dxbs?	DVBS
	BYTE(1) WRITE	dxbm?	dxbm?	dxbm?	DVBM
	BYTE(3) WRITE	dxbm?	dxbm?	dxbm?	DVBM
D16	Double-byte transfers				
	BYTE(0-1) READ	dxbs?	dxbs?	DVBS	DVBS
	BYTE(2-3) READ	dxbs?	dxbs?	DVBS	DVBS
	BYTE(0-1) WRITE	dxbm?	dxbm?	DVBM	DVBM
	BYTE(2-3) WRITE	dxbm?	dxbm?	DVBM	DVBM
D32	Quad-byte transfers				
	BYTE(0-3) READ	DVBS	DVBS	DVBS	DVBS
	BYTE(0-3) WRITE	DVBM	DVBM	DVBM	DVBM
D08(EO):BLT	Single-byte block transfers				
	SINGLE-BYTE BLOCK READ	dxbs?	dxbs?	— See NOTE —	
	SINGLE-BYTE BLOCK WRITE	dxbm?	dxbm?	— See NOTE —	
D16:BLT	Double-byte block transfers				
	DOUBLE-BYTE BLOCK READ	dxbs?	dxbs?	DVBS	DVBS
	DOUBLE-BYTE BLOCK WRITE	dxbm?	dxbm?	DVBM	DVBM
D32:BLT	Quad-byte block transfers				
	QUAD-BYTE BLOCK READ	DVBS	DVBS	DVBS	DVBS
	QUAD-BYTE BLOCK WRITE	DVBM	DVBM	DVBM	DVBM
D08(EO):RMW	Single-byte RMW transfers				
	BYTE(0) READ-MODIFY-WRITE	dxbb?	dxbb?	DVBB	dxbb?
	BYTE(1) READ-MODIFY-WRITE	dxbb?	dxbb?	dxbb?	DVBB
	BYTE(2) READ-MODIFY-WRITE	dxbb?	dxbb?	DVBB	dxbb?
	BYTE(3) READ-MODIFY-WRITE	dxbb?	dxbb?	dxbb?	DVBB

Table 21 (*Continued*)
Use of the Data Lines to Transfer Data

Mnemonic	Type of Cycles	D24-D31	D16-D23	D08-D15	D00-D07
D16:RMW	Double-byte RMW transfers				
	BYTE(0-1) READ-MODIFY-WRITE	dxbb?	dxbb?	DVBB	DVBB
	BYTE(2-3) READ-MODIFY-WRITE	dxbb?	dxbb?	DVBB	DVBB
D32:RMW	Quad-byte RMW transfers				
	BYTE(0-3) READ-MODIFY-WRITE	DVBB	DVBB	DVBB	DVBB
D32:UAT	Unaligned transfers				
	BYTE(0-2) READ	DVBS	DVBS	DVBS	dxbs?
	BYTE(1-3) READ	dxbs?	DVBS	DVBS	DVBS
	BYTE(1-2) READ	dxbs?	DVBS	DVBS	dxbs?
	BYTE(0-2) WRITE	DVBM	DVBM	DVBM	dxbm?
	BYTE(1-3) WRITE	dxbm?	DVBM	DVBM	DVBM
	BYTE(1-2) WRITE	dxbm?	DVBM	DVBM	dxbm?

NOTE: During single-byte block transfers, data is transferred 8 bits at a time over D00-D07 or D08-D15. A single-byte block read example is given below:

	D08-D15	D00-D07
First data transfer	DVBS	dxbs?
	dxbs?	DVBS
	DVBS	dxbs?
	dxbs?	DVBS
	DVBS	dxbs?
↓	dxbs?	DVBS
Last data transfer	DVBS	dxbs?

Table 22
Master, Slave, and Location-Monitor Timing Parameters

Parameter Number	Master (See also Table 24)		Slave (See also Table 25)		Location Monitor (See also Table 25)	
	min	max	min	max	min	max
1	0					
2	0					
3	60					
4	35		10		10	
5	40		30		30	
6	0		0			
7	0		0			
8	35		10			
9	0		0			
10	0		-10		-10	
11	40		30		30	
12	35		10		10	
13		10		20		20
14	0		0			
15	0		0			
16	0		0			
17	40		30		30	
18	0		0			
19	40		30		30	
20	0		0			
21	0		0			
22	0		0			
23	10		0		0	
24A	0					
24B	0					
25		25				
26	0		0			
27	-25		0			
28	30	2T	30			
29	0		0			
30	0		0			
31	0		0			
32			10		10	
33			30		30	

NOTES: (1) All times are in nanoseconds (2) T = time-out value, microseconds

Table 23
Bus-Timer Timing Parameters

Parameter Number	Bus Timer	
	min	max
28	T	2T
30	0	

NOTE: T = time-out value, microseconds
See also Table 27

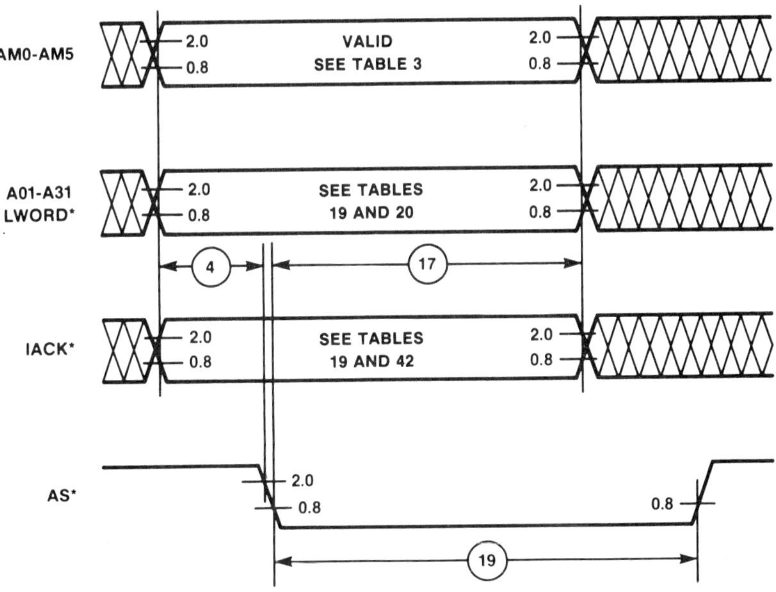

Parameter Number	Master min	Master max	Slave min	Slave max	Location Monitor min	Location Monitor max
4	35		10		10	
17	40		30		30	
19	40		30		30	

NOTE: All times are in nanoseconds

Fig 15
Address Broadcast Timing
All Cycles

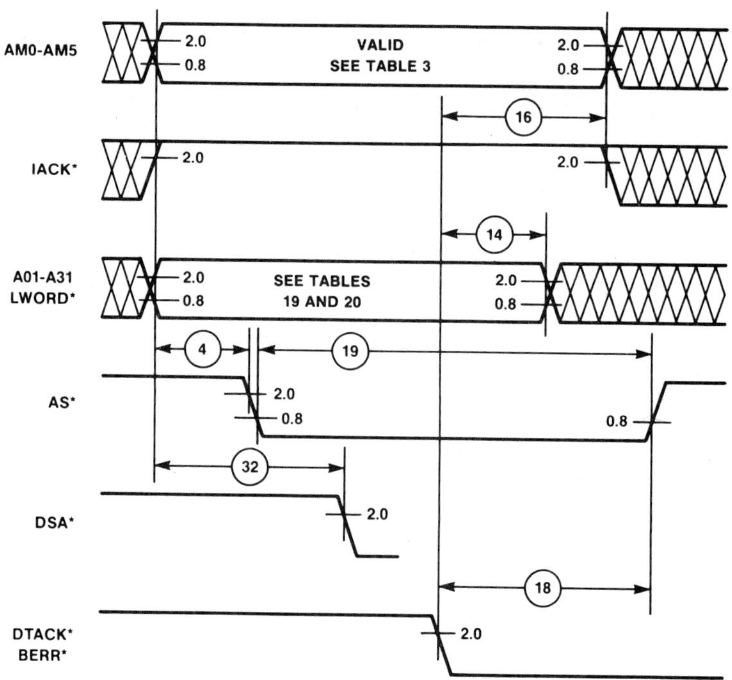

Parameter Number	Master min	Master max	Slave min	Slave max	Location Monitor min	Location Monitor max
4	35		10		10	
14	0		0			
16	0		0			
18	0		0			
19	40		30		30	
32			10		10	

NOTE: All times are in nanoseconds

Fig 16
Master, Slave, and Location Monitor — Address Broadcast Timing Single-Even-Byte Transfers, Single-Odd-Byte Transfers, Double-Byte Transfers,Quad-Byte Transfers, Unaligned Transfers

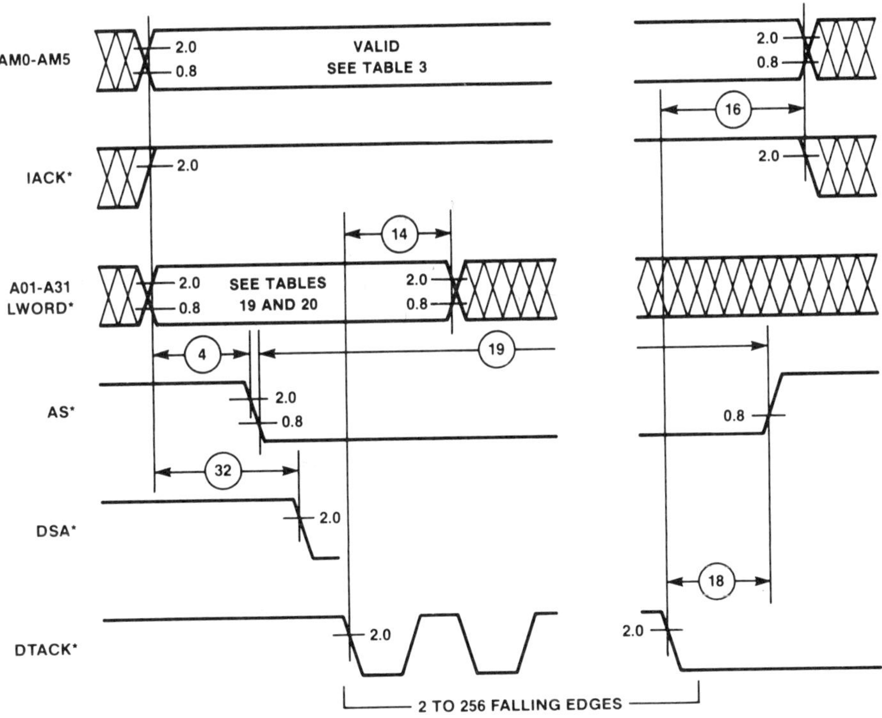

Parameter Number	Master min	Master max	Slave min	Slave max	Location Monitor min	Location Monitor max
4	35		10		10	
14	0		0			
16	0		0			
18	0		0			
19	40		30		30	
32			10		10	

NOTE: All times are in nanoseconds

Fig 17
Master, Slave, and Location Monitor — Address Broadcast Timing Single-Byte Block Transfers, Double-Byte Block Transfers, Quad-Byte Block Transfers

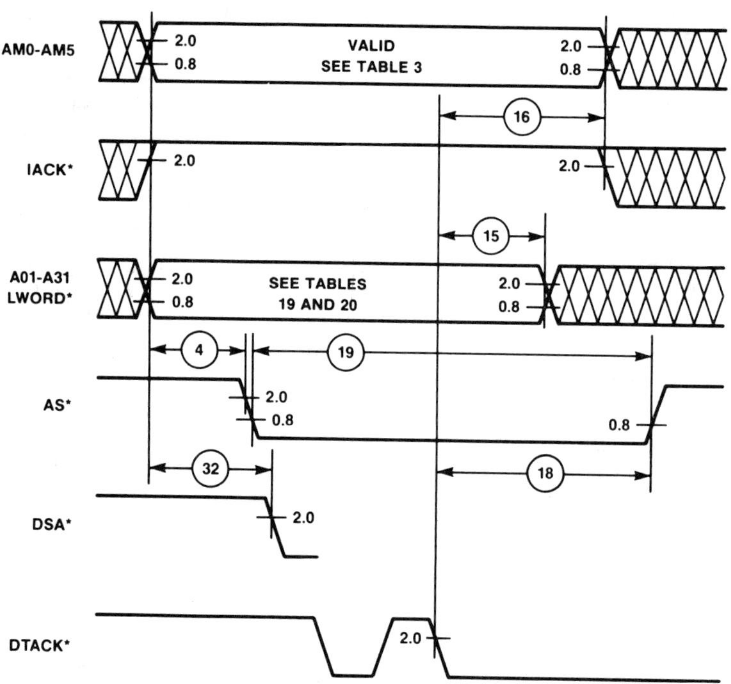

Parameter Number	Master min	Master max	Slave min	Slave max	Location Monitor min	Location Monitor max
4	35		10		10	
15	0		0			
16	0		0			
18	0		0			
19	40		30		30	
32			10		10	

NOTE: All times are in nanoseconds

Fig 18
Master, Slave, and Location Monitor — Address Broadcast Timing Single-Byte RMW Cycles, Double-Byte RMW Cycles, Quad-Byte RMW Cycles

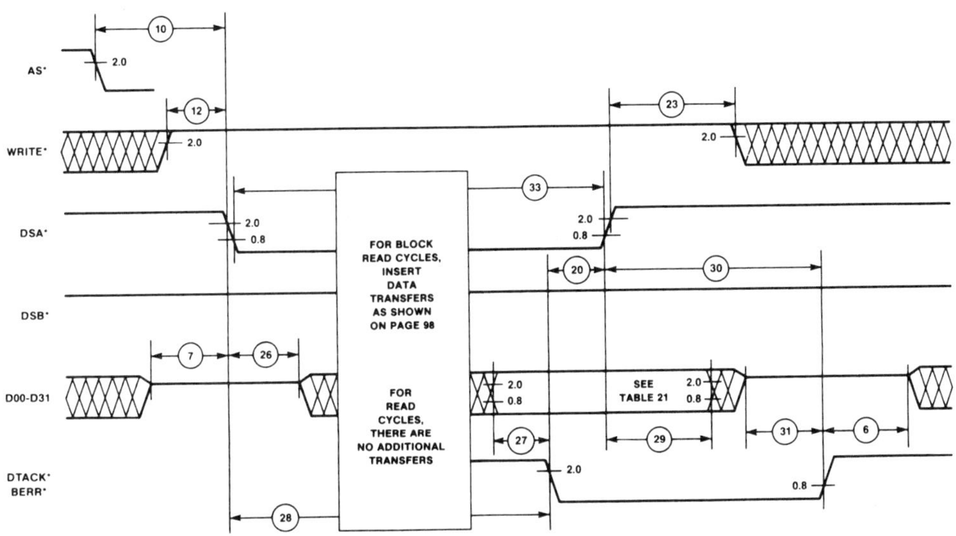

Parameter Number	Master min	Master max	Slave min	Slave max	Location Monitor min	Location Monitor max
6	0		0			
7	0		0			
10	0		-10		-10	
12	35		10		10	
20	0		0			
23	10		0		0	
26	0		0			
27	-25		0			
28	30	2T	30			
29	0		0			
30	0		0			
31	0		0			
33			30		30	

NOTES: (1) All times are in nanoseconds
(2) T = time-out value, microseconds

Fig 19
Master, Slave, and Location Monitor — Data Transfer Timing
BYTE(0) READ, BYTE(1) READ, BYTE(2) READ, BYTE(3) READ
BYTE(0-2) READ, BYTE(1-3) READ, SINGLE-BYTE BLOCK READ

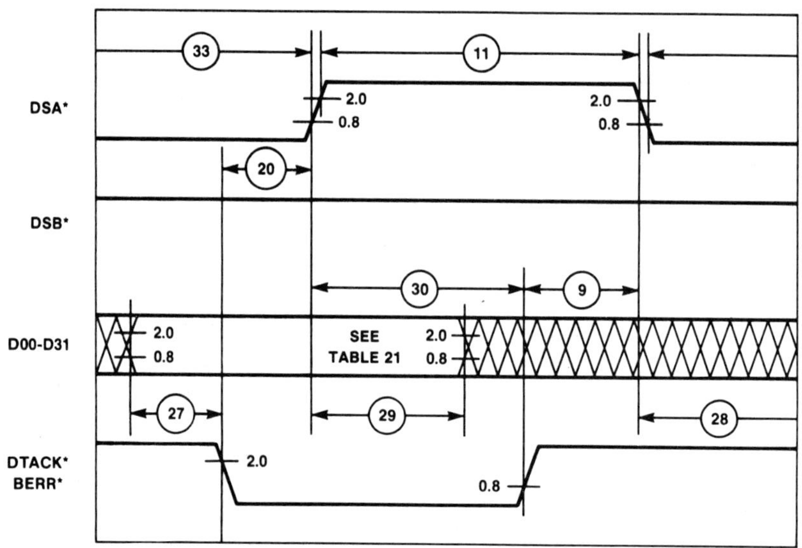

Parameter Number	Master min	Master max	Slave min	Slave max	Location Monitor min	Location Monitor max
9	0		0			
11	40		30		30	
20	0		0			
27	-25		0			
28	30	2T	30			
29	0		0			
30	0		0			
33			30		30	

NOTES: (1) All times are in nanoseconds
(2) T = time-out value, microseconds

Fig 19 (*Continued*)
Master, Slave, and Location Monitor — Data Transfer Timing BYTE(0) READ, BYTE(1) READ, BYTE(2) READ, BYTE(3) READ BYTE(0-2) READ, BYTE(1-3) READ, SINGLE-BYTE BLOCK READ

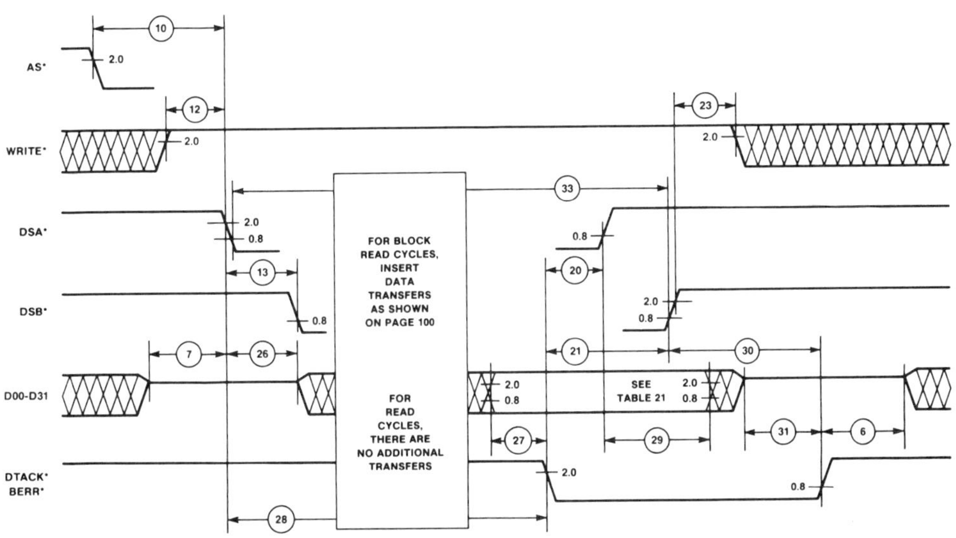

Parameter Number	Master min	Master max	Slave min	Slave max	Location Monitor min	Location Monitor max
6	0		0			
7	0		0			
10	0		-10		-10	
12	35		10		10	
13		10		20		20
20	0		0			
21	0		0			
23	10		0		0	
26	0		0			
27	-25		0			
28	30	2T	30			
29	0		0			
30	0		0			
31	0		0			
33			30		30	

NOTES: (1) All times are in nanoseconds
(2) T = time-out value, microseconds

Fig 20
Master, Slave, and Location Monitor — Data Transfer Timing
BYTE(0-1) READ, BYTE(2-3) READ, BYTE(0-3) READ, BYTE(1-2) READ
DOUBLE-BYTE BLOCK READ, QUAD-BYTE BLOCK READ

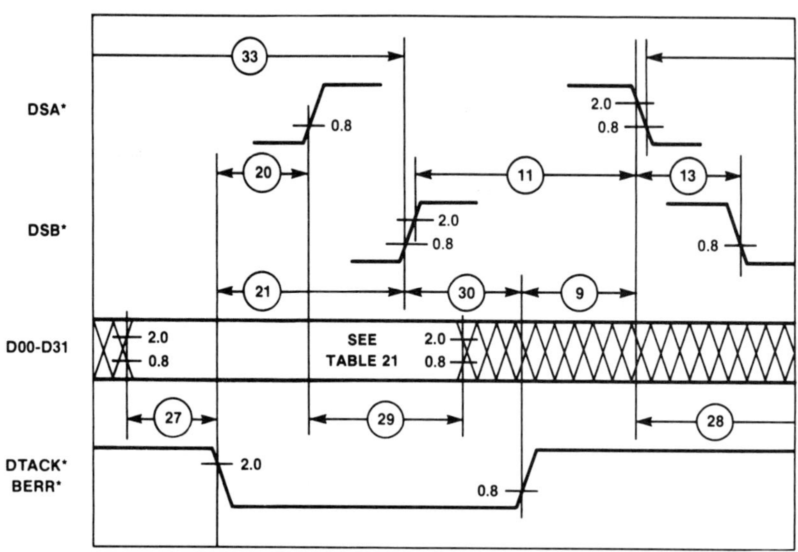

Parameter Number	Master min	Master max	Slave min	Slave max	Location Monitor min	Location Monitor max
9	0		0			
11	40		30		30	
13		10		20		20
20	0		0			
21	0		0			
27	-25		0			
28	30	2T	30			
29	0		0			
30	0		0			
33			30		30	

NOTES: (1) All times are in nanoseconds
(2) T = time-out value, microseconds

Fig 20 (*Continued*)
Master, Slave, and Location Monitor — Data Transfer Timing
BYTE(0-1) READ, BYTE(2-3) READ, BYTE(0-3) READ, BYTE(1-2) READ
DOUBLE-BYTE BLOCK READ, QUAD-BYTE BLOCK READ

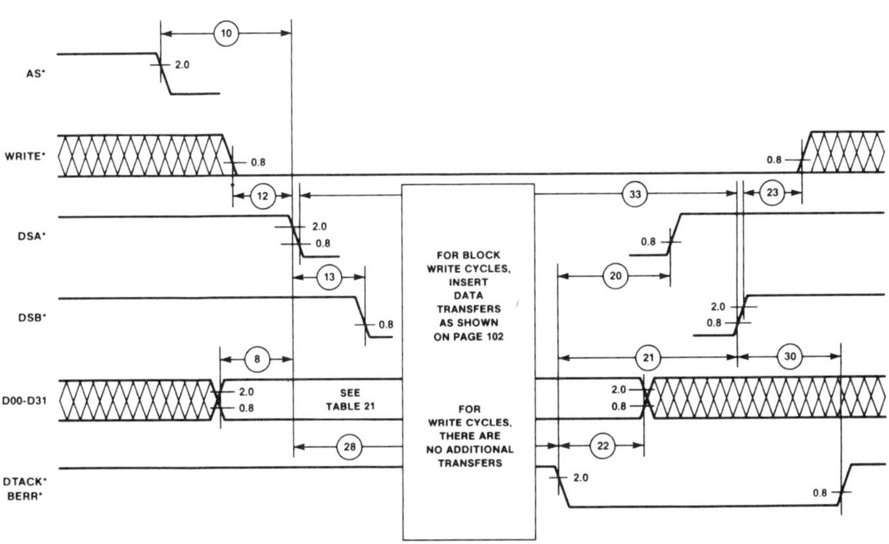

Parameter Number	Master min	Master max	Slave min	Slave max	Location Monitor min	Location Monitor max
8	35		10			
10	0		-10		-10	
12	35		10		10	
20	0		0			
22	0		0			
23	10		0		0	
28	30	2T	30			
30	0		0			
33			30		30	

NOTES: (1) All times are in nanoseconds
(2) T = time-out value, microseconds

Fig 21
Master, Slave, and Location Monitor — Data Transfer Timing
BYTE(0) WRITE, BYTE(1) WRITE, BYTE(2) WRITE, BYTE(3) WRITE
BYTE(0-2) WRITE, BYTE(1-3) WRITE, SINGLE-BYTE BLOCK WRITE

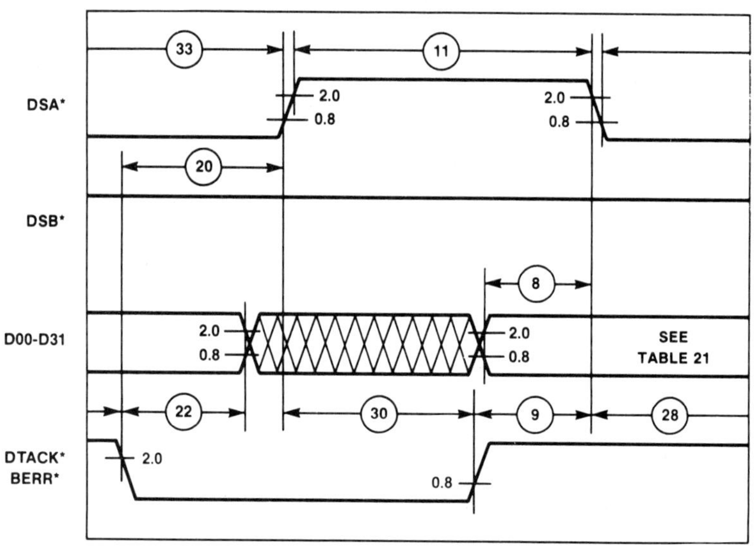

Parameter Number	Master min	Master max	Slave min	Slave max	Location Monitor min	Location Monitor max
8	35		10			
9	0		0			
11	40		30		30	
20	0		0			
22	0		0			
28	30	2T	30			
30	0		0			
33			30		30	

NOTES: (1) All times are in nanoseconds
(2) T = time-out value, microseconds

Fig 21 (*Continued*)
Master, Slave, and Location Monitor — Data Transfer Timing BYTE(0) WRITE, BYTE(1) WRITE, BYTE(2) WRITE, BYTE(3) WRITE BYTE(0-2) WRITE, BYTE(1-3) WRITE, SINGLE-BYTE BLOCK WRITE

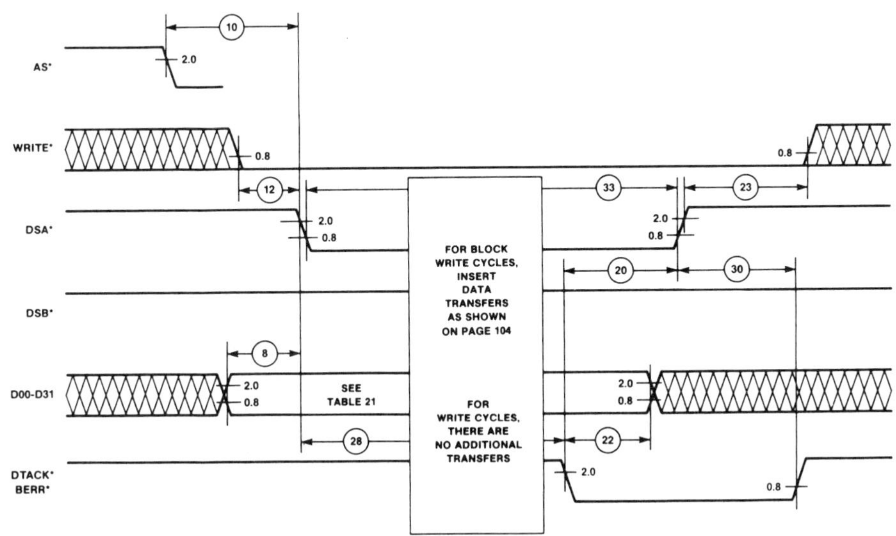

Parameter Number	Master min	Master max	Slave min	Slave max	Location Monitor min	Location Monitor max
8	35		10			
10	0		-10		-10	
12	35		10		10	
13		10		20		20
20	0		0			
21	0		0			
22	0		0			
23	10		0		0	
28	30	2T	30			
30	0		0			
33			30		30	

NOTES: (1) All times are in nanoseconds
T = time-out value, microseconds

Fig 22
Master, Slave, and Location Monitor — Data Transfer Timing BYTE(0-1) WRITE, BYTE(2-3) WRITE, BYTE(0-3) WRITE, BYTE(1-2) WRITE DOUBLE-BYTE BLOCK WRITE, QUAD-BYTE BLOCK WRITE

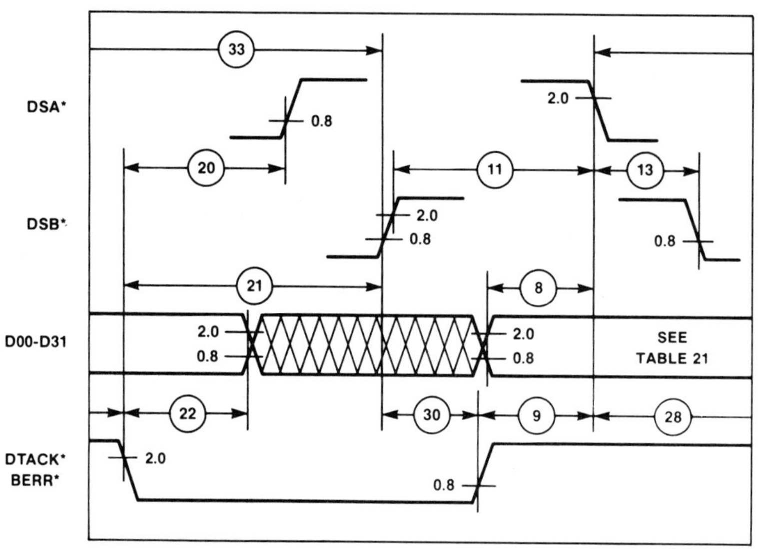

Parameter Number	Master min	Master max	Slave min	Slave max	Location Monitor min	Location Monitor max
8	35		10			
9	0		0			
11	40		30		30	
13		10		20		20
20	0		0			
21	0		0			
22	0		0			
28	30	2T	30			
30	0		0			
33			30		30	

NOTES: (1) All times are in nanoseconds
(2) T = time-out value, microseconds

Fig 22 (*Continued*)
Master, Slave, and Location Monitor — Data Transfer Timing BYTE(0-1) WRITE, BYTE(2-3) WRITE, BYTE(0-3) WRITE, BYTE(1-2) WRITE DOUBLE-BYTE BLOCK WRITE, QUAD-BYTE BLOCK WRITE

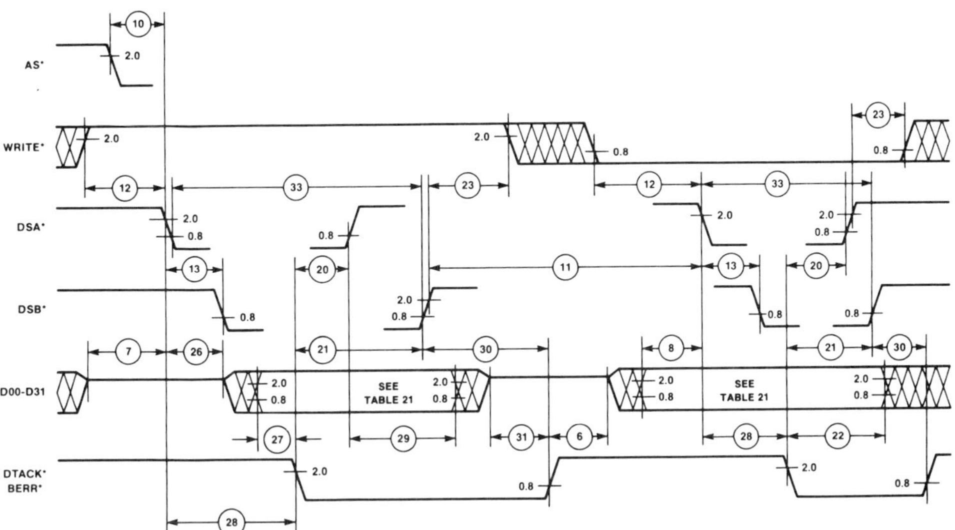

Parameter Number	Master min	Master max	Slave min	Slave max	Location Monitor min	Location Monitor max
6	0		0			
7	0		0			
8	35		10			
10	0		-10		-10	
11	40		30		30	
12	35		10		10	
20	0		0			
22	0		0			
23	10		0		0	
26	0		0			
27	-25		0			
28	30	2T	30			
29	0		0			
30	0		0			
31	0		0			
33			30		30	

NOTES: (1) All times are in nanoseconds
(2) T = time-out value, microseconds

Fig 23
Master, Slave, and Location Monitor Data Transfer Timing Single-Byte RMW Cycles

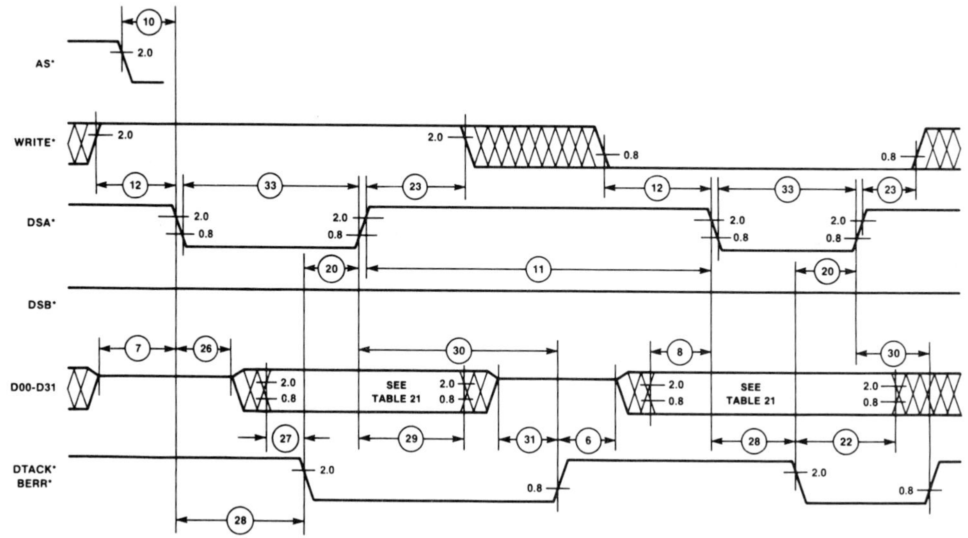

Parameter Number	Master min	Master max	Slave min	Slave max	Location Monitor min	Location Monitor max
6	0		0			
7	0		0			
8	35		10			
10	0		-10		-10	
11	40		30		30	
12	35		10		10	
13		10		20		20
20	0		0			
21	0		0			
22	0		0			
23	10		0		0	
26	0		0			
27	-25		0			
28	30	2T	30			
29	0		0			
30	0		0			
31	0		0			
33			30		30	

NOTES: (1) All times are in nanoseconds
(2) T = time-out value, microseconds

Fig 24
Master, Slave, and Location Monitor — Data Transfer Timing Double-Byte RMW Cycles, Quad-Byte RMW Cycles

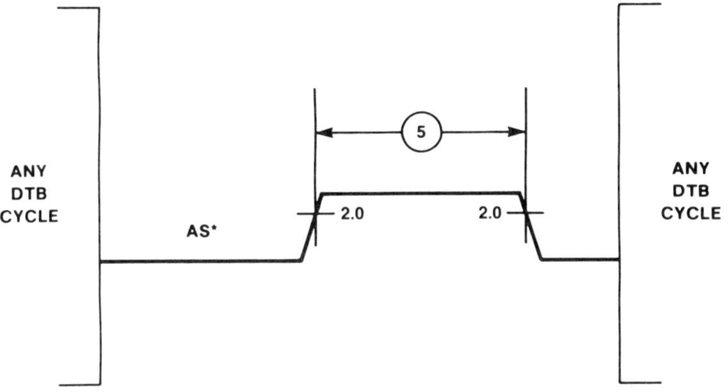

Parameter Number	Master min	Master max	Slave min	Slave max	Location Monitor min	Location Monitor max
5	40		30		30	

NOTE: All times are in nanoseconds

Fig 25
Address Strobe Inter-Cycle Timing

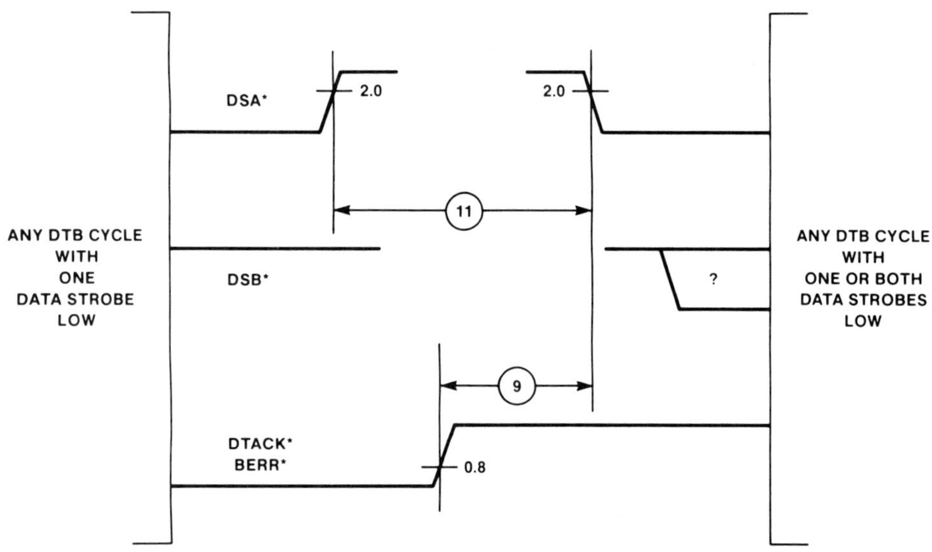

A cycle where both data strobes go low followed by a cycle where one or both data strobes go low.

Parameter Number	Master min	Master max	Slave min	Slave max	Location Monitor min	Location Monitor max
9	0		0			
11	40		30		30	

NOTE: All times are in nanoseconds

Fig 26
Data Strobe Inter-Cycle Timing

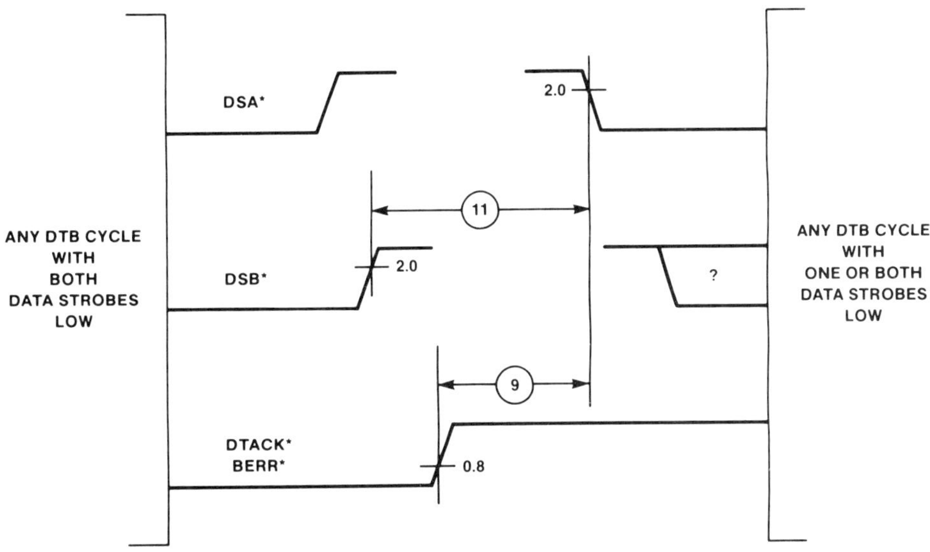

A cycle where one data strobe goes low followed by a cycle where one or both data strobes go low.

Parameter Number	Master min	Master max	Slave min	Slave max	Location Monitor min	Location Monitor max
9	0		0			
11	40		30		30	

NOTE: All times are in nanoseconds

Fig 27
Data Strobe Inter-Cycle Timing

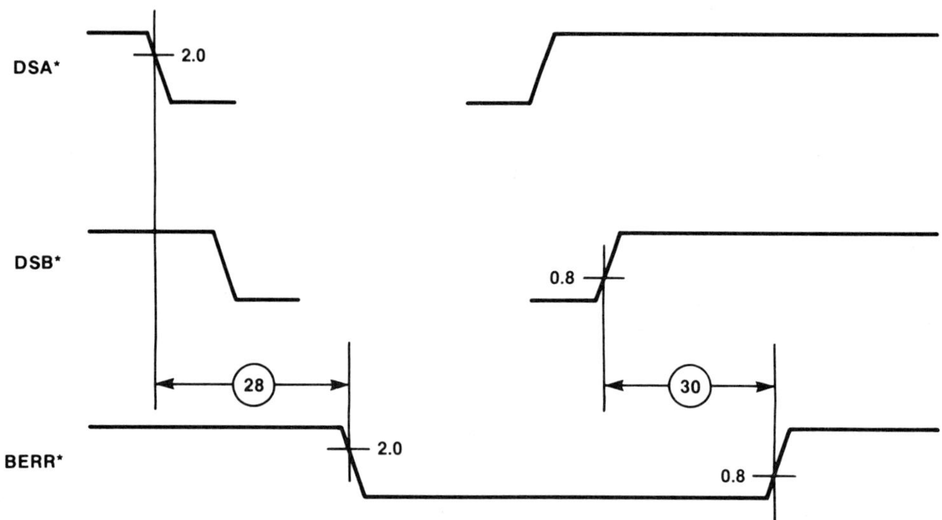

Parameter Number	Master min	Master max	Slave min	Slave max	Location Monitor min	Location Monitor max
28	30	2T	30			
30	0		0			

NOTES: (1) All times are in nanoseconds
(2) T = time-out value, microseconds

Fig 28
Master, Slave, and Bus Timer — Data Transfer Timing
Timed-Out Cycle

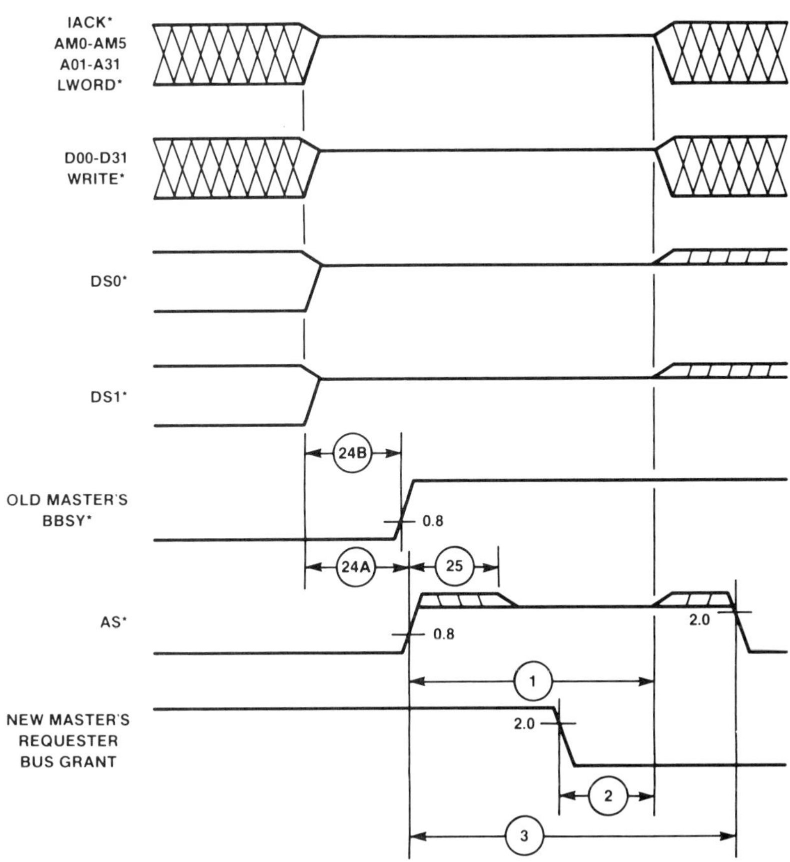

Parameter Number	Master min	Master max	Slave min	Slave max	Location Monitor min	Location Monitor max
1	0					
2	0					
3	60					
24A	0					
24B	0					
25		25				

NOTE: All times are in nanoseconds

Fig 29
Master — DTB Control Transfer Timing

Table 24
Master, Timing Rules and Observations

Timing Parameters Specified in Table 22	Rules and Observations
1	**Rule 2.27** When taking control of the DTB, the master shall not drive any of IACK*, AM0-AM5, A01-A31, LWORD*, D00-D31, WRITE*, DS0*, DS1*, or AS* until after the previous master allows AS* to rise above the low level.
	Observation 2.35 Section 3 describes how a master's requester is granted use of the DTB.
2	**Rule 2.28** When taking control of the DTB, the master shall not drive any of IACK*, AM0-AM5, A01-A31, LWORD*, D00-D31, WRITE*, DS0*, DS1*, or AS* until after its requester is granted the bus.
	Observation 2.36 Section 3 describes how a master's requester is granted use of the DTB.
3	**Rule 2.29** When taking control of the DTB, the master shall not drive AS* low until this time after the previous master allows AS* to rise above the low level.
	Observation 2.37 Rule 2.29 ensures that timing parameter 5 for slaves is guaranteed when there is an interchange of the DTB mastership.
4	**Rule 2.30** The master shall not drive AS* low until IACK* has been high, and the required lines among A01-A31, AM0-AM5, and LWORD* have been valid for this minimum time.
	Observation 2.38 Table 19 specifies the lines among A01-A31 that the master is required to drive. Table 3 specifies how it uses AM0-AM5, and Table 20 how it uses LWORD*.
5	**Rule 2.31** When using the DTB for two consecutive cycles, the master shall not drive AS* low until it has been high for this minimum time.
6	**Rule 2.32** After a read cycle, the master shall not drive any of D00-D31 until both DTACK* and BERR* are high.
7	**Rule 2.33** During read cycles, the master shall not drive DSA* low until it has released all of D00-D31.
8	**Rule 2.34** During write cycles, the master shall not drive DSA* low until the required lines among D00-D31 have been valid for this minimum time.
	Observation 2.39 Table 21 specifies the lines among D00-D31 that a master is required to drive.
9	**Rule 2.35** The master shall not drive DSA* low until both DTACK* and BERR* are high.

Table 24 (*Continued*)
Master, Timing Rules and Observations

Timing Parameters Specified in Table 22	Rules and Observations
10	**Rule 2.36** The master shall not drive DSA* low until it has driven AS* low.
11	**Rule 2.37** The master shall not drive DSA* low until DS0* and DS1* have both been simultaneously high for this minimum time.
12	**Rule 2.38** The master shall not drive DSA* low until WRITE* has been valid for this minimum time.
13	**Rule 2.39** During cycles where the master drives both DS0* and DS1* low, it shall drive DSB* low within this maximum time after it drives DSA* low.
	Observation 2.40 Timing parameter 13 does not apply to transfers where either DS0* or DS1* is driven low, but not both.
14	**Rule 2.40** During all data transfer cycles, except read-modify-write cycles, the master shall hold A01-A31 valid and maintain the appropriate level on LWORD* until it detects the first falling edge on DTACK* or BERR*.
	Observation 2.41 During all data transfer cycles, except block transfer and read-modify-write cycles, there will be only one falling edge on DTACK* or BERR*.
15	**Rule 2.41** During read-modify-write cycles, the master shall hold A01-A31 valid and maintain the appropriate level on LWORD* until it detects the second falling edge on DTACK* or BERR*.
16	**Rule 2.42** During all data transfer cycles, the master shall maintain a valid AM code, and ensure that IACK* stays high until it detects the last falling edge on DTACK* or BERR*.
	Observation 2.42 During all data transfer cycles, except block transfer and read-modify-write cycles, there will be only one falling edge on DTACK* or BERR*.
17	**Rule 2.43** The master shall not change the levels on IACK*, A01-A31, AM0-AM5, or LWORD* for this minimum time after it drives AS* low.
18	**Rule 2.44** During all data transfer cycles, the master shall hold AS* low until it detects the last falling edge on DTACK* or BERR*.
19	**Rule 2.45** The master shall hold AS* low for this minimum time.
20	**Rule 2.46** Once a master has driven DSA* low, it shall maintain that line low until it detects DTACK* or BERR* low.
21	**Rule 2.47** Once a master has driven DSB* low, it shall maintain that line low until it detects DTACK* or BERR* low.

Table 24 (*Continued*)
Master, Timing Rules and Observations

Timing Parameters Specified in Table 22	Rules and Observations
22	**Rule 2.48** During write cycles, once the master has driven DSA* low, it shall not change any of D00-D31 until it detects DTACK* or BERR* low.
23	**Rule 2.49** Once a master has driven DSA* low, it shall not change the level of the WRITE* line until this minimum time after both DS0* and DS1* are high.
24A	**Rule 2.50** When the master drives or releases AS* high after its requester releases BBSY*, then it shall release IACK*, AM0-AM5, A01-A31, LWORD*, D00-D31, WRITE*, DS0*, and DS1* before allowing AS* to rise above the low level.
	Observation 2.43 Section 3 describes how a master's requester releases the BBSY* line.
24B	**Rule 2.51** When the master drives or releases AS* high before its requester releases BBSY*, then it shall release AS*, IACK*, AM0-AM5, A01-A31, LWORD*, D00-D31, WRITE*, DS0*, and DS1* before allowing its requester to release BBSY*.
	Observation 2.44 Section 3 describes how a master's requester releases the BBSY* line.
25	**Rule 2.52** When the master drives or releases AS* high after its requester releases BBSY*, then it shall release AS* within this time after allowing it to rise above the low level.
	Observation 2.45 Section 3 describes how a master's requester releases the BBSY* line.
26	**Observation 2.46** Timing parameter 26 guarantees that during read cycles, the data bus will not be driven until the master drives DSA* low.
27	**Observation 2.47** During read cycles, the master is guaranteed that the data bus will be valid within this time after DTACK* goes low. This time does not apply to cycles where the slave drives BERR* low instead of DTACK*.
28	**Observation 2.48** The master is guaranteed that neither DTACK* nor BERR* will go low until this minimum time after it drives DSA* low. The bus timer guarantees the master that if DTACK* is not detected low after its time-out period has elapsed, and within twice its time-out period, then the bus timer will drive BERR* low.
29	**Observation 2.49** During read cycles, the master is guaranteed that the data bus will remain valid until it drives DSA* high.
30	**Observation 2.50** Timing parameter 30 guarantees that neither DTACK* nor BERR* will go high until the master drives both DS0* and DS1* high.
31	**Observation 2.51** During read cycles, the master is guaranteed that the data bus has been released by the time DTACK* and BERR* are high.

Table 25
Slave, Timing Rules and Regulations

Timing Parameters Specified in Table 22	Rules and Regulations
4	**Observation 2.52** All slaves are guaranteed that IACK*, A01-A31, AM0-AM5, and LWORD* have been valid for this minimum time when they detect a falling edge on AS*.
5	**Observation 2.53** All slaves are guaranteed this minimum high time on AS* between DTB cycles.
6	**Observation 2.54** During read cycles, the responding slave is guaranteed that none of D00-D31 will be driven by any other module until the responding slave releases DTACK* and BERR* to high.
7	**Observation 2.55** During read cycles, the responding slave is guaranteed that the data bus will be released by all other modules by the time DSA* goes low.
8	**Observation 2.56** During write cycles, the responding slave is guaranteed that the data bus has been valid for this minimum time when it detects a falling edge on DSA*.
9	**Observation 2.57** The responding slave is guaranteed that neither DS0* nor DS1* will go low until DTACK* and BERR* from the previous cycle have gone high.
10	**Observation 2.58** Due to bus skew, slaves on the DTB might detect a falling edge on DSA* before detecting the falling edge on AS*. However, slaves are guaranteed that a falling edge on DSA* will not precede the falling edge on AS* by more than this time.
11	**Observation 2.59** Slaves are guaranteed this minimum time during which both DS0* and DS1* are simultaneously high between consecutive data transfers.
12	**Observation 2.60** Slaves are guaranteed that WRITE* has been valid for this minimum time before a falling edge on DSA*.
13	**Observation 2.61** When the master drives both DS0* and DS1* low, then the responding slave is guaranteed that DSB* will go low within this maximum time after DSA* has gone low.
14	**Observation 2.62** During all data transfer cycles except read-modify-write cycles, the responding slave is guaranteed that A01-A31 and LWORD* remain valid until it drives DTACK* or BERR* low for the first time, provided that it does so within the bus time-out period.
15	**Observation 2.63** During all read-modify-write cycles, the responding SLAVE is guaranteed that A01-A31 and LWORD* remain valid until it drives DTACK* or BERR* low for the second time, provided that it does so within the bus time-out period.

Table 25 (*Continued*)
Slave, Timing Rules and Regulations

Timing Parameters Specified in Table 22	Rules and Regulations
16	**Observation 2.64** The responding slave is guaranteed that IACK* and AM0-AM5 remain valid until it drives DTACK* or BERR* low for the last time, provided that it does so within the bus time-out period.
17	**Observation 2.65** Slaves are guaranteed that IACK*, A01-A31, AM0-AM5, and LWORD* will remain valid for this minimum time after the falling edge of AS*. During address-only cycles this time is guaranteed by the master. During all other cycle types, this time is derived from timing parameters 10, 14, 16, and 28.
18	**Observation 2.66** The responding slave is guaranteed that AS* will remain low until it drives DTACK* or BERR* low, provided that it does so within the bus time-out period.
19	**Observation 2.67** Slaves are guaranteed that the AS* will remain low for this minimum time.
20	**Observation 2.68** The responding slave is guaranteed that once DSA* goes low, it will remain low until it drives DTACK* or BERR* low, provided that it does so within the bus time-out period.
21	**Observation 2.69** The responding slave is guaranteed that once DSB* goes low, it will remain low until it drives DTACK* or BERR* low, provided that the slave does so within the bus time-out period.
22	**Observation 2.70** During write cycles, the responding slave is guaranteed that the data bus will remain valid until it drives DTACK* or BERR* low, provided that it does so within the bus time-out period.
23	**Observation 2.71** The responding slave is guaranteed that the WRITE* line remains valid until both data strobes are high.
26	**Rule 2.53** During read cycles, the responding slave shall not drive the data bus until DSA* goes low.
27	**Rule 2.54** During read cycles, the responding slave shall not drive DTACK* before it drives the data lines with valid data.
	Observation 2.72 Rule 2.54 does not apply to cycles where the responding slave drives BERR* low instead of DTACK*.
28	**Rule 2.55** The responding slave shall wait this minimum time after DSA* goes low before driving DTACK* or BERR* low.
29	**Rule 2.56** During read cycles, once the responding slave has driven DTACK* low, it shall not change D00-D31 until DSA* goes high.

Table 25 (*Continued*)
Slave, Timing Rules and Regulations

Timing Parameters Specified in Table 22	Rules and Regulations
30	**Rule 2.57** Once the responding slave has driven DTACK* or BERR* low, it shall not release it until it detects both DS0* and DS1* high.
31	**Rule 2.58** During read cycles, the responding slave shall release all of D00-D31 before releasing DTACK* or BERR* to high.
32	**Observation 2.73** Slaves are guaranteed that IACK*, LWORD*, A00-A31, and AM0-AM5 have been valid for this minimum time when they detect a falling edge on DSA*. This time is derived from timing parameters 4 and 10.
33	**Observation 2.74** During data transfer cycles, slaves are guaranteed that either DS0* or DS1* or both will remain low for at least this minimum time. This time is derived from timing parameter 28, where the responding slave is required to wait a minimum time before driving BERR* or DTACK* to low.

Table 26
Location Monitor, Timing Observations

Timing Parameters Specified in Table 22	Observations
4	**Observation 2.75** Location monitors are guaranteed that IACK*, A01-A31, AM0-AM5, and LWORD* have been valid for this minimum time when they detect a falling edge on AS*.
5	**Observation 2.76** Location monitors are guaranteed this minimum high time on AS* between DTB cycles.
10	**Observation 2.77** Due to bus skew, location monitors on the DTB might detect a falling edge on DSA* before detecting the falling edge on AS*. However, they are guaranteed that the falling edge on DSA* will not precede the falling edge on AS* by more than this time.
11	**Observation 2.78** Location monitors are guaranteed this minimum time during which both DS0* and DS1* are simultaneously high between consecutive data transfers.
12	**Observation 2.79** Location monitors are guaranteed that WRITE* has been valid for this minimum time when they detect a falling edge on DSA*.
13	**Observation 2.80** When the master will drive both DS0* and DS1* low, then location monitors are guaranteed that DSB* will go low within this maximum time after DSA* has gone low.
17	**Observation 2.81** Location monitors are guaranteed that IACK*, A01-A31, AM0-AM5, and LWORD* will remain valid for this minimum time after the falling edge of AS*. During address-only cycles this time is guaranteed by the master. During all other cycle types, this time is derived from timing parameters 10, 14, 16, and 28.
19	**Observation 2.82** Location monitors are guaranteed that AS* will remain low for this minimum time.
23	**Observation 2.83** Location monitors are guaranteed that the WRITE* line remains valid until both DS0* and DS1* go high.
32	**Observation 2.84** Location monitors are guaranteed that IACK*, LWORD*, A01-A31, and AM0-AM5 have been valid for this minimum time when they detect a falling edge on DSA*.
33	**Observation 2.85** During data transfer cycles, location monitors are guaranteed that either or both of DS0* and DS1* will remain low for at least this minimum time. This time is derived from timing parameter 28, where the responding slave is required to wait a minimum time before driving BERR* or DTACK* to low.

Table 27
Bus Timer, Timing Rules

Timing Parameters Specified in Table 23	Rules
28	**Rule 2.59** The bus timer shall wait at least its time-out time, but no longer than twice its time-out time, after DSA* goes low before driving BERR* low.
30	**Rule 2.60** Once it has driven BERR* low, the bus timer shall not release BERR* until it detects both DS0* and DS1* high.

3. DTB Arbitration Bus

3.1 Introduction. As microprocessor costs decrease, it is becoming more cost effective to design systems with multiple processors sharing global resources.

The most fundamental of these global resources is the data transfer bus through which all other global resources are accessed. Therefore, any system that supports multiprocessing must provide an efficient allocation method for the data transfer bus. Because speed of allocation is vital, a hardware allocation scheme is the only practical alternative. The arbitration subsystem provides this service (see Fig 30).

The arbitration subsystem:

(1) Prevents simultaneous use of the bus by two masters

(2) Schedules requests from multiple masters for optimum bus use

3.1.1 Types of Arbitration. When several boards request use of the DTB simultaneously, the arbitration subsystem detects these requests and grants the bus to one board at a time. The decision of which board is granted the bus first depends on the scheduling algorithm used. Three algorithms are described: prioritized, round-robin, and single level.

(1) Prioritized arbitration assigns the bus according to a fixed priority scheme where each of four bus request lines has a priority from highest (BR3*) to lowest (BR0*).

(2) Round-robin arbitration assigns the bus on a rotating priority basis. When the bus is granted to the requester on bus request line "BR(n)*", then the highest priority for the next arbitration is assigned to bus request line "BR(n-1)*".

(3) Single-level arbitration only accepts requests on BR3*, and relies on BR3*'s bus grant daisy-chain to arbitrate the requests.

> **Permission 3.1** Scheduling algorithms other than priority, round-robin, or single level may be used. For example, an arbiter's algorithm might give highest priority to BR3*, but grant the bus to BR0* through BR2* on a round-robin basis.

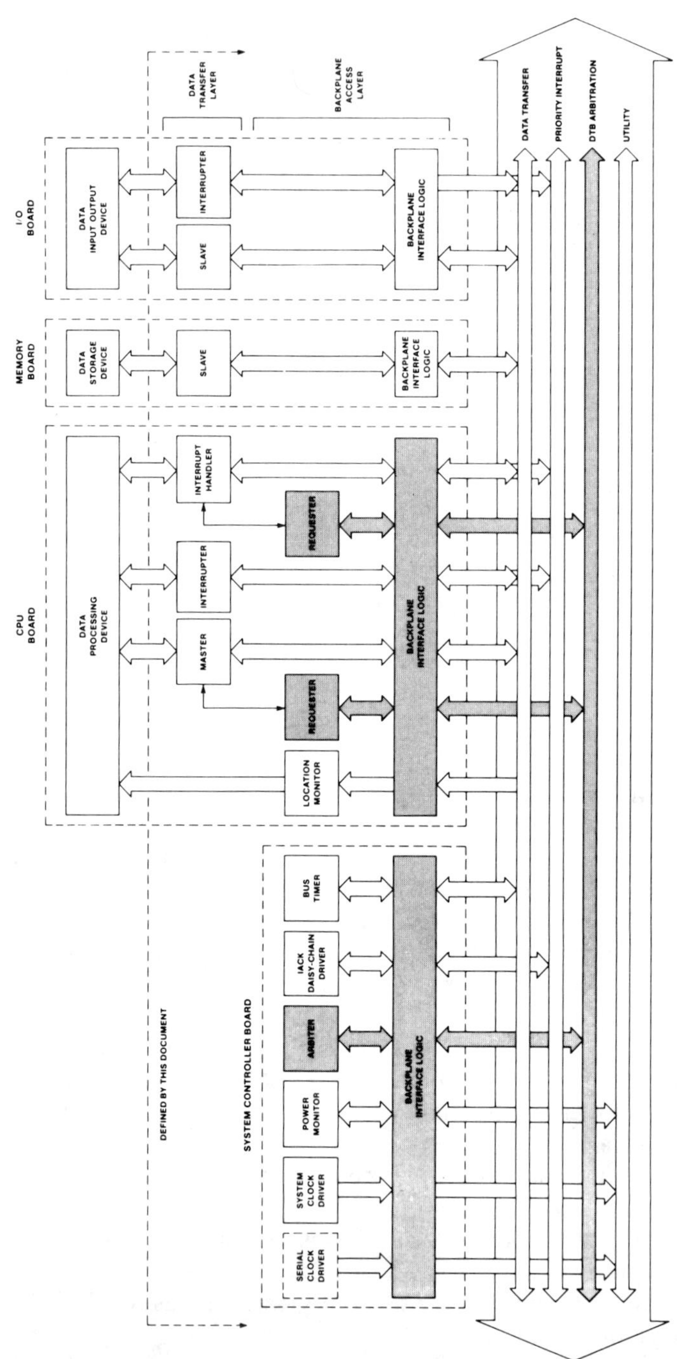

Fig 30
Arbitration Bus Functional Block Diagram

3.2 Arbitration Bus Lines. The arbitration bus consists of six bused lines and four daisy-chained lines. The daisy-chained lines require special signal names. The signals entering each board are called *Bus Grant IN* lines (BGxIN*), while the signals leaving each board are called *Bus Grant OUT* lines (BGxOUT*). The lines that leave slot n as BGxOUT* enter slot n+1 as BGxIN*. This is shown in Fig 31.

Observation 3.1 The terms BRx*, BGxIN*, and BGxOUT* are used to describe the bus request and bus grant lines, where x takes on any value from 0 to 3.

In the arbitration system, a requester module drives the following lines:

1 bus request line	(one of BR0* through BR3*)
1 bus grant out line	(one of BG0OUT* through BG3OUT*)
1 bus busy line	(BBSY*)

Rule 3.1 If a board does not generate bus requests on some bus request levels, then it shall propagate the daisy-chain signals for those levels from its BGxIN* lines to its respective BGxOUT* lines.

Permission 3.2 The unused lines of the bus grant daisy-chain may be propagated using jumpers or active logic. The latter approach allows selection of the request level under software control, while the former results in faster propagation through the daisy-chain.

Three types of arbiters are described:

Prioritized	(PRI)
Round-Robin-Select	(RRS)
Single level	(SGL)

The operation of these three types of arbiters is described in 3.3.

A PRI arbiter drives the following lines:

1 bus clear line	(BCLR*)
4 bus grant lines	(Slot 1 BG0IN* through BG3IN*)

An RRS arbiter drives the four BGxIN* lines of slot 1 and, optionally, the BCLR* line.

A SGL arbiter drives BG3IN* at slot 1 and optionally, the BCLR* line.

Two additional lines are intimately associated with the arbitration system during power-up and power-down sequencing: SYSRESET*, and ACFAIL*. While their impact on the arbitration system is included in this section, these lines are discussed further in Section 5.

Fig 31
Illustration of the Bus Grant Daisy-Chain

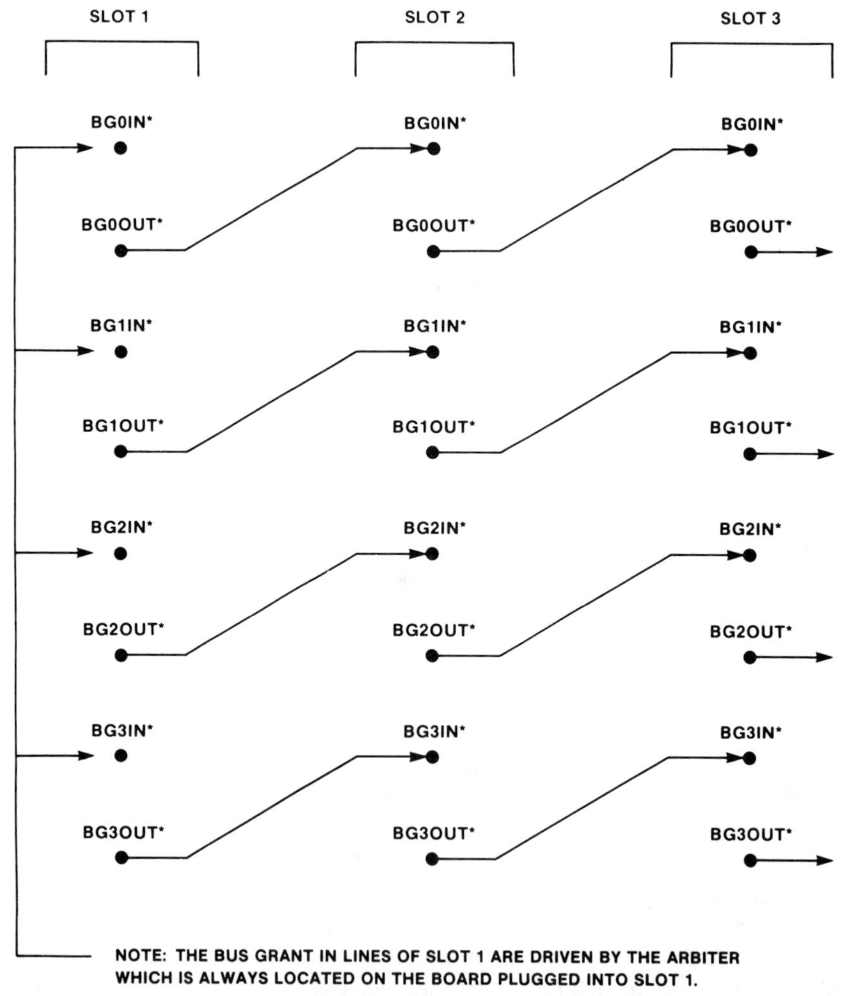

3.2.1 Bus Request and Bus Grant Lines. The bus request lines are used by each requester to request use of the DTB. They allow the arbiter to award use of the bus by driving a bus grant daisy-chain line low. This low level propagates down the daisy-chain, typically passing through several boards in the process. If a board never uses a particular request/grant level, the signal is passed through that board. Where the board uses a request/grant level x, the corresponding signal BGxIN* is gated on board. If its on-board requester is currently requesting the DTB on that level, it does not pass the low level on to its BGxOUT*. Otherwise, it passes on the low level.

Rule 3.2 If a backplane slot is not occupied by a board, and if there are boards farther down the daisy-chain, then jumpers shall be installed at the empty slot to pass through the daisy-chain signal.

Observation 3.2 The backplane mechanical specification in Section 7 describes a provision for the installation of jumpers at each slot.

Rule 3.3 The arbiter shall be located in slot 1.

3.2.2 Bus Busy Line (BBSY*). Once a requester has been granted control of the DTB by way of the bus grant daisy-chain, it drives BBSY* low. It then has control of the DTB until it releases BBSY*. The release of BBSY* allows the arbiter to grant the DTB to some other requester.

3.2.3 Bus Clear Line (BCLR*). The PRI arbiter drives BCLR* low to inform the master, currently in control of the DTB, when a higher priority request is pending. The current master is not required to relinquish the bus within any prescribed time limit. It can continue transferring data until it reaches an appropriate stopping point, and then allow its on-board requester to release BBSY*.

Permission 3.3 Although RRS and SGL arbiters are not required to drive the BCLR* line they may do so.

Suggestion 3.1 If a RRS arbiter drives the BCLR* line low, then design it to do so whenever there is a request pending on any of the nongranted bus request lines.

3.3 Functional Modules. The arbitration subsystem is composed of several modules:

(1) One arbiter

(2) One or more requesters

Figures 32 and 33 provide block diagrams for the two types of arbitration bus modules.

Rule 3.4 Output signal lines shown with solid lines in Figs 32 and 33 shall be driven by the module, unless it would always drive them high.

Rule 3.5 Input signal lines shown with solid lines in Figs 32 and 33 shall be monitored and responded to in the appropriate fashion.

Observation 3.3 Rules and permissions for driving and monitoring the signal lines shown with dotted lines in Figs 32 and 33 are given in Tables 28 and 29.

Observation 3.4 If an output signal line is not driven, then terminators on the backplane ensure that it is high.

Observation 3.5 Although SYSRESET* and ACFAIL* are not specified as part of the arbitration bus, they are important here because masters, which are paired with requesters, respond to these signal lines (The power monitor module discussed in Section 5 drives these signal lines.)

3.3.1 Arbiter. The arbiter is the functional module that decides which requester should be granted control of the DTB when several request it simultaneously. Three types of arbiters are described: a prioritized (PRI) arbiter, a round-robin-select (RRS) arbiter, and a single-level (SGL) arbiter.

The arbiter responds to incoming bus requests and grants the DTB to the appropriate requester. When the arbiter detects BBSY* high, and after it detects one or more of BRx* driven low, it drives low the bus grant line that corresponds to the highest priority pending bus request.

The bus request lines might be in transition from high to low just at the time that the arbiter is capturing their state. If the line is sampled during the transition, the output of the sampling device might not be stable for some time. This phenomenon is sometimes referred to as metastability. Appendix D provides a sample arbiter circuit that deals with this phenomenon.

When the requester receives the bus grant, it drives BBSY* low and signals to its on-board master or interrupt handler that it has been granted the DTB. After its on-board master or interrupt handler finishes using the DTB, the requester releases BBSY*. The resulting rising edge of BBSY* enables the arbiter to issue another bus grant, based upon the levels of the bus request lines at that time.

In addition to the arbitration provided by the arbiter, a secondary level of arbitration is provided by the bus grant daisy-chains. Because of these daisy-chains, requesters sharing a common request line are prioritized by slot position. The requester closest to slot 1 has the highest priority.

The SGL arbiter responds only to bus requests on BR3*, relying on the BG3IN*/BG3OUT* daisy-chain to do the arbitration.

The PRI arbiter prioritizes the four bus request lines, from BR0* (the lowest) to BR3* (the highest), and responds with BG0IN* through BG3IN*, as appropriate. A PRI arbiter also informs the master currently in control of the bus, when a higher level request is pending by driving BCLR* low.

To visualize an RRS arbiter, consider a mechanical switch being driven by a stepping motor. Each position on the switch connects a bus request line to its corresponding bus grant line. When the bus is busy, the switch is stopped on the current level. Upon release of the bus, the switch steps one position lower (that is, from BR(n)* to BR(n-1)*) and tests for a request. It continues this scanning operation until a request is found, sending a bus grant over the appropriate line.

Permission 3.4 An arbiter may be designed with a built-in time-out feature that causes it to withdraw a bus grant if BBSY* is not driven low by a requester within a prescribed time.

Observation 3.6 The time-out period used by the arbiter allowed by Permission 3.4 needs to be longer than the longest possible bus grant daisy-chain propagation delay time, plus the time the slowest requester takes to generate BBSY*.

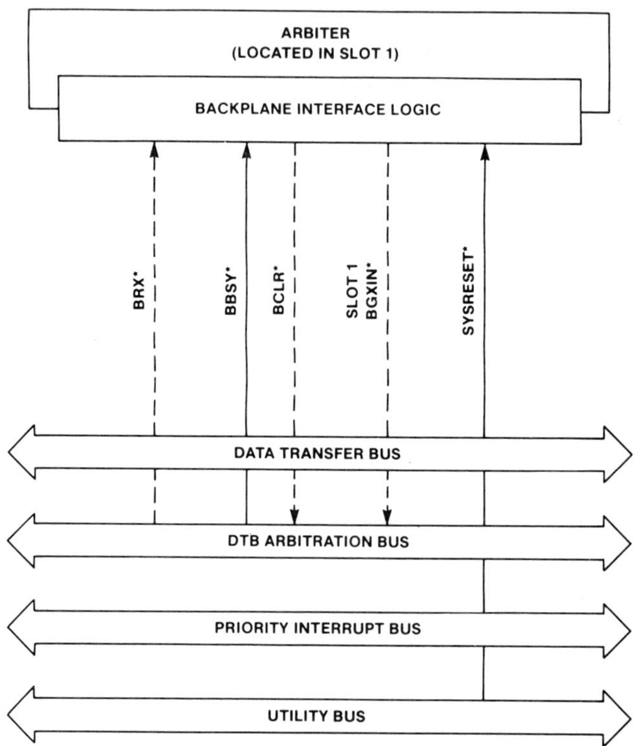

NOTE: The rules and permissions for monitoring and driving the dotted lines are given in Table 28.

Fig 32
Block Diagram: ARBITER

Suggestion 3.4 Specify the maximum propagation delay time from the BGxIN* to the BGxOUT* in the data sheets of products. In addition, specify the maximum time it would take the requester to generate BBSY*. This will allow users to determine the required value of the arbitration time-out.

Table 28
Arbiters: Rules and Permissions for Driving and Monitoring the Dotted Lines

Type of Arbiter	Rules and Permissions
SGL	Shall drive slot 1 BG3IN* Shall ensure slot 1 BG0IN*-BG2IN* are high Shall monitor BR3* May or may not drive BCLR* or slot 1 BG0IN*-BG2IN* May or may not monitor BR0*-BR2*
RRS	Shall drive slot 1 BG0IN*-BG3IN* Shall monitor BR0*-BR3* May or may not drive BCLR*
PRI	Shall drive slot 1 BG0IN*-BG3IN* and BCLR* Shall monitor BR0*-BR3*

Rule 3.6 Except for a time-out situation where no requester responds, once the arbiter grants the bus to a requester it shall not generate a new bus grant before that requester generates a rising edge on the BBSY* line. (The requester generates a rising edge by driving BBSY* low and then releasing it. The arbiter generates a new bus grant by driving all BGxIN* lines of slot 1 to high, and then issuing the new bus grant by driving the appropriate BGxIN* line to low.)

Observation 3.7 If an arbiter uses a *snapshot* of the request lines taken prior to the rising edge of BBSY*, then it might grant the bus to a requester that has since removed its request.

3.3.2 Requester. Each requester in the system

(1) Monitors the DEVICE WANTS BUS signal from its on-board master or interrupt handler and generates a bus request when the DTB is needed.

(2) If it detects a low level on its BGxIN* line, and its on-board master or interrupt handler does not need the DTB, then it passes on that low level to its BGxOUT*.

(3) If it detects a low level on its BGxIN* line, and its on-board master or interrupt handler needs the DTB, it generates an on-board DEVICE GRANTED BUS signal to indicate the DTB is available, and drives the BBSY* signal low.

Three types of requesters are described: a release-when-done (RWD) requester, a release-on-request (ROR) requester, and a FAIR requester.

The RWD requester releases BBSY* when its master or interrupt handler drives the on-board DEVICE WANTS BUS signal false.

The ROR requester does not release BBSY* when its on-board DEVICE WANTS BUS signal goes false unless some other requester on the bus drives one of the bus request lines low. It monitors the four bus request lines and releases BBSY* only if another bus request is pending. ROR requesters reduce the number of arbitrations initiated by a master that is generating a large percentage of the bus traffic.

As long as a system has no more than four masters or interrupt handlers (one per bus request line), the RRS arbitration algorithm assures fairness (that is, no master will be prevented from accessing the bus indefinitely by higher level requests). In systems with more than four masters or interrupt handlers, fairness can be provided by FAIR requesters. After it has been granted the bus, the FAIR requester refrains from requesting the bus again as long as there are any active bus requests pending on its own request level.

> **Observation 3.17** When configuring a system to provide fairness for more than four masters or interrupt handlers, all the requesters in the system should be FAIR requesters. If one or more of the requesters are not fair requesters, then fairness can still be guaranteed if the sum total of bus traffic generated by the nonFAIR requesters does not exceed the capacity of the bus.

> **Observation 3.18** The RWD and ROR capabilities describe under what conditions a requester relinquishes control of the DTB. On the other hand, the FAIR capability describes under what conditions the requester requests control of the DTB. And therefore, both the RWD and the ROR requesters can include the FAIR capability as well.

Assuming that its DEVICE WANTS BUS input is true and that it drives its BRx* line low, when a requester detects its BGxIN* driven low it does 3 things:

(1) It drives BBSY* low

(2) It releases its BRx* line high

(3) It drives the DEVICE GRANTED BUS on-board signal true, allowing its master or interrupt handler to initiate bus transfers.

It is even possible that the master or interrupt handler might not use the bus in response to this particular grant. However, the following rules apply:

Rule 3.7 In response to a falling edge on BGxIN*, the requester shall drive BBSY* to low for at least 90 ns.

Rule 3.8 In response to a falling edge on BGxIN*, the requester shall release BRx* high.

Rule 3.9 In response to a falling edge on BGxIN*, the requester shall maintain BBSY* low for at least 30 ns after it releases BRx*.

Observation 3.8 The 30 ns delay between the rising edge on BRx* and the rising edge on BBSY* ensures that the arbiter does not mistakenly interpret the old bus request as a new one and issues another grant.

Rule 3.10 The requester shall maintain BBSY* low until its BGxIN* goes high.

Observation 3.9 Rule 3.10 ensures that the BBSY* transition to low has been detected by the arbiter and that all segments of the bus grant daisy-chain have returned to high, in preparation for the next arbitration.

Permission 3.5 If a requester drives its BRx* line low and, if it sees some other requester drive BBSY* low, then it may withdraw its request by releasing its BRx* line to high.

> **Rule 3.11** If a requester withdraws a bus request without having first been granted the bus, then it shall wait to do so until BBSY* goes low, and it shall do so within 50 ns after BBSY* goes low.

Suggestion 3.2 Design requesters so that they pass on the bus grant daisy-chain as fast as possible after receipt of a bus grant. This will improve system performance.

Fig 33
Block Diagram: REQUESTER

NOTE: The rules and permissions for monitoring the dotted lines are given in Table 29.

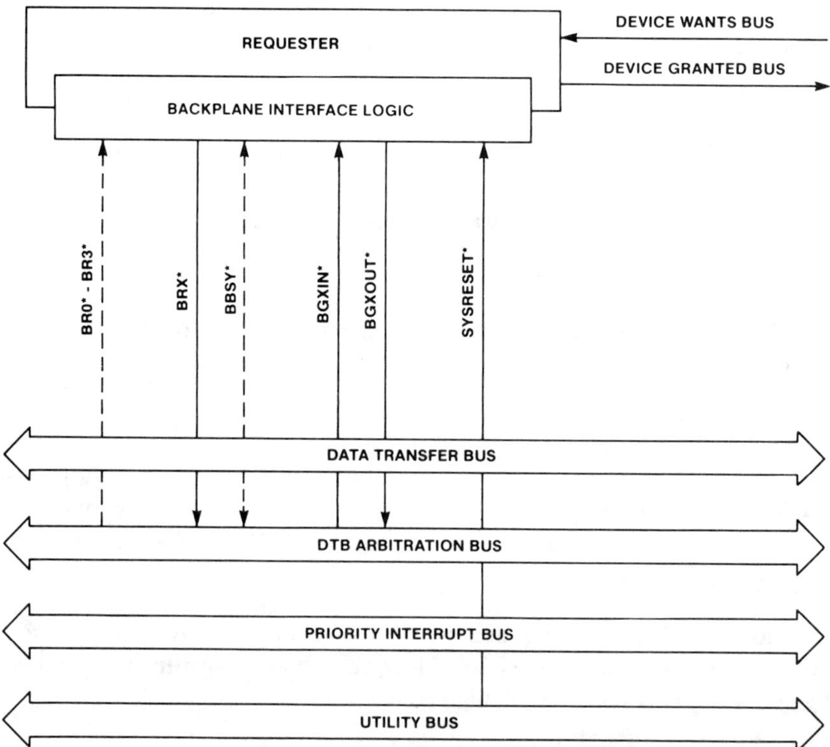

Rule 3.14 Before issuing a bus request, a fair requester shall sample its bus request line when BBSY* is detected high.

Table 29
Requesters: Rules and Permissions for Driving and Monitoring the Dotted Lines

Type of Requester	Rules and Permissions
RWD	May or may not monitor BR0*-BR3* May or may not monitor BBSY*
ROR	Shall monitor BR0*-BR3* May or may not monitor BBSY*
FAIR	Shall monitor the bus request line it uses Shall monitor BBSY*

3.3.3 Data-Transfer-Bus Master

3.3.3.1 Release of the DTB. The bus arbitration protocol determines how and when the DTB is granted to the various masters and interrupt handlers in the system. It does not, however, control when masters and interrupt handlers release the DTB. Masters give up the bus when they finish their data transfers. Interrupt handlers give up the bus after the interrupt acknowledge cycle.

Some masters monitor the ACFAIL* and BCLR* signals, which inform the master that the DTB is needed for some higher priority activity. In the case of BCLR*, the master's design determines how long it takes to release the bus. For example, a master on a disk controller board might not be able to relinquish the bus during a disk sector transfer without loss of data, so it might keep the bus until the sector transfer is finished. ACFAIL* informs the master that an ac power loss has been detected, and whatever problems the master will face in surrendering the bus are insignificant compared to the needs of the total system.

Recommendation 3.1 Design masters to release the DTB within 200 μs after ACFAIL* goes low, except to participate in the ensuing power failure activities.

Observation 3.10 The 200 μs specified in **Recommendation 3.1** is intended to provide time for an orderly shutdown of the system.

Masters and interrupt handlers use several criteria in deciding when to release the DTB. Whatever criteria are used to decide when to release the DTB, arbitration is done before some other master or interrupt handler begins using it. This arbitration takes place either during the last data transfer or after that transfer, depending on how much notice the master or interrupt handler gives to its on-board requester.

Permission 3.6 Masters and interrupt handlers may release the DTB either during or after their last data transfer.

For example, if the master notifies its on-board requester that it no longer needs the bus during its last data transfer, the requester releases BBSY* and arbitration takes place during the last transfer. But if the master waits until the last transfer has completed before signaling its on-board requester, the DTB remains idle while the arbitration is done (This was illustrated in 2.5.1). Sections 2 and 4 contain rules that pertain to the release of the DTB.

Suggestion 3.3 Design master boards that have block transfer capability to signal their requester to release BBSY* during the last data transfer of the block transfer. If it is released at the beginning of the block transfer, high priority bus requests initiated during the block transfer might not be taken into account by the arbiter until the next arbitration cycle.

3.3.3.2 Acquisition of the DTB. To ensure that no DTB line is ever driven to opposite states by two masters or interrupt handlers, these modules are constrained by certain rules when they take control of the DTB.

Rule 3.12 When a master or interrupt handler is given control of the DTB by its on-board requester, it shall wait until it detects AS* high before turning on its DTB drivers.

Observation 3.11 If the previous master or interrupt handler releases the bus during its last data transfer, then Rule 3.12 ensures that the data transfer will be finished before the new master or interrupt handler starts using the DTB (If the previous master or interrupt handler waited until the data transfer was finished before releasing the bus, AS* will already be high).

3.3.3.3 Other Information

Recommendation 3.2 To allow for prompt servicing of interrupt requests and for optimum use of the DTB, design masters to release the DTB as soon as possible after they detect BCLR* low.

Permission 3.7 A master or interrupt handler may have more than one requester, where each requester generates bus requests on a different bus request line.

Observation 3.12 Where a master or interrupt handler has two or more requesters, it can do high priority data transfers using one requester and low priority transfers using the other.

3.4 Typical Operation

3.4.1 Arbitration of Two Different Levels of Bus Request. Figures 34 and 35 illustrate the sequence of events that takes place when two requesters send simultaneous bus requests to a PRI arbiter on different bus request lines. When the sequence begins requester A drives BR1* low and requester B drives BR2* low. The arbiter detects BR1* and BR2* low simultaneously, and drives BG2IN* low to its own slot (slot 1). That BG2IN* signal is monitored by requester B (also in slot 1). When requester B detects BG2IN* low, it responds by driving BBSY* low. Requester B then releases the BR2* line and informs its on-board master (master B) that the DTB is available.

When BBSY* goes low, the arbiter drives BG2IN* of slot 1 high.

When master B completes its data transfer(s), it signals that fact to its requester B by driving DEVICE WANTS BUS false. Requester B then releases BBSY*, provided that its BG2IN* has been received high and 30 ns have elapsed since it released BR2*.

The arbiter interprets the release of BBSY* as a signal to arbitrate any current bus requests. Since BR1* is the only bus request driven low, the arbiter grants the DTB to requester A by driving BG1IN* low. Requester A responds by driving BBSY* low and releasing BR1* high. When master A completes its data

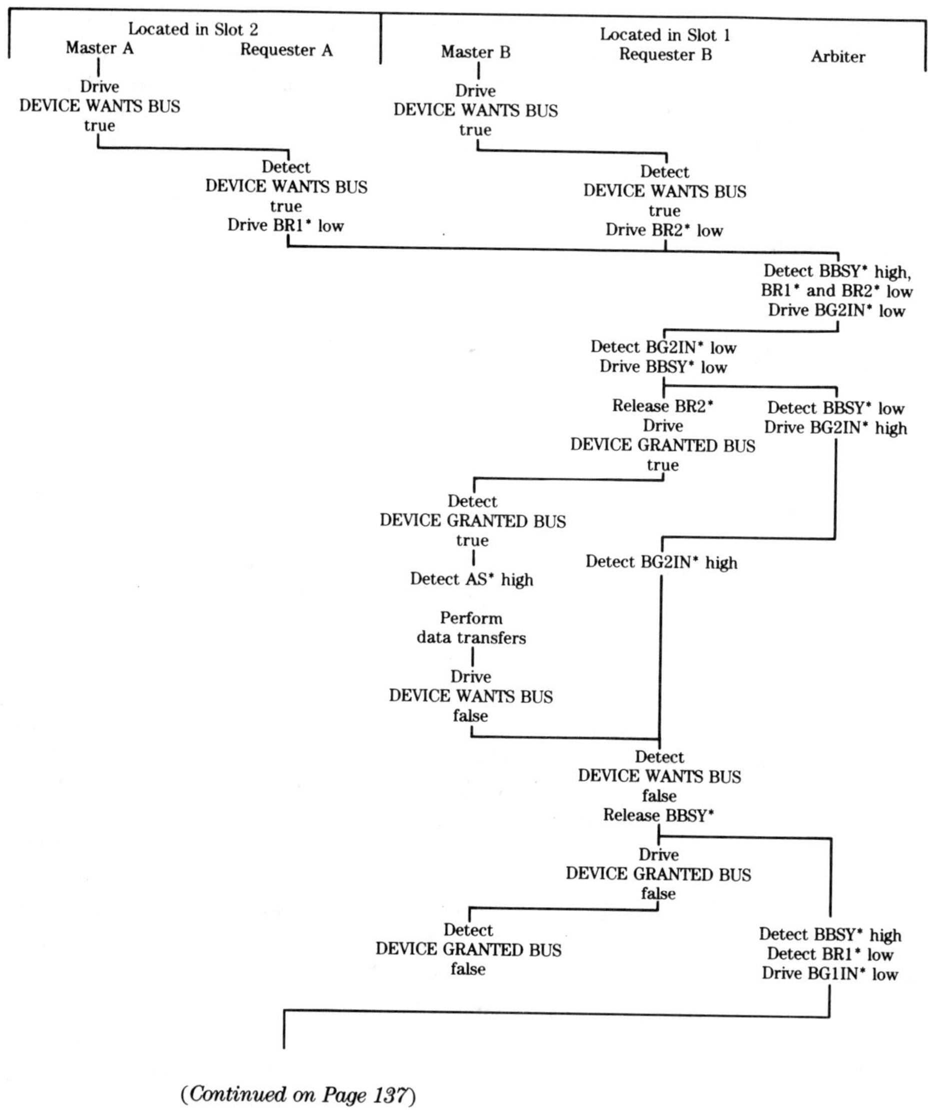

(*Continued on Page 137*)

NOTE: DEVICE WANTS BUS and DEVICE GRANTED BUS are on-board signals between the master and its requester (See Fig 33).

Fig 34
Arbitration Flow Diagram: Two Requesters, Two Request Levels

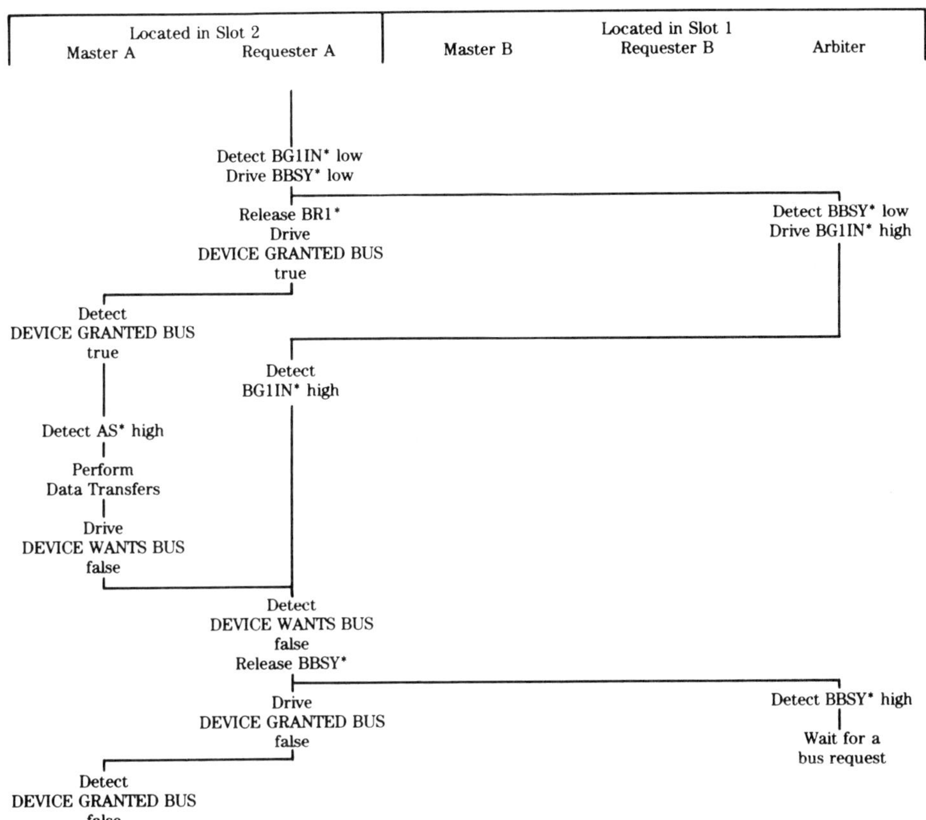

Fig 34 (*Continued*)
Arbitration Flow Diagram: Two Requesters, Two Request Levels

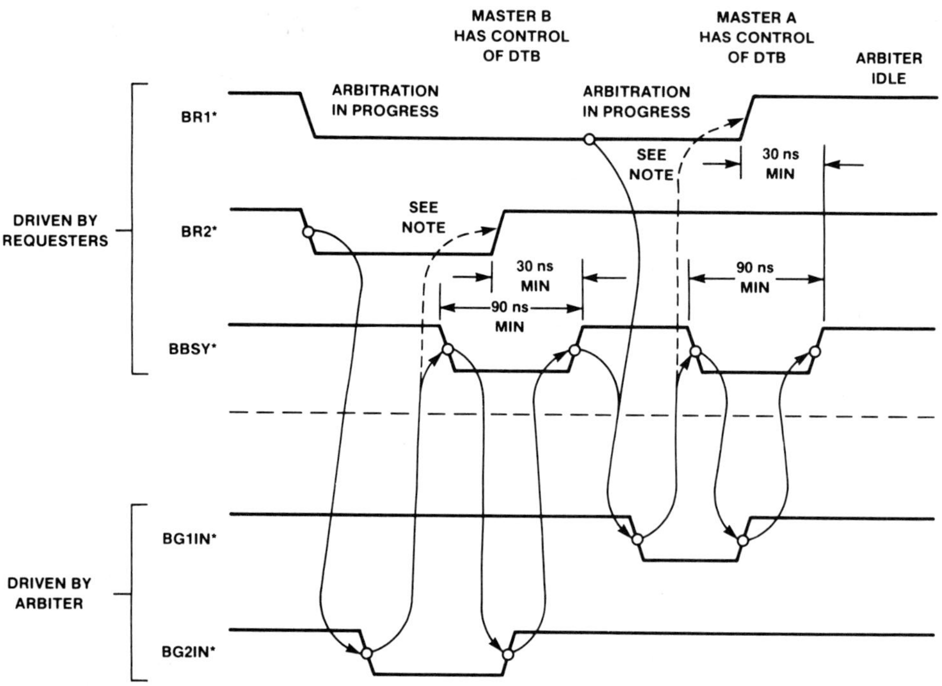

NOTE: In this example each requester maintains its bus request line low until it is granted the DTB. In some cases a requester might release its bus request line without receiving a bus grant (see 3.3.2).

Fig 35
Arbitration Sequence Diagram: Two Requesters, Two Request Levels

transfer(s), and signals that fact by driving DEVICE WANTS BUS false, requester A releases BBSY*, provided that its BG1IN* has been received high and 30 ns have elapsed since it released BR1*.

In this example, since no bus request lines are low when requester A releases BBSY*, the arbiter waits until it detects a bus request.

Observation 3.13 The description illustrated in Figs 34 and 35 would hold for both PRI and RRS arbiters, unless we consider an RRS arbiter where the last active request was level BR2*. In this case, the arbiter would process the BR1* request first and then proceed to the BR2* request.

Observation 3.14 BBSY* and the bus grants are fully interlocked as shown in Fig 35.

(1) The arbiter does not drive the bus grant high until it detects BBSY* low.

(2) The requester does not release BBSY* to high until it detects the bus grant high.

(3) The arbiter does not drive the next bus grant low until it detects BBSY* high.

(4) The next requester does not drive BBSY* low until it detects the bus grant low.

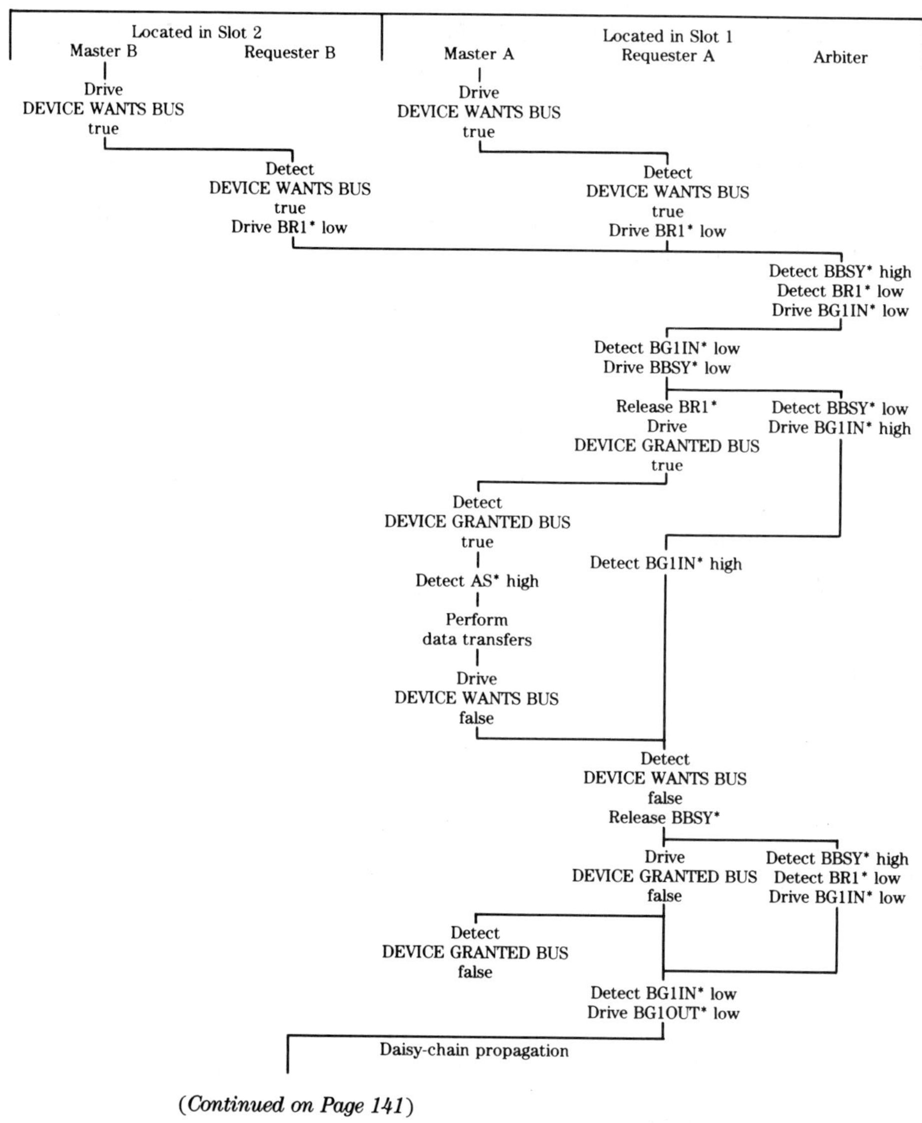

(*Continued on Page 141*)

NOTE: DEVICE WANTS BUS and DEVICE GRANTED BUS are on-board signals between the master and its requester (See Fig 33).

Fig 36
Arbitration Flow Diagram: Two Requesters, Same Request Level

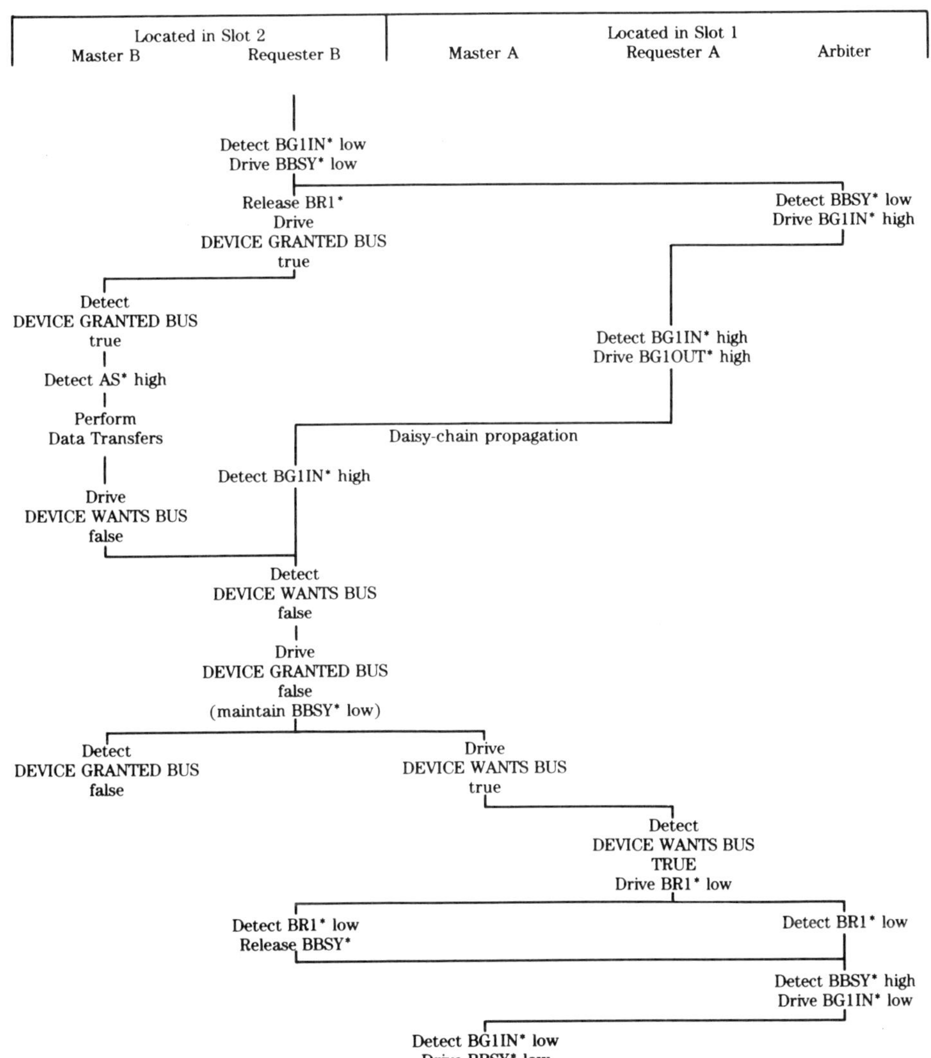

Fig 36 *(Continued)*
Arbitration Flow Diagram: Two Requesters, Same Request Level

3.4.2 Arbitration of Two Bus Requests on the Same Bus Request Line. Figures 36 and 37 illustrate the sequence of events which take place when an ROR requester and an RWD requester send simultaneous requests to a PRI arbiter on a common bus request line. In this example, the arbiter and RWD requester are located on the system controller board in slot 1, with the ROR requester located in slot 2. When the sequence begins, both of the requesters drive BR1* low simultaneously. The arbiter then drives BG1IN* low to its own slot (slot 1). That BG1IN* signal is monitored by requester B (also in slot 1). When requester B detects BG1IN* low, it responds by driving BBSY* low. Requester B then releases BR1* and informs master B that the DTB is available.

Observation 3.15 Even though requester B releases BR1*, requester A continues to drive it low (see Figs 36 and 37).

After detecting BBSY* low, the arbiter drives BG1IN* high. When master B has completed its data transfer(s), it drives DEVICE WANTS BUS false. When requester B detects this, and when the 30 ns delay since the release of BR1* has been satisfied, requester B releases BBSY*.

The arbiter interprets the release of BBSY* as a signal to arbitrate any current bus requests. Since the BR1* line is still low, the arbiter drives BG1IN* low again. When requester B detects BG1IN* low, it drives its BG1OUT* low because it does not need the DTB. Requester A then detects the low on its BG1IN* and responds by driving BBSY* low and BR1* high. When the arbiter detects the low on BBSY*, it drives BG1IN* high, which causes requester B to drive its BG1OUT* high.

Some time later, when master A has finished its data transfers, it drives DEVICE WANTS BUS false, indicating that it has finished using the DTB.

Since requester A is an ROR requester, it does not release BBSY*, but keeps it driven low. In the event that master A needs to use the DTB again, no arbitration will be required. In this example, however, requester B drives BR1* low, indicating a need to use the DTB, and requester A (which is monitoring the bus request lines) releases the BBSY* line. The arbiter then grants the DTB to requester B.

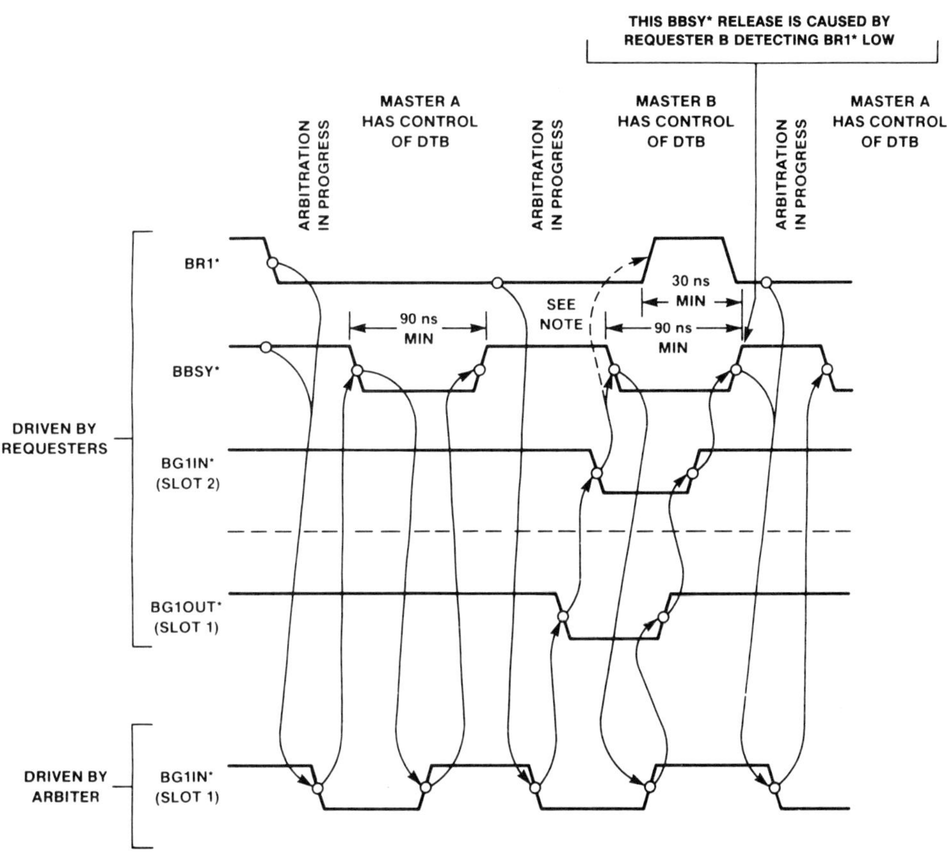

NOTE: In this example each requester maintains its bus request line low until it is granted the DTB. In some cases a requester might release its bus request line without receiving a bus grant (see 3.3.2).

Fig 37
Arbitration Sequence Diagram: Two Requesters, Same Request Level

3.5 Race Conditions Between Master Requests and Arbiter Grants. Suppose that there are two requesters: requester A and requester B, that share a common bus request line. Requester B, which is further down the daisy-chain, requests the bus and the arbiter drives the corresponding bus grant line low. This low level on the bus grant arrives at requester A just as master A signals that it wants the bus. If requester A is improperly designed, this situation might cause it to momentarily drive its BGxOUT* line low and then high again resulting in a low-going transient.

Rule 3.13 Requesters shall be designed to ensure that no momentary low-going transients are generated on their BGxOUT* line.

Observation 3.16 If the requester is designed so that it latches the state of the on-board DEVICE WANTS BUS line upon the falling edge of its BGxIN* line, and if that signal is in transition when the falling edge occurs, the outputs of the latch will sometimes oscillate, or remain in the threshold region between the high and low levels, for a short time. Because of this, no time is specified for the requester to pass along the bus grant. It is only prohibited from generating a low-going transient on its BGxOUT* line which might be interpreted as a bus grant by a requester further down the daisy-chain.

Permission 3.8 If a requester detects that its on-board master needs the bus between the time that it receives a bus grant intended for another requester and the time it would pass that bus grant on, then it may treat the bus grant as its own. In this case the other requester will maintain its bus request until another bus grant is issued.

4. Priority Interrupt Bus

4.1 Introduction. This standard defines a priority interrupt bus, which provides the signal lines needed to generate and service interrupts. Figure 38 shows a typical system. Interrupters use the priority interrupt bus to send interrupt requests to interrupt handlers, which respond to these requests. Any system that has interrupt capability includes software routines that are called interrupt service routines, and are invoked by the interrupts.

Interrupt subsystems can be classified into two groups

(1) Single handler systems, which have only one interrupt handler that receives and services all bus interrupts.

(2) Distributed systems, which have two or more interrupt handlers that receive and service bus interrupts.

4.1.1 Single Handler Systems. In a single handler system, all interrupts are received by one interrupt handler, and all interrupt service routines executed by one processor. Figure 39 shows the interrupt structure of a single handler system. This type of architecture is well suited to machine or process control applications, where a supervisory processor coordinates the activities of dedicated processors. The dedicated processors are typically interfaced to the machine or process being controlled.

The supervisory processor is the destination for all bus interrupts, servicing them in a prioritized manner. The dedicated processors are not required to service interrupts from the bus, and can give primary attention to controlling the machine or the process.

4.1.2 Distributed Systems. Figure 40 shows the interrupt structure of a distributed system. This system includes two or more interrupt handlers, each servicing only a subset of the bus interrupts. In a typical implementation, each of the interrupt handlers resides on a different processor board. This architecture is well suited to distributed computing applications, where multiple, co-equal processors execute the application software. As each of the co-equal processors executes part of the system software, it might need to communicate with the other processors. In the distributed system, each processor services only those interrupts directed to it, establishing dedicated communication paths among all processors.

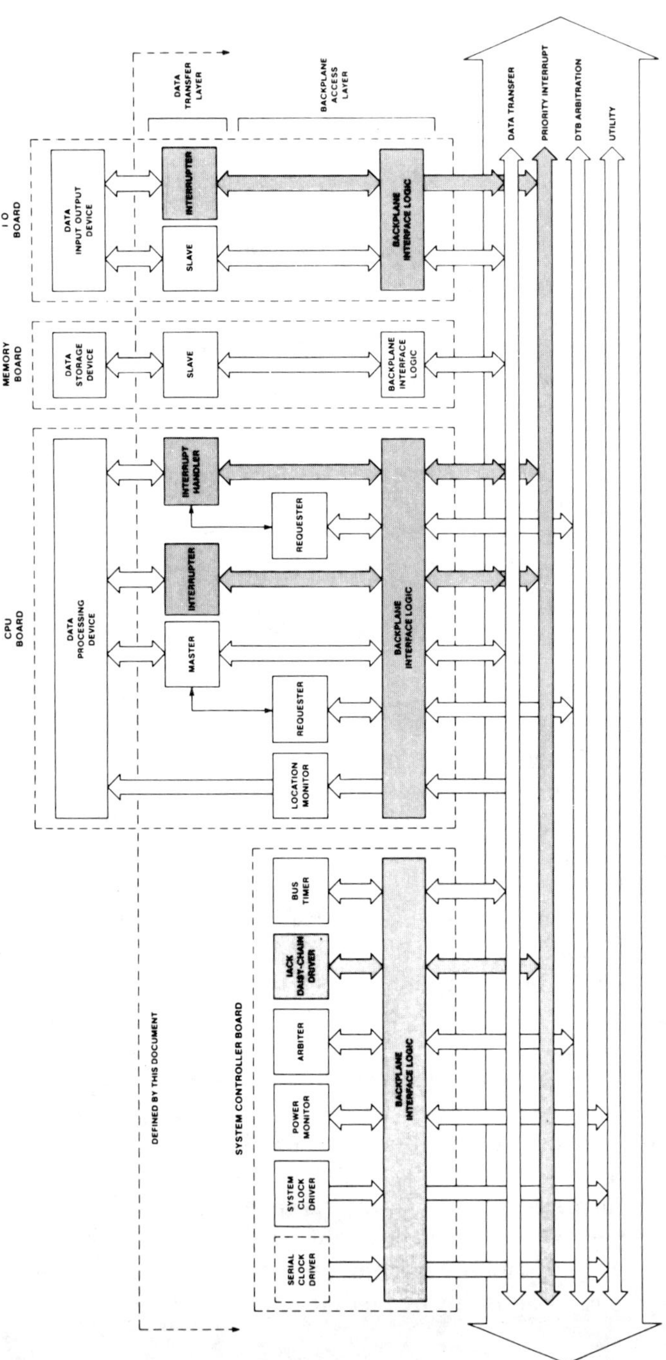

Fig 38
Priority Interrupt Bus Functional Block Diagram

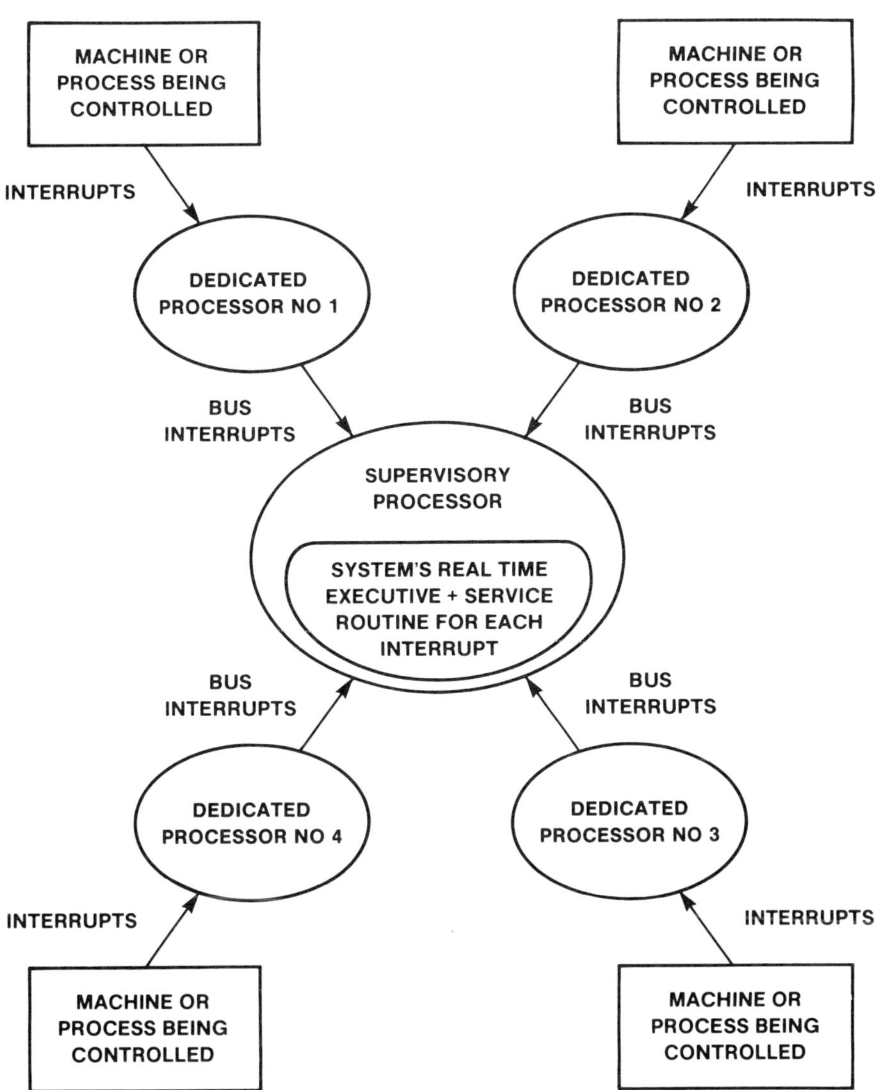

Fig 39
Interrupt Subsystem Structure: Single Handler System

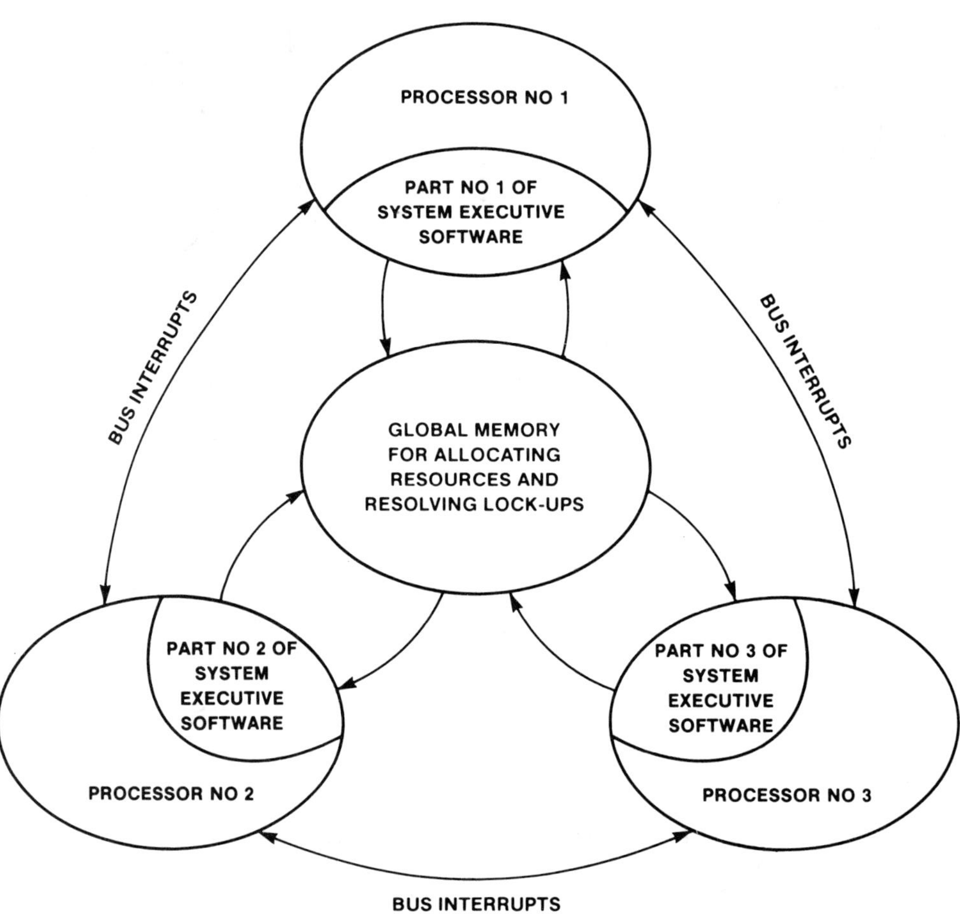

Fig 40
Interrupt Subsystem Structure: Distributed Handler System

4.2 Priority Interrupt Bus Lines. The data transfer bus, the arbitration bus, and the priority interrupt bus are all used in the process of generating and handling bus interrupts.

The following discussion of the priority interrupt bus assumes that the reader understands the operation of the data transfer bus described in Section 2, and the arbitration bus described in Section 3.

The priority interrupt bus consists of seven interrupt request lines, one interrupt acknowledge line, and one interrupt acknowledge daisy-chain.

IRQ1*	Interrupt Request 1
IRQ2*	Interrupt Request 2
IRQ3*	Interrupt Request 3
IRQ4*	Interrupt Request 4
IRQ5*	Interrupt Request 5
IRQ6*	Interrupt Request 6
IRQ7*	Interrupt Request 7
IACK*	Interrupt Acknowledge
IACKIN*/IACKOUT*	Interrupt Acknowledge Daisy-Chain

4.2.1 Interrupt Request Lines. Interrupters request interrupts by driving an interrupt request line low. In a single handler system, these interrupt request lines are prioritized, with IRQ7* having the highest priority.

4.2.2 Interrupt Acknowledge Line. The IACK* line runs the full length of the backplane and is connected to the IACKIN* pin of slot 1 (see Fig 41). When driven low, the IACKIN* pin causes the IACK daisy-chain driver, located in slot 1, to propagate a falling edge down the interrupt acknowledge daisy-chain.

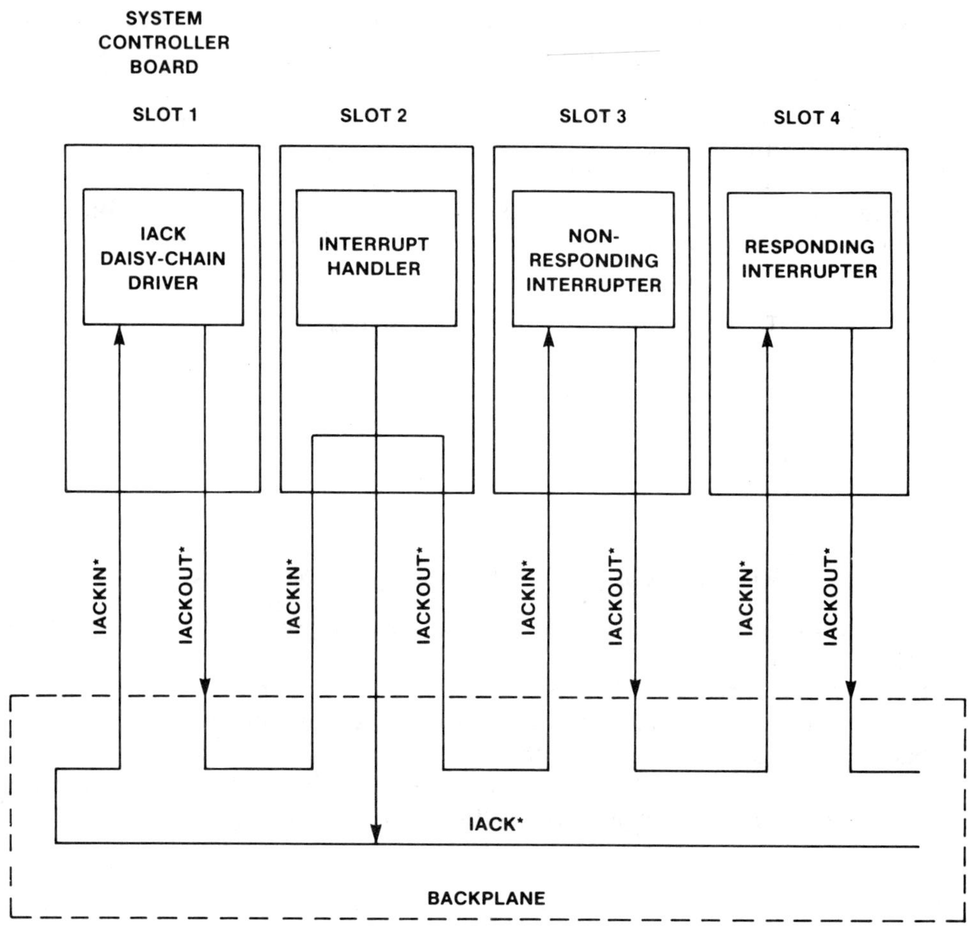

Fig 41
IACKIN*/IACKOUT* Daisy-Chain

4.2.3 Interrupt Acknowledge Daisy-Chain. Each of the seven interrupt request lines can be shared by two or more interrupter modules. The interrupt acknowledge daisy-chain ensures that only one interrupter responds to the interrupt acknowledge cycle. This daisy-chain line passes through each board in the system. Each interrupter that is driving an interrupt request line low waits for a falling edge to arrive at its IACKIN* daisy-chain input. Only upon receiving this falling edge does an interrupter respond to an interrupt acknowledge cycle. It does not pass the falling edge on down the daisy-chain, preventing other interrupters from responding to the interrupt acknowledge cycle.

Rule 4.1 If a backplane slot is not occupied by a board, and if there are boards farther down the interrupt acknowledge daisy-chain, then jumpers shall be installed at the empty slot to pass through the daisy-chain signal.

4.3 Priority Interrupt Bus Modules — Basic Description. There are three types of functional modules associated with the priority interrupt bus: interrupters, interrupt handlers, and IACK daisy-chain drivers. The capabilities of interrupt handlers and interrupters are described by a list of mnemonics that show what types of interrupt acknowledge cycles they can generate and accept, respectively.

Sections 4.3.1 through 4.3.3 provide block diagrams for the three types of priority interrupt bus modules: interrupt handler, interrupter, and IACK daisy-chain driver.

Rule 4.2 Output signal lines shown with solid lines in Figs 42 through 44 shall be driven by the module, unless it would always drive them high.

Observation 4.1 If an output line is not driven, then terminators on the backplane ensure that it is high.

> **Rule 4.3** Input signal lines shown with solid lines in Figs 42 through 44 shall be monitored and responded to in the appropriate fashion.

Observation 4.2 Rules and permissions for driving and monitoring signal lines shown with dotted lines in Figs 42 and 43, are given in Tables 30 and 31.

4.3.1 Interrupt Handlers. The interrupt handler is used to accomplish several tasks:

(1) It prioritizes the incoming interrupt requests within its assigned group of interrupt request lines (highest of IRQ1*-IRQ7*).

(2) It uses its on-board requester to request the DTB and, when granted use of the DTB, initiates an interrupt acknowledge cycle, reading a status/ID from the interrupter being acknowledged.

(3) It initiates the appropriate interrupt servicing sequence, based on the information received in the status/ID.

Observation 4.3 The actions taken during the interrupt servicing sequence are not specified. Servicing of the interrupt might or might not involve use of the bus.

The interrupt handler uses the DTB to read a status/ID from the interrupter. In this respect, the interrupt handler acts like a master and the interrupter acts like a slave. However, there are four important differences. The interrupt handler

(1) Always drives IACK* low
(2) Is not required to drive the address modifier lines
(3) Only uses the lowest three address lines (A01-A03)
(4) Never drives the data bus

The interrupt handler always drives IACK* low when it accesses the bus. The master either drives it high or does not drive it at all.

The interrupt handler does not have to drive the address modifier lines with a valid code, and it only drives the lowest three address lines (A01-A03) with valid information. The levels of these three address lines indicate which of the seven interrupt request lines is being acknowledged, as shown in Table 36. A master drives 15, 23, or 31 address lines (depending on the addressing mode) with the address of the slave being accessed, and provides an address modifier code on the address modifier lines.

The interrupt handler does not drive the data lines (that is, it does not *write* to the interrupter) and, since it never drives it low, does not have to drive the WRITE* line. A master uses the data lines to a slave bidirectionally and, during normal use, drives WRITE* low or high as required.

A block diagram of the interrupt handler is shown in Fig 42. The rules and permissions for monitoring and driving the dotted lines are given in Table 30.

4.3.2 Interrupters. The interrupter functions as follows:

(1) It requests an interrupt from the interrupt handler that monitors its interrupt request line.

(2) If it receives a falling edge on the interrupt acknowledge daisy-chain input, then if it is requesting an interrupt and the levels on the three valid address lines correspond to the interrupt request line it is using, and the width of the requested status/ID is either equal to, or greater than the size it can supply, then it supplies a status/ID, or else it passes the falling edge down the interrupt acknowledge daisy-chain.

Each interrupter module drives only one interrupt request line. A board that generates interrupt requests on several interrupt lines is described as having several interrupter modules.

> **Permission 4.1** Since the interrupter is just a conceptual model, logic on a board may be shared between several interrupter modules.

The interrupter uses one of seven lines to request an interrupt. It then monitors the lowest three lines of the address bus A01-A03, IACKIN*, and optionally IACK*, to determine when its interrupt is being acknowledged. When acknowledged, it places its status/ID on the data bus and signals the interrupt handler that the status/ID is valid by driving DTACK* low.

There are five primary differences in the use of the DTB by the interrupter and the slave. The interrupter

(1) Only responds when its IACKIN* is low

(2) Does not have to monitor the address modifier lines

(3) Only monitors the lowest three address lines

(4) Does not monitor the WRITE* line

(5) Is permitted to respond with data of a different size than that requested

The slave monitors AS*, and interprets a falling edge on AS* as the signal that a valid bus cycle is in progress. It then proceeds to decode the appropriate number of address lines (15, 23, or 31), and the address modifier lines, and based on this information determines whether it was addressed. However, the slave responds only if IACK* is high.

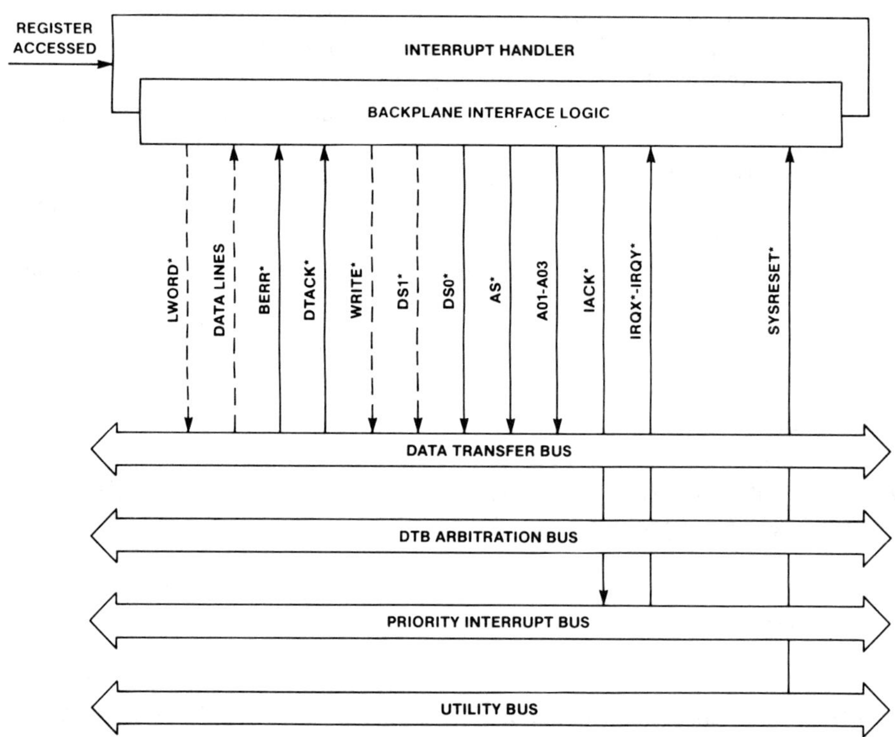

Fig 42
Block Diagram: Interrupt Handler

The interrupter, on the other hand, interprets the falling edge on its IACKIN* line as a signal that it can respond to the interrupt acknowledge cycle in progress. It decodes only the lowest three address lines (A01-A03), ignoring the address modifier lines.

Table 30
Interrupt Handler: Rules and Permissions for Driving and Monitoring the Dotted Lines

Type of Interrupt Handler	Rules and Permissions
D08(O)	Shall monitor D00-D07
	May or may not drive LWORD* and DS1* May or may not monitor D08-D31
D16	Shall drive DS1* Shall monitor D00-D15
	May or may not drive LWORD* May or may not monitor D16-D31
D32	Shall drive DS1* and LWORD* Shall monitor D00-D31
ALL	Shall not drive WRITE* low

NOTE: The mnemonics D08(O), D16, and D32 are defined in Table 34.

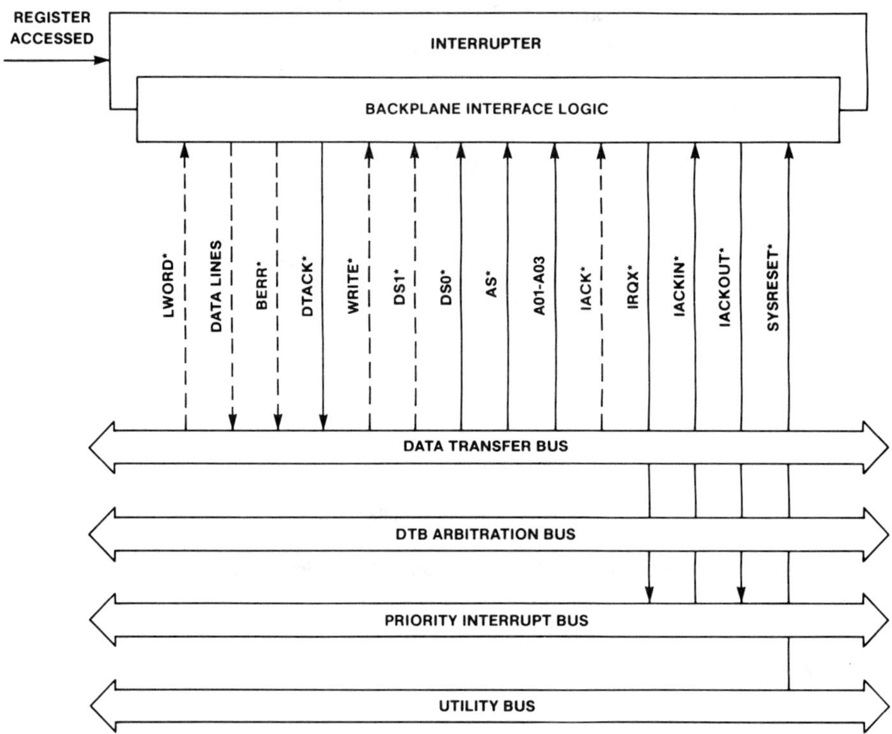

NOTE: This input signal is present on RORA interrupters only.

Fig 43
Block Diagram: Interrupter

Table 31
Interrupters: Rules and Permissions for Driving and Monitoring the Dotted Lines

Type of Interrupter	Rules and Permissions
D08(O)	Shall drive D00-D07 Shall not drive D08-D31 low May or may not monitor LWORD* or DS1*
D16	Shall monitor DS1* Shall drive D00-D15 Shall not drive D16-D31 low May or may not monitor LWORD*
D32	Shall monitor DS1* and LWORD* Shall drive D00-D31
ALL	May or may not monitor WRITE* and IACK* May or may not drive BERR*

NOTE: The mnemonics D08(O), D16, and D32 are defined in Table 34.

The interrupter does not need to monitor WRITE*, since it is never written to. Slaves need to monitor WRITE* so that they can distinguish read cycles from write cycles.

The interrupter places a status/ID on the bus, and responds with DTACK*, even if the LWORD*, DS1*, and DS0* lines call for a status/ID whose width is greater than it is able to provide. For example, the interrupt handler might drive LWORD* and both DS0* and DS1* low, indicating that it wishes to read 32 bits of status/ID from D00-D31, but a D08(O) interrupter would still respond with its 8-bit status/ID on D00-D07. In contrast, when a slave cannot provide the requested data width, it either responds with BERR* or does not respond at all, typically resulting in a bus time-out.

Observation 4.4 When an interrupter places a status/ID on the data bus, any undriven data lines are read by the interrupt handler as high because of the bus terminators. For example, if a D16 interrupt handler initiates a double-byte interrupt acknowledge cycle, a D08(O) interrupter would place an 8-bit status/ID on D00-D07. The upper 8 bits, read by the interrupt handler from D08-D15, are read as ones (high), since they are not driven by the D08(O) interrupter.

Rule 4.4 Before responding to an interrupt acknowledge cycle, the interrupter

(1) Shall have an interrupt request pending

(2) The level of that request shall match the level indicated on A01-A03

(3) The width of the requested status/ID shall be equal to or greater than the size it can respond with

(4) It shall have received an incoming falling edge on its IACKIN* daisy-chain input.

If any of these four conditions are not met, then the interrupter shall not respond to the interrupt acknowledge cycle. If condition (4) is met, but either (1), (2), or (3) is not, then the interrupter shall pass the falling edge of IACKIN* to the next interrupter module in the daisy-chain by driving IACKOUT* low.

A block diagram of the interrupter is shown in Fig 35. The rules and permissions for driving and monitoring the dotted lines are given in Table 31.

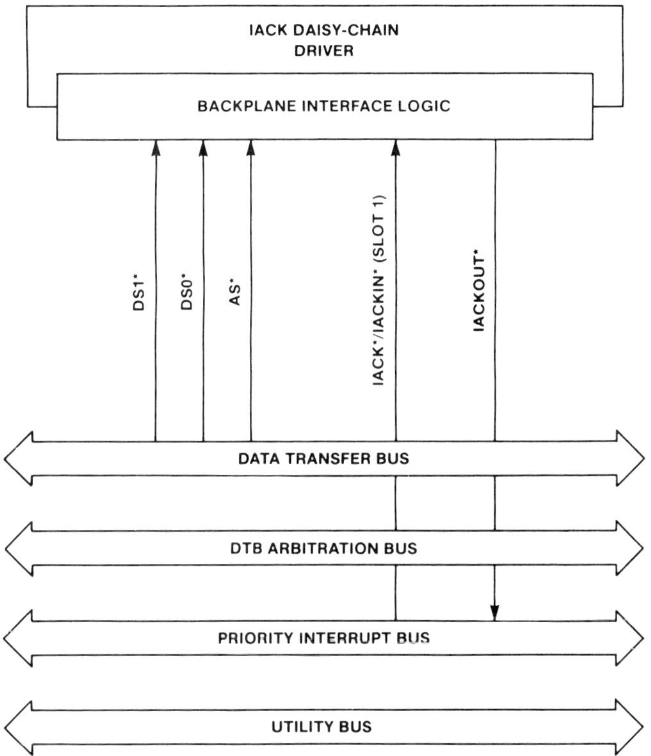

Fig 44
Block Diagram: IACK Daisy-Chain Driver

4.3.3 IACK Daisy-Chain Driver. The IACK daisy-chain driver is another module that interacts with interrupt handlers and interrupters to coordinate the servicing of interrupts. It generates a falling edge on the interrupt acknowledge daisy-chain each time an interrupt handler initiates an interrupt acknowledge cycle.

The block diagram of the IACK daisy-chain driver is given in Fig 44.

Table 32
Use of the IH( ) Mnemonic to Specify Interrupt Handling Capabilities

The Following Mnemonic	When Applied to a	Means that It
IH(x-y)	Interrupt handler	Can generate interrupt acknowledge cycles in response to interrupt requests on lines IRQx* through IRQy*
IH(x)	Interrupt handler	Can generate interrupt acknowledge cycles in response to interrupt requests on line IRQx*

4.3.4 Interrupt Handling Capabilities. Interrupt handlers can be designed to handle interrupt requests received on one to seven interrupt request lines. Table 32 shows how the IH( ) mnemonic is used to describe the interrupt handling capabilities of interrupt handlers.

4.3.5 Interrupt Request Capabilities. Interrupters can be designed to generate an interrupt request on any of the seven interrupt request lines. Table 33 shows how the I( ) mnemonic is used to describe the interrupt request generation capabilities of interrupters.

Table 33
Use of the I( ) Mnemonic to Specify Interrupt Request Capabilities

The Following Mnemonic	When Applied to a	Means that It
I(x)	Interrupter	Can generate an interrupt request on line IRQx*

Table 34
Mnemonics that Specify Status/ID Transfer Capabilities

The Following Mnemonic	When Applied to an	Means that It
D08(O)	Interrupter	Responds to 8 bit, 16 bit, and 32 bit interrupt acknowledge cycles by providing an 8 bit status/ID on D00-D07
	Interrupter handler	Generates 8 bit interrupt acknowledge cycles in response to the requests on the interrupt request line(s) and reads an 8 bit status/ID from D00-D07
D16	Interrupter	Responds to 16 bit and 32 bit interrupt acknowledge cycles by providing a 16 bit status/ID on D00-D15
	Interrupt handler	Generates 16 bit interrupt acknowledge cycles in response to the requests on the interrupt request line(s) and reads a 16 bit status/ID from D00-D15
D32	Interrupter	Responds to 32 bit interrupt acknowledge cycles by providing a 32 bit status/ID on D00-D31
	Interrupter handler	Generates 32 bit interrupt acknowledge cycles in response to the requests on the interrupt request line(s) and reads a 32 bit status/ID from D00-D31

4.3.6 Status/ID Transfer Capabilities. There are three status/ID transfer capabilities: D08(O), D16, and D32. Table 34 shows how these mnemonics are used to describe the status/ID transfer capabilities of interrupt handlers and interrupters.

4.3.7 Interrupt Release Capabilities. Many widely used peripheral IC generate interrupt requests. Unfortunately, there is no standard method for indicating to these IC when it is time for them to remove their interrupt request from the bus. Three methods are used:

(1) When the relevant processor senses an interrupt request from a peripheral device, it enters an interrupt service routine, and reads a status register in the device. The peripheral device interprets this read cycle on its status register as a signal to remove its interrupt request.

(2) When the relevant processor senses an interrupt request from a peripheral device, it enters an interrupt service routine, and writes to a control register in the device. The peripheral device interprets this write cycle to its control register as a signal to remove its interrupt request.

(3) When the relevant processor senses an interrupt request from a peripheral device, it reads a status/ID from the device. The peripheral device interprets this read cycle as a signal to remove its interrupt request.

Interrupters that use methods 1 and 2 are called Release On Register Access (RORA) interrupters, and those that use method 3 are called Release On Acknowledge (ROAK) interrupters. Figure 45 shows how an ROAK interrupter releases its interrupt request line when the interrupt handler reads its status/ID, and how an RORA interrupter releases its interrupt request upon an access to a control or status register.

Fig 45
Release of the Interrupt Request Lines by ROAK and RORA Interrupters

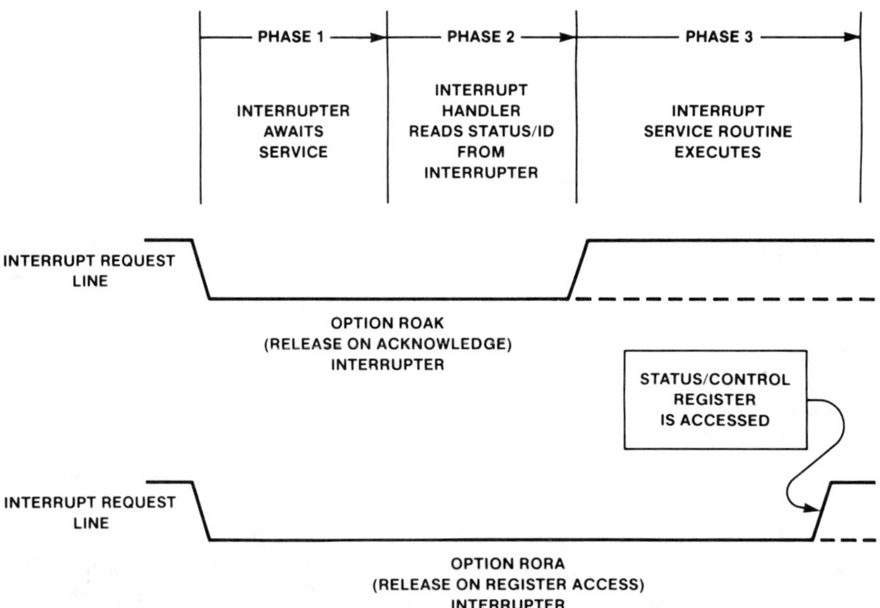

Observation 4.5 The slave that provided the access to the interrupter's control or status register is typically on the same board as the interrupter, and generates an on-board signal to the interrupter when it has completed the register access.

Rule 4.5 A RORA interrupter shall not release its interrupt request line before it detects a falling edge on DSA* during the register access cycle. It shall release the interrupt request line within 2 μs after DSB* goes high at the end of the register access cycle.

Rule 4.6 A ROAK interrupter shall not release its interrupt request line before it detects a falling edge on DSA* during the interrupt acknowledge cycle that acknowledges its interrupt, and it shall release its interrupt request line within 500 nanoseconds after DSB* goes high at the end of the status/ID read cycle.

Rule 4.7 Both RORA and ROAK interrupters shall provide a status/ID during the interrupt acknowledge cycle that was initiated in response to their interrupt request.

Rule 4.8 After an interrupt handler initiates an interrupt acknowledge cycle and reads the status/ID from a RORA interrupter, it shall ignore the low level on the interrupt request line for 2 μs after its on-board signal register accessed goes true.

Observation 4.6 Rule 4.8 prevents the interrupt handler from misinterpreting the low level on that line as a new interrupt request.

Observation 4.7 The master that accesses the interrupter's control or status register is typically on the same board as the interrupt handler, and it generates an on-board signal to the interrupt handler when it has completed the register access.

Permission 4.2 If a procedure is established to allow the master to signal the interrupt handler an access to the interrupter's control or status registers, then the master and interrupt handler may reside on different boards.

Table 35 shows how the RORA and ROAK mnemonics are used to describe interrupters.

Table 35
Mnemonics that Specify Interrupt Release Capabilities

The Following Mnemonic	When Applied to an	Means that It
RORA	Interrupter	Releases its interrupt request line when some master accesses an on-board status or control register
ROAK	Interrupter	Releases its interrupt request line when its status/ID is read during an interrupt acknowledge cycle

4.3.8 Interaction Between Priority Interrupt Bus Modules. In the following discussion, several on-board signals are defined to describe the interaction between the interrupter modules, interrupt handler modules, and other on-board logic. These signals are only intended to illustrate the information that is passed to and from the modules, rather than to define their designs.

Permission 4.3 Boards may be designed with on-board signals that differ from those used in the following discussions.

Figure 41 (See page 150) shows how the IACKIN*/IACKOUT* daisy-chain is routed through a typical configuration of boards in a system. The IACK* line runs the full length of the backplane and can be driven by any interrupt handler that has control of the DTB. The backplane connects IACK* to the IACKIN* pin of slot 1. The IACK daisy-chain driver resides in slot 1 and monitors the level of slot 1's IACKIN* line.

When an interrupt handler drives IACK* (and slot 1's IACKIN*) low, and then drives DSA* low, the IACK daisy-chain driver generates a falling edge on its IACKOUT* pin. This pin is connected to the IACKIN* pin of slot 2. A jumper on the board in slot 2 routes the falling edge on the IACKIN* pin to the IACKOUT* pin, and through the backplane to the IACKIN* pin of the board in slot 3. The interrupter in slot 3 does not have a pending interrupt request, so it passes on the falling edge to its IACKOUT* pin. The interrupter in slot 4 then detects the falling edge on its IACKIN* line and responds by placing its status/ID on the data bus, and then driving DTACK* low.

Permission 4.4 An interrupter may reside on the system controller board, installed in slot 1, along with the IACK daisy-chain driver. Figure 46 shows how the two modules are connected.

Fig 46
An IACK Daisy-Chain Driver and an Interrupter on the Same Board

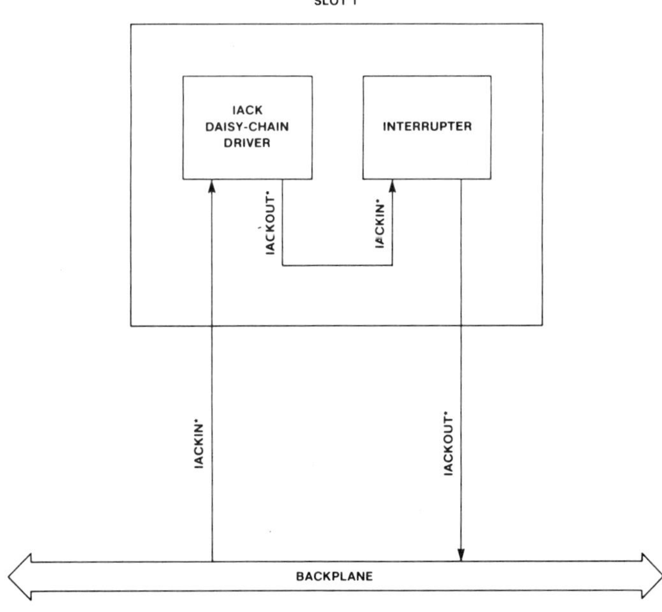

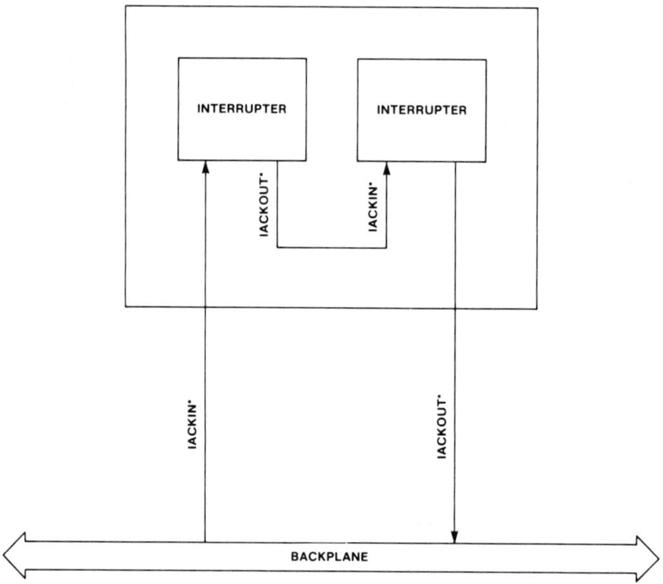

Fig 47
Two Interrupters on the Same Board

Permission 4.5 More than one interrupter may reside on a board. Figure 47 shows how this might be done.

Observation 4.8 In some cases, designers might not know whether or not the board they are designing will be installed in slot 1, or in some other slot of the system.

Recommendation 4.1 If a board includes both an IACK daisy-chain driver and an interrupter, and might or might not be installed in slot 1, then design it as shown in Fig 46.

Permission 4.6 Several boards containing IACK daisy-chain drivers may be installed in a system.

4.4 Typical Operation. A typical interrupt sequence is divided into the following three phases:

Phase 1: The interrupt request phase

Phase 2: The interrupt acknowledge phase

Phase 3: The interrupt servicing phase

Figure 48 illustrates the timing relationships between the three phases.

Phase 1 starts when an interrupter drives an interrupt request line low and ends when the interrupt handler gains control of the DTB.

During phase 2 the interrupt handler uses the DTB to read the interrupter's status/ID.

During phase 3 an interrupt service routine is executed (This might or might not involve data transfers on the bus).

The protocol for the interrupt subsystem describes the module interaction required during phases 1 and 2. Any data transfers that take place during phase 3 will follow the data transfer bus protocol described in Section 2.

Fig 48
The Three Phases of an Interrupt Sequence

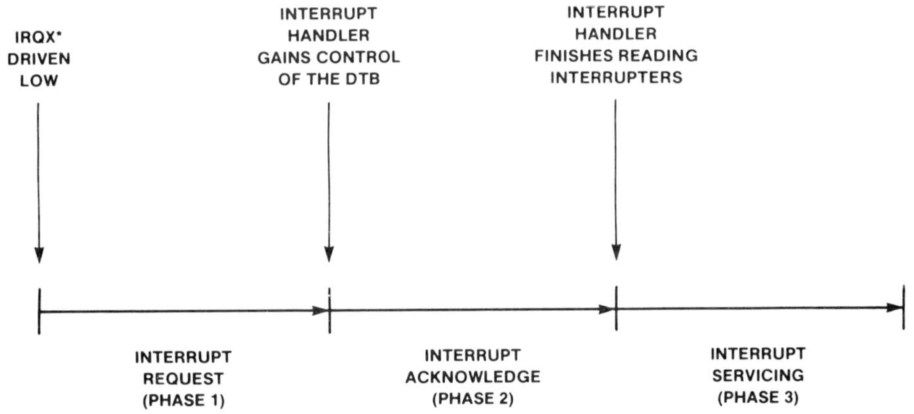

4.4.1 Single Handler Interrupt Operation. In single handler interrupt systems, the seven interrupt request lines are all monitored by a single interrupt handler. The interrupt request lines are prioritized so that IRQ7* has the highest priority, and IRQ1* has the lowest. When the interrupt handler detects simultaneous requests on two interrupt request lines, it acknowledges the highest priority request first.

4.4.2 Distributed Interrupt Operation. Distributed interrupt systems contain from two to seven interrupt handlers. For purposes of the following discussion, distributed interrupt systems will be considered in two groups:

(1) Distributed interrupt systems with seven interrupt handlers

(2) Distributed interrupt systems with two to six interrupt handlers

4.4.2.1 Distributed Interrupt Systems with Seven Interrupt Handlers. In distributed interrupt systems with seven interrupt handlers, each of the interrupt request lines is monitored by a separate interrupt handler. Each interrupt handler gains control of the DTB before it reads the status/ID from the interrupter that is driving its interrupt request line.

Observation 4.9 There is no specified relationship between the interrupt request line that an interrupt handler services and the bus request line used by its associated requester. For example, an interrupt handler that services IRQ7* might have a requester that uses BR0*, and an interrupt handler that services IRQ1* might have a requester that uses BR3*.

Fig 49
Two Interrupt Handlers, Each Monitoring One Interrupt Request Line

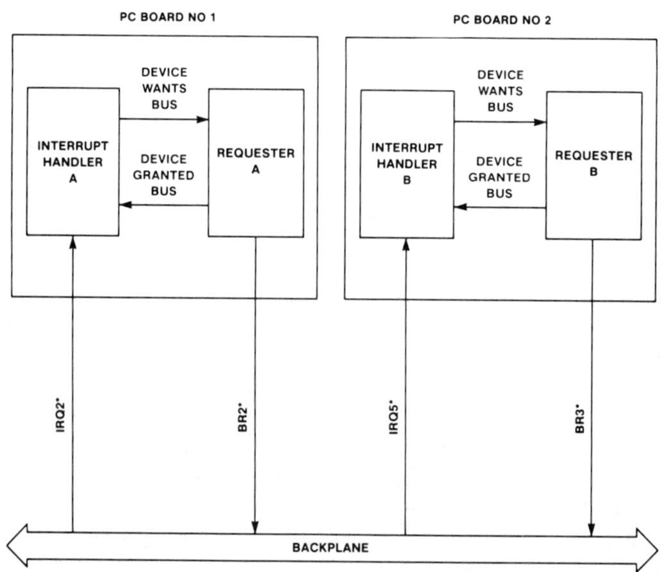

Figure 49 illustrates a distributed interrupt system where interrupt handler A monitors IRQ2* and has an associated requester that requests the DTB on BR2*. Interrupt handler B monitors IRQ5* and has an associated requester that requests the DTB on BR3*. Two interrupters simultaneously drive IRQ2* and IRQ5* low, and the two interrupt handlers cause their on-board requesters to drive BR2* and BR3* low simultaneously. In this example priority arbitration is used and, since both bus requests go low together, the arbiter first grants control of the DTB to interrupt handler B's requester, and interrupt handler A waits until B finishes using the DTB.

Observation 4.10 If round-robin arbitration is used, either of the interrupt handlers described in Fig 49 might be granted the bus first.

4.4.2.2 Distributed Interrupt Systems with Two to Six Interrupt Handlers. It is also possible to configure a distributed interrupt system in which two or more of the interrupt request lines are monitored by a single interrupt handler. Figure 50 illustrates a system configured with two interrupt handlers. Interrupt

Fig 50
Two Interrupt Handlers, Each Monitoring Several Interrupt Request Lines

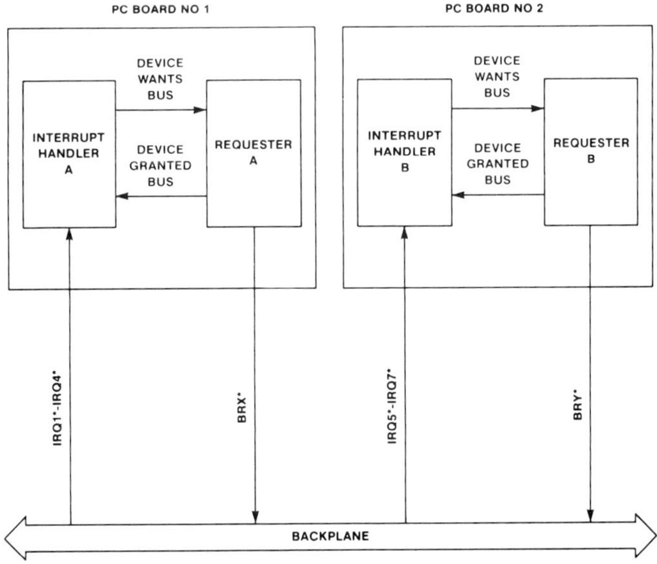

handler A monitors IRQ1*-IRQ4*, and interrupt handler B monitors IRQ5*-IRQ7*. In this case, the IRQ1*-IRQ4* lines are prioritized; IRQ4* = highest priority for interrupt handler A, and the IRQ5*-IRQ7* lines are prioritized; IRQ7* = highest priority for interrupt handler B. The DTB arbitration still determines which interrupt handler is granted use of the DTB first.

4.4.3 Example: Typical Single Handler Interrupt System Operation. Figure 51 illustrates the operation of a single handler interrupt system in which one interrupt handler monitors and prioritizes all seven interrupt lines. At the top of the diagram, a master, whose requester was granted the bus using BR2*, is using the DTB. An interrupter in slot 4 requests an interrupt by driving IRQ4* low. When the interrupt handler detects the low level on IRQ4* it drives true the DEVICE WANTS BUS signal to its on-board requester, indicating that it needs the bus. This requester then drives BR3* low. Upon detecting the bus request, the arbiter drives BCLR* low, indicating that a higher priority requester is waiting for the DTB (This example assumes a PRI arbiter). When master A detects the low level on BCLR*, it stops moving data and allows its requester to relinquish control of the DTB by releasing BBSY* high.

> **Observation 4.11** The active master is not required to relinquish the DTB within any specified time, but a prompt response to the BCLR* line allows the interrupt to be serviced quicker.

When the arbiter detects BBSY* high, it grants the DTB to requester B, which informs its interrupt handler that the DTB is available. The interrupt handler then drives 3-bit code on address lines A01-A03 to indicate that it is acknowledging the interrupt request on the IRQ4* line (see Table 36), and drives IACK* low to indicate that it is acknowledging an interrupt. The interrupt handler then drives AS* low.

Table 36
3-Bit Interrupt Acknowledge Code

Interrupt Line Being Acknowledged	A03	A02	A01
IRQ1*	low	low	high
IRQ2*	low	high	low
IRQ3*	low	high	high
IRQ4*	high	low	low
IRQ5*	high	low	high
IRQ6*	high	high	low
IRQ7*	high	high	high

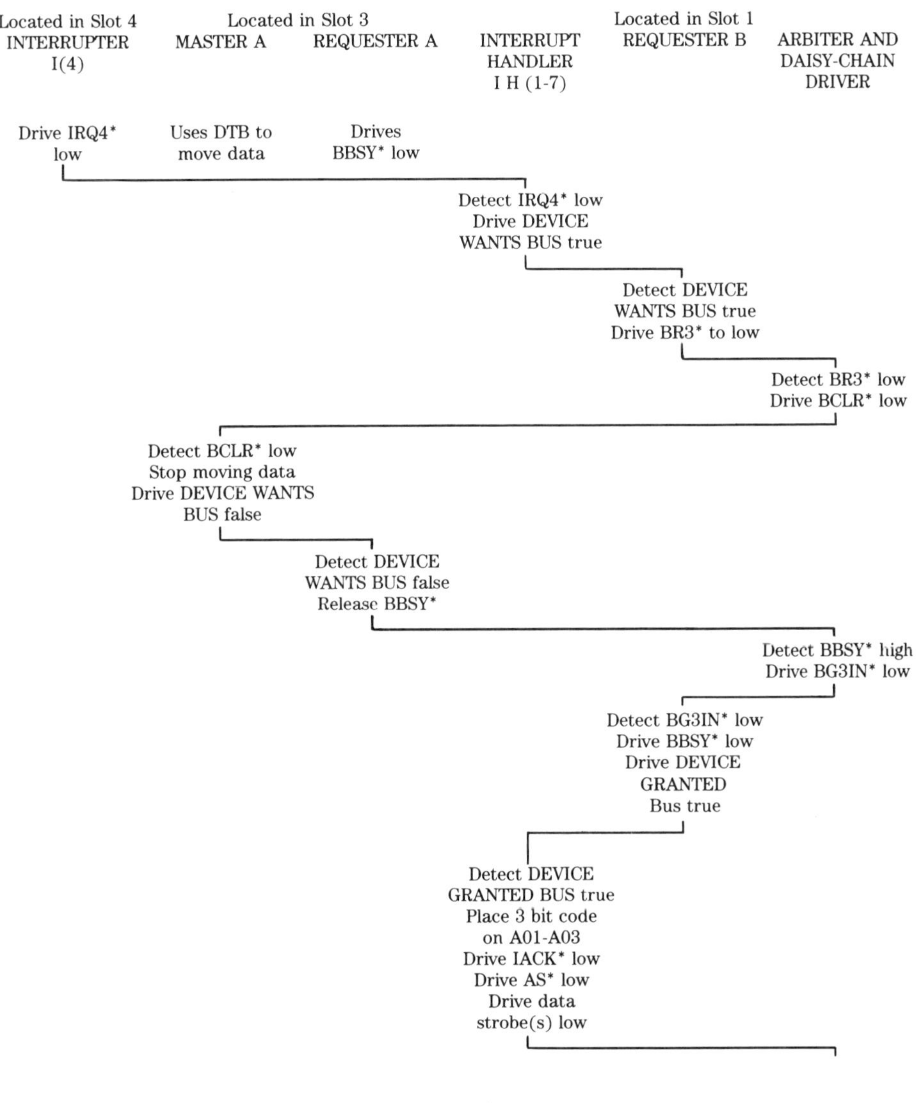

(*Continued on Page 172*)

Fig 51
Operation of a Single Handler Interrupt System

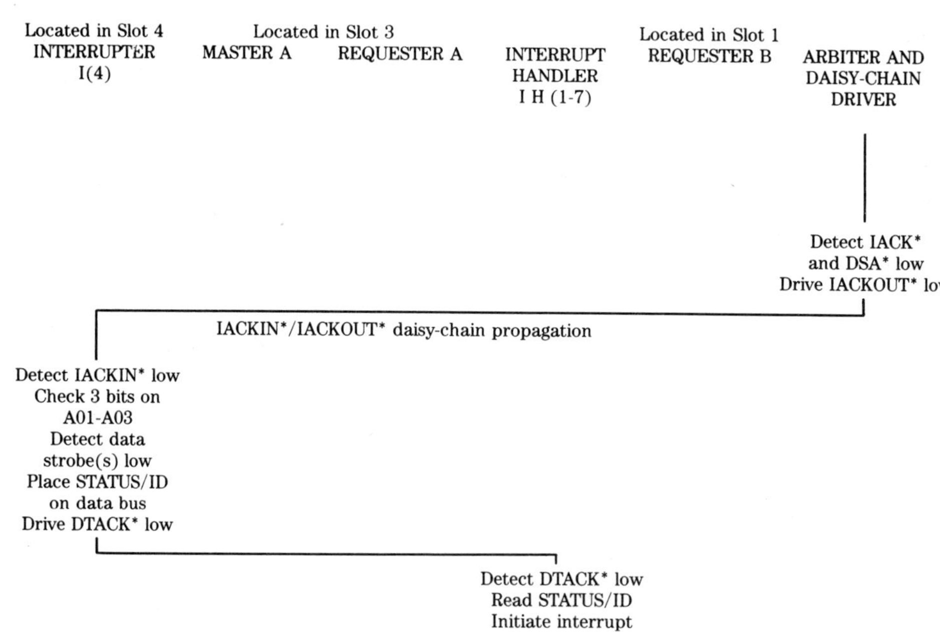

Fig 51 *(Continued)*
Operation of a Single Handler Interrupt System

The low level on IACK* is connected by a signal trace in the backplane to the IACKIN* pin of slot 1, and causes the IACK daisy-chain driver to generate a falling edge down the IACKIN*/IACKOUT* daisy-chain.

When the interrupter detects a falling edge on IACKIN* it checks the levels of A01-A03 to see if they match the interrupt request line it is driving low. Since the 3-bit code matches the line on which it is making its interrupt request, the interrupter places its status/ID on the data bus and drives the DTACK* line low, after detecting the data strobe(s) low. When the interrupt handler detects DTACK* low, it reads the status/ID and activates the appropriate interrupt service routine.

4.4.4 Example: Prioritization of Two Interrupts in a Distributed Interrupt System. Figure 52 illustrates the operation of a distributed interrupt system with two interrupt handlers. Interrupt handler A monitors IRQ1*-IRQ4*, while interrupt handler B monitors IRQ5*-IRQ7*. Interrupt handler A treats IRQ4* as its highest priority interrupt, while interrupt handler B treats IRQ7* as its highest priority interrupt. At the top of the diagram, interrupter C drives IRQ3* low, and interrupter D drives IRQ6* low. Both interrupt handlers detect their respective interrupt request lines low, and both simultaneously indicate to their on-board requesters that they need the DTB. Both requesters drive BR3* low. Upon detecting BR3* low, the arbiter drives BG3IN* low on slot 1. This low signal is

Fig 52
Operation of a Distributed Interrupt System with Two Interrupt Handlers

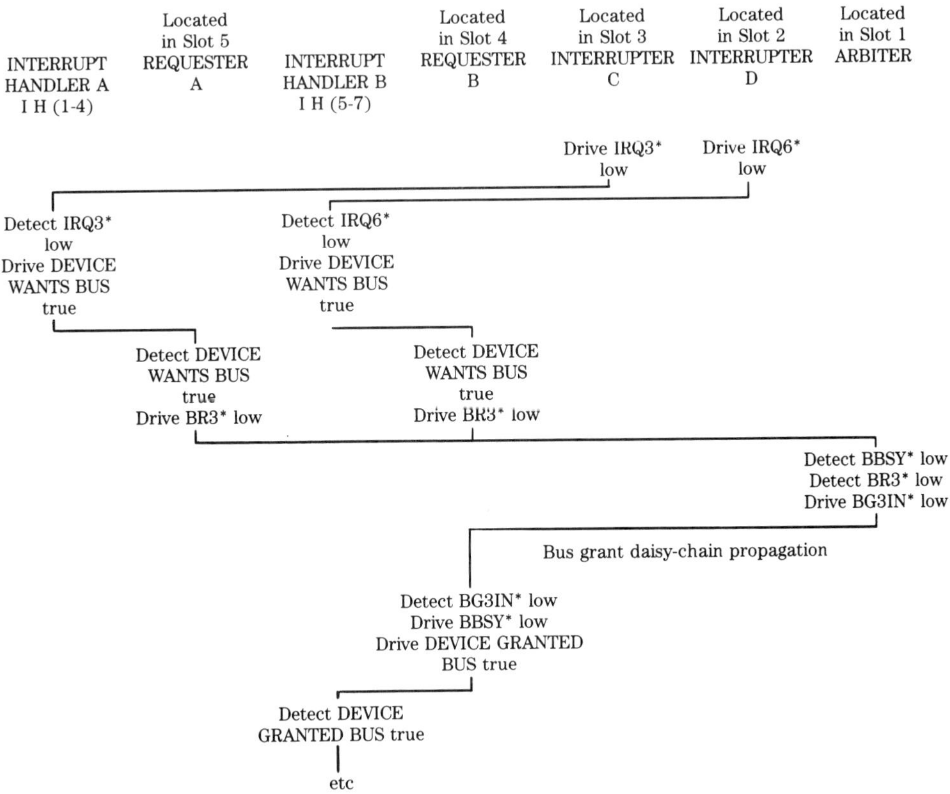

passed down the BG3IN*/BG3OUT* daisy-chain until it is detected by requester B in slot 4. This requester then signals its on-board interrupt handler B that the DTB is available. Interrupt handler B then reads the status/ID from interrupter D.

4.5 Race Conditions. Suppose that there are two interrupters: interrupter A and interrupter B. Interrupter B, which is further down the interrupt acknowledge daisy-chain, requests an interrupt. After the relevant interrupt handler is granted the bus, it acknowledges the interrupt request by driving the IACK* line low. The resulting low-going edge on the interrupt acknowledge daisy-chain arrives at interrupter A just as it is about to drive its own interrupt request line low. If interrupter A is improperly designed, this situation might cause it to momentarily drive its IACKOUT* line low, and then high again, resulting in a low-going transient on the interrupt acknowledge daisy-chain.

Rule 4.49 Interrupters shall be designed to ensure that no momentary low-going transients are generated on their IACKOUT* line.

Observation 4.50 If the interrupter is designed so that it latches the state of an on-board generated interrupt request line upon the falling edge of its IACKIN* line, and if that signal is in transition when the falling edge occurs, the outputs of the latch will sometimes oscillate, or remain in the threshold region between the high and low levels, for a short time. Because of this, no time limit is set for the interrupter to pass along the interrupt acknowledge. It is only prohibited from generating a low-going transient on its IACKOUT* line, which might be interpreted as an acknowledge by an interrupter further down the daisy-chain. Appendix D provides a sample circuit for the IACK daisy-chain logic.

Permission 4.11 If an interrupter is about to drive an interrupt request line low between the time it receives an interrupt acknowledge intended for another interrupter, and the time it would pass the interrupt acknowledge on, then it may treat the interrupt acknowledge as its own. In this case the other interrupter maintains its interrupt request until another acknowledge is issued.

4.6 Priority Interrupt Bus Timing Rules and Observations. This section describes the timing rules and observations that govern the behavior of interrupt handlers, interrupters, and IACK daisy-chain drivers during the selection of the responding interrupter (that is, the interrupter that is to provide its status/ID in response to the interrupt acknowledge cycle). This timing information is in the form of figures and tables.

The interrupt acknowledge cycle begins with the selection of the responding interrupter. This is called the interrupter selection phase of the cycle. Once an interrupter responds, the interrupt handler reads the status/ID from it. This is called the status/ID transfer phase of the cycle.

When the interrupt handler initiates an interrupt acknowledge cycle, there might be interrupters between it and the interrupter being acknowledged that do not have an interrupt pending, or have an interrupt pending, but are on a different interrupt request line than the one being acknowledged.

Although these interrupters do not respond with a status/ID, they do participate in the interrupt acknowledge cycle by passing the falling edge from their IACKIN* line on to their IACKOUT* line. For this reason, these interrupters are called participating interrupters.

The first interrupter in the daisy-chain that has an interrupt pending on the interrupt request line that is being acknowledged responds with a status/ID. For this reason it is called the responding interrupter. All other interrupters are called nonparticipating interrupters.

(1) Table 37 lists a timing tables and timing diagrams that specify interrupt handler and interrupter operation.

(2) Table 38 lists timing tables and timing diagrams that specify IACK daisy-chain driver operation.

(3) Table 39 lists timing tables and timing diagrams that specify participating interrupter operation.

(4) Table 40 lists timing tables and timing diagrams that specify responding interrupter operation.

(5) Table 41 defines the mnemonics that are used in Tables 42 through 44.

(6) Tables 42 through 44 specify the use of bus signal lines by the priority interrupt bus functional modules.

(7) Tables 45 through 48 specify the timing parameters for the priority interrupt bus functional modules (The reference numbers used in Tables 46 through 48 correspond to the timing parameter numbers in Table 45).

(8) Figures 53 through 60 are timing diagrams that specify the timing during interrupt acknowledge cycles.

(9) Figure 61 specifies additional inter-cycle timing for the IACKIN*/IACK-OUT* daisy-chain.

All of the rules and observations associated with the figures listed below also apply to interrupt handlers, interrupters, and IACK daisy-chain drivers.

(10) Figures 25 through 27 in Section 2 specify the timing for the address and data strobes between data transfer cycles.

(11) Figure 28 specifies the timing of a timed-out cycle.

(12) Figure 29 specifies the timing during bus mastership transfer.

To meet the specified timing, board designers have to take into account the worst case propagation delays of the bus drivers and receivers used on their boards. The propagation delay of the drivers depends on their output loads, however, manufacturers' specifications do not always give enough information to calculate the propagation delays under various loads. To help the board designer, some suggestions are offered in Section 6.

The observations specify the timing of incoming signal transitions. These times can be relied upon as long as the backplane loading rules in Section 6 are not violated. The rules for the bus terminators in Section 6 guarantee that the timing parameters for signal lines that are released after they have been driven, are met.

Typically, for each timing rule there is a corresponding timing observation. However, the time that is guaranteed in the observations might differ from the time specified by the rule. For example, a careful inspection of the timing diagrams shows that the interrupt handler is required to provide 35 ns of address setup time, but the interrupter is only guaranteed 10 ns. This is because the address drivers are not always able to drive the backplane's signal lines completely through the low to high threshold region, until the transition propagates to the end of the backplane and is reflected back. The falling edge of the address strobe, however, typically crosses the 0.8 V threshold without waiting for a reflection. And therefore, the resulting setup time at the interrupter is the interrupt handler's setup time less two bus propagation times.

A special notation has been used to describe the timing of the data strobes. The two data strobes (DS0* and DS1*) do not always make their transitions simultaneously. For purposes of these timing diagrams, DSA* represents the first data strobe to make its transition (whether that is DS0* or DS1*). DSB* represents the second data strobe to make its transition (whether that is DS1* or DS0*). The broken line shown while the data strobes are stable indicates that the first data strobe to make a falling transition might not be the first to make its rising transition, that is, DSA* might represent DS0* on its falling edge and DS1* on its rising edge.

Table 37
Timing Diagrams that Define Interrupt Handler and Interrupter Operation

Mnemonic	Type of Cycle	Interrupter Selection Timing Diagram	Status/ID Transfer Timing Diagram
D08(O)	Single-Byte Status/ID Read	Figs 15 and 53	Fig 57
D16	Double-Byte Status/ID Read	Figs 15 and 53	Fig 57
D32	Quad-Byte Status/ID Read	Figs 15 and 53	Fig 57

Table 38
Timing Diagrams that Define IACK Daisy-Chain Driver Operation

Type of Cycle	Interrupter Selection Timing Diagram
Single-Byte Status/ID Read	Fig 54
Double-Byte Status/ID Read	Fig 54
Quad-Byte Status/ID Read	Fig 54

Table 39
Timing Diagrams that Define Participating Interrupter Operation

Type of Cycle	Interrupter Selection Timing Diagram
Single-Byte Status/ID Read	Fig 55
Double-Byte Status/ID Read	Fig 55
Quad-Byte status/ID Read	Fig 55

Table 40
Timing Diagrams that Define Responding Interrupter Operation

Mnemonic	Type of Cycle	Interrupter Selection Timing Diagram	Status/ID Transfer Timing Diagram
D08(O)	Single-Byte Status/ID Read	Fig 56	Fig 59
D16	Double-Byte Status/ID Read	Fig 56	Fig 59
D32	Quad-Byte Status/ID Read	Fig 56	Fig 59

Table 41
Definitions of Mnemonics Used in Tables 50, 51, and 52

Mnemonic	Description	Comments
DLBIH	Driven Low by Interrupt Handler	**Rule 4.10** The interrupt handler shall drive DLBIH lines to a low level.
DHBIH	Driven High by Interrupt Handler	**Rule 4.11** The interrupt handler shall drive DHBIH lines to a high level.
dhbih?	Driven High by Interrupt Handler?	**Permission 4.7** The interrupt handler may drive dhbih? lines high.
		Rule 4.12 The interrupt handler shall not drive dhbih? lines low during the cycle.
DVBI	Driven Valid by Interrupter	**Rule 4.13** The interrupter shall drive DVBI lines to a valid level.
dhbi?	Driven by Interrupter?	**Permission 4.9** The interrupter may drive dhbi? lines high.
		Rule 4.14 The interrupter shall not drive dhbi? lines low.

Table 42
Use of A01-A03 and IACK* During Interrupt Acknowledge Cycles

Interrupt Line Being Acknowledged	A03	A02	A01	IACK*
IRQ1*	DLBIH	DLBIH	DHBIH	DLBIH
IRQ2*	DLBIH	DHBIH	DLBIH	DLBIH
IRQ3*	DLBIH	DHBIH	DHBIH	DLBIH
IRQ4*	DHBIH	DLBIH	DLBIH	DLBIH
IRQ5*	DHBIH	DLBIH	DHBIH	DLBIH
IRQ6*	DHBIH	DHBIH	DLBIH	DLBIH
IRQ7*	DHBIH	DHBIH	DHBIH	DLBIH

Table 43
Use of DS1*, DS0*, LWORD*, and WRITE* During Interrupt Acknowledge Cycles

Mnemonic	Type of Cycle	DS1*	DS0*	LWORD*	WRITE*
D08(O)	Single-byte interrupt acknowledge	dhbih?	DLBIH	dhbih?	dhbih?
D16	Double-byte interrupt acknowledge	DLBIH	DLBIH	dhbih?	dhbih?
D32	Quad-byte interrupt acknowledge	DLBIH	DLBIH	DLBIH	dhbih?

Table 44
Use of the Data Lines to Transfer the Status/ID

Mnemonic	Type of Cycle	D24-D31	D16-D23	D08-D15	D00-D07
D08(O)	Single-, double-, and quad-byte interrupt acknowledge	dhbi?	dhbi?	dhbi?	DVBI
D16	Double- and quad-byte interrupt acknowledge	dhbi?	dhbi?	DVBI	DVBI
D32	Quad-byte interrupt acknowledge	DVBI	DVBI	DVBI	DVBI

Table 45
Interrupt Handler, Interrupter, and IACK Daisy-Chain Driver Timing Parameters

Parameter Number	Interrupt Handler See Table 46		Interrupter See Table 47		IACK Daisy-Chain Driver See Table 48	
	min	max	min	max	min	max
1	0					
2	0					
3	60					
4	35		10			
5	40		30		30	
6			0			
7			0			
9	0		0			
10	0		-10			
11	40		30			
12	35		10			
13		10		20		
14	0		0			
16	0		0			
18	0		0			
19	40		30		30	
20	0		0			
21	0		0			
23	10		0			
24A	0					
24B	0					
25		25				
26	0		0			
27	-25		0			
28	30	2T	30			
29	0		0			
30	0		0			
31	0		0			
32			10		10	
34			30		40	
35			0	30	0	30
36			0			
37			0			
38A			0			
38B			0			
39				40		
40			30		30	
41			0			
42					30	
43			0			

NOTES: (1) All times are in nanoseconds
(2) T = the time-out value

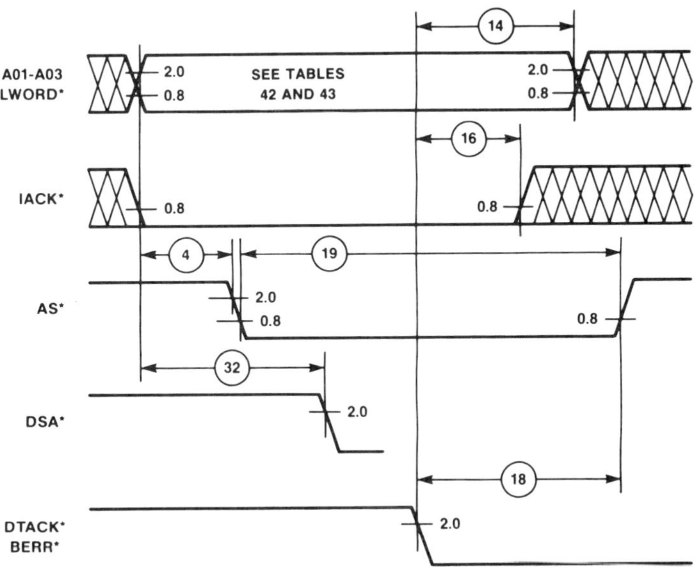

Parameter Number	Interrupt Handler min	Interrupt Handler max	Interrupter min	Interrupter max	IACK Daisy-Chain Driver min	IACK Daisy-Chain Driver max
4	35		10			
14	0		0			
16	0		0			
18	0		0			
19	40		30		30	
32			10		10	

NOTE: All times are in nanoseconds

Fig 53
Interrupt Handler and Interrupter—Interrupter Selection Timing
Single-Byte, Double-Byte, and Quad-Byte Interrupt Acknowledge Cycles

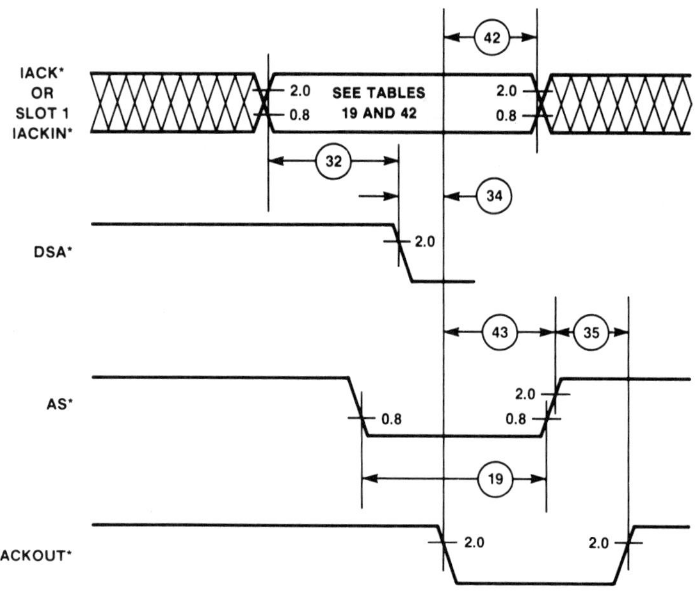

Parameter Number	Interrupt Handler min	Interrupt Handler max	Interrupter min	Interrupter max	IACK Daisy-Chain Driver min	IACK Daisy-Chain Driver max
19	40		30		30	
32			10		10	
34			30		40	
35			0	30	0	30
42					30	
43			0			

NOTE: All times are in nanoseconds

Fig 54
IACK Daisy-Chain Driver—Interrupter Selection Timing
Single-Byte, Double-Byte, and Quad-Byte Interrupt Acknowledge Cycles

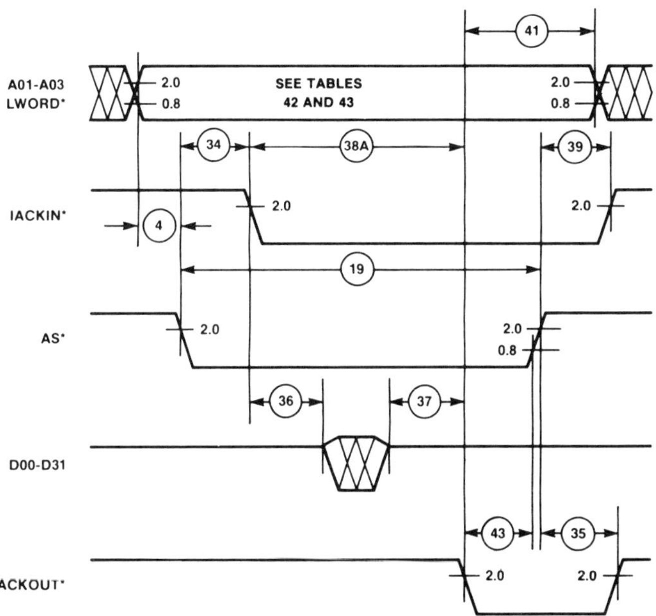

Parameter Number	Interrupt Handler min	Interrupt Handler max	Interrupter min	Interrupter max	IACK Daisy-Chain Driver min	IACK Daisy-Chain Driver max
4	35		10			
19	40		30		30	
34			30		40	
35			0	30	0	30
36			0			
37			0			
38A			0			
39				40		
41			0			
43			0			

NOTE: All times are in nanoseconds

Fig 55
Participating Interrupter—Interrupter Selection Timing
Single-Byte, Double-Byte, and Quad-Byte Interrupt Acknowledge Cycles

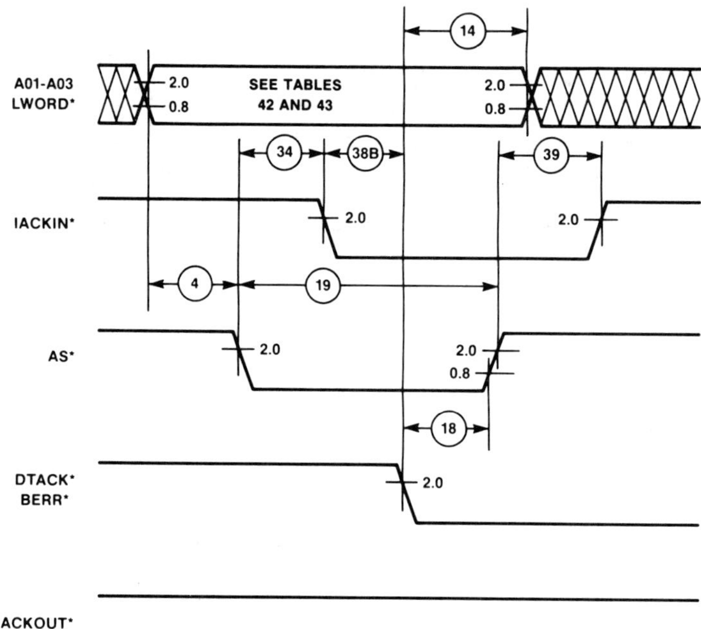

Parameter Number	Interrupt Handler min	Interrupt Handler max	Interrupter min	Interrupter max	IACK Daisy-Chain Driver min	IACK Daisy-Chain Driver max
4	35		10			
14	0		0			
18	0		0			
19	40		30		30	
34			30		40	
38B			0			
39				40		

NOTE: All times are in nanoseconds

Fig 56
Responding Interrupter — Interrupter Selection Timing
Single-Byte, Double-Byte, and Quad-Byte Interrupt Acknowledge Cycles

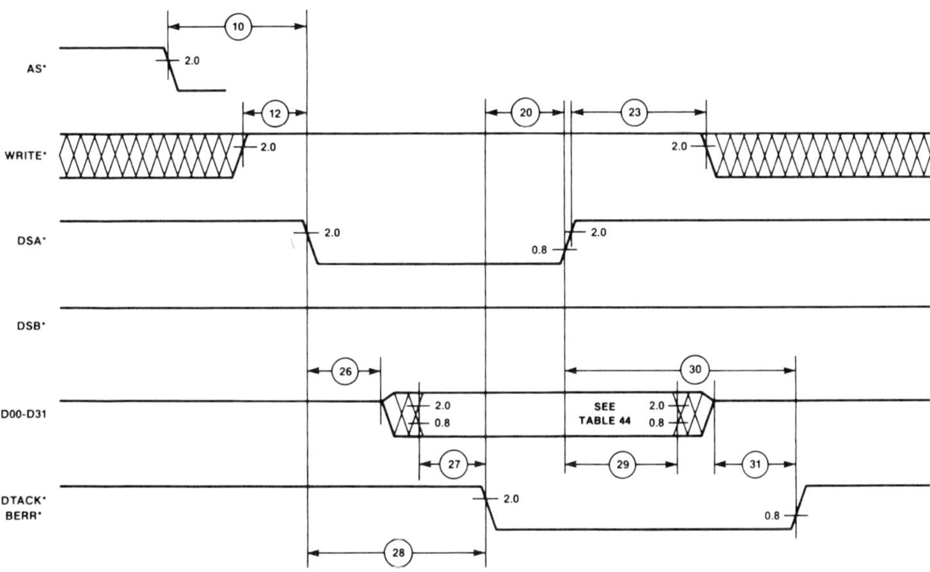

Parameter Number	Interrupt Handler min	Interrupt Handler max	Interrupter min	Interrupter max	IACK Daisy-Chain Driver min	IACK Daisy-Chain Driver max
10	0		-10			
12	35		10			
20	0		0			
23	10		0			
26	0		0			
27	-25		0			
28	30	2T	30			
29	0		0			
30	0		0			
31	0		0			

NOTES: (1) All times are in nanoseconds
(2) T = the time-out value

Fig 57
Interrupt Handler—Status/ID Transfer Timing
Single-Byte Interrupt Acknowledge Cycle

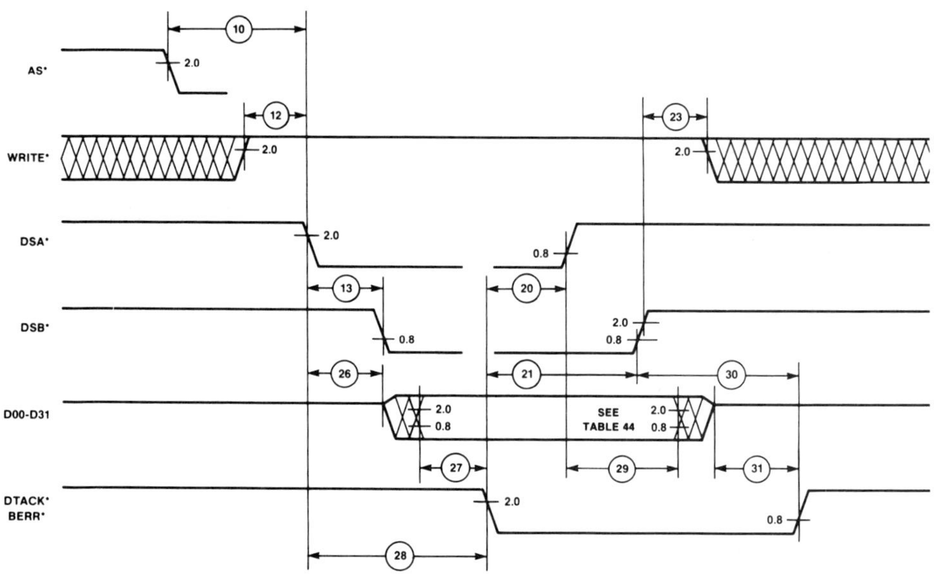

Parameter Number	Interrupt Handler min	Interrupt Handler max	Interrupter min	Interrupter max	IACK Daisy-Chain Driver min	IACK Daisy-Chain Driver max
10	0		-10			
12	35		10			
13		10		20		
20	0		0			
21	0		0			
23	10		0			
26	0		0			
27	-25		0			
28	30	2T	30			
29	0		0			
30	0		0			
31	0		0			

NOTES: (1) All times are in nanoseconds
(2) T = the time-out value

Fig 58
Interrupt Handler—Status/ID Transfer Timing
Double-Byte and Quad-Byte Interrupt Acknowledge Cycles

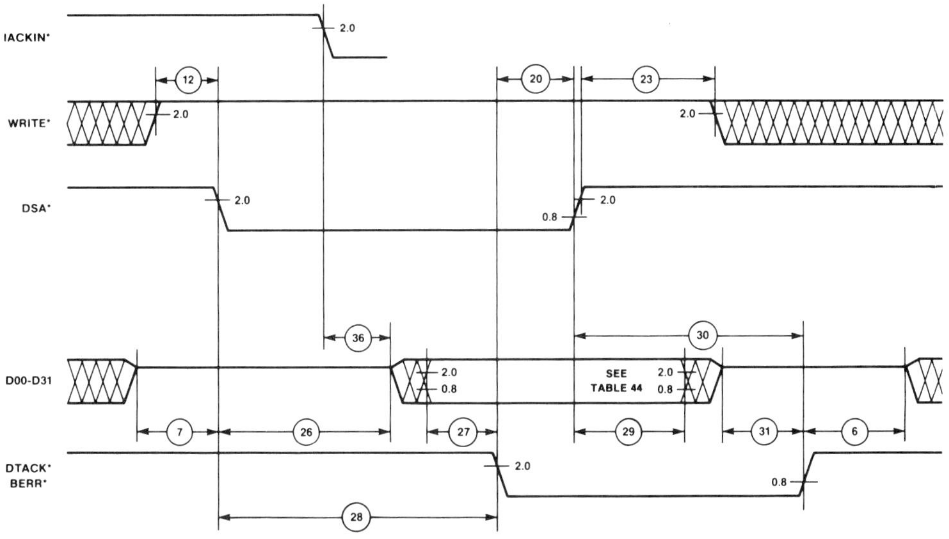

Parameter Number	Interrupt Handler min	Interrupt Handler max	Interrupter min	Interrupter max	IACK Daisy-Chain Driver min	IACK Daisy-Chain Driver max
6			0			
7			0			
12	35		10			
20	0		0			
23	10		0			
26	0		0			
27	-25		0			
28	30	2T	30			
29	0		0			
30	0		0			
31	0		0			
36			0			

NOTES: (1) All times are in nanoseconds
(2) T = the time-out value

Fig 59
Responding Interrupter—Status/ID Transfer Timing
Single-Byte Interrupt Acknowledge Cycle

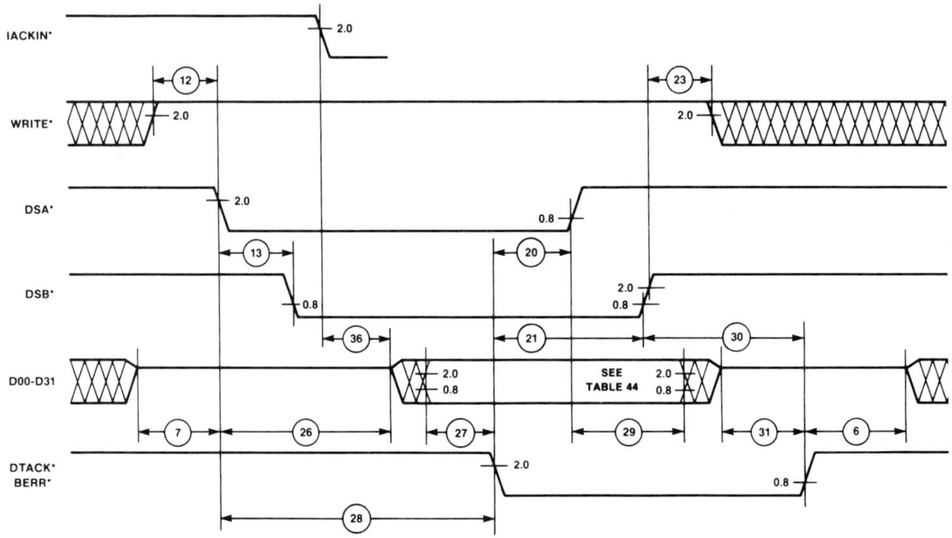

Parameter Number	Interrupt Handler min	Interrupt Handler max	Interrupter min	Interrupter max	IACK Daisy-Chain Driver min	IACK Daisy-Chain Driver max
6			0			
7			0			
12	35		10			
13		10		20		
20	0		0			
21	0		0			
23	10		0			
26	0		0			
27	-25		0			
28	30	2T	30			
29	0		0			
30	0		0			
31	0		0			
36			0			

NOTES: (1) All times are in nanoseconds
(2) T = the time-out value

Fig 60
Responding Interrupter—Status/ID Transfer Timing
Double-Byte and Quad-Byte Interrupt Acknowledge Cycle

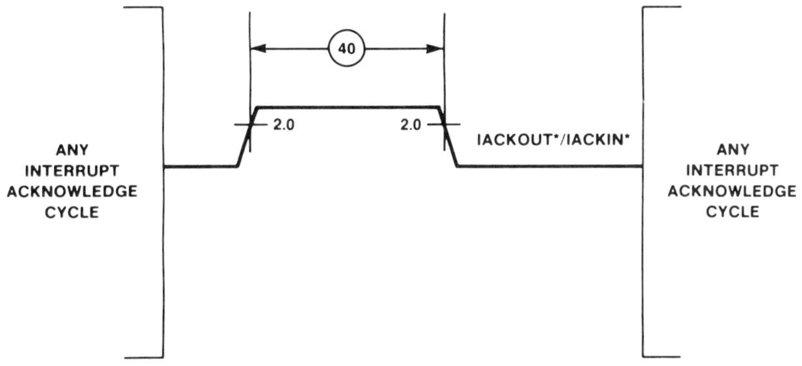

Parameter Number	Interrupt Handler min	Interrupt Handler max	Interrupter min	Interrupter max	IACK Daisy-Chain Driver min	IACK Daisy-Chain Driver max
40			30		30	

NOTES: (1) All times are in nanoseconds
(2) T = the time-out value

Fig 61
IACK Daisy-Chain Driver, Responding Interrupter, and Participating Interrupter IACK Daisy-Chain Inter-Cycle Timing

Table 46
Interrupt Handler, Timing Rules and Observations

Timing Parameters Specified in Table 45	Rules and Observations
1	**Rule 4.15** When taking control of the DTB, the interrupt handler shall not drive any of IACK*, A01-A03, LWORD*, WRITE*, DS0*, DS1* or AS* until after the previous master or interrupt handler allows AS* to rise above the low level.
	Observation 4.12 Section 3 describes how an interrupt handler's requester is granted use of the DTB.
2	**Rule 4.16** When taking control of the DTB, the interrupt handler shall not drive any of IACK*, A01-A03, LWORD*, WRITE*, DS0*, DS1*, or AS* until after it receives DEVICE GRANTED BUS true.
	Observation 4.13 Section 3 describes how an interrupt handler's requester is granted use of the DTB.
3	**Rule 4.17** When taking control of the DTB, the interrupt handler shall not drive AS* low until this time after the previous master or interrupt handler allows AS* to rise above the low level.
	Observation 4.14 **Rule 4.17** ensures that timing parameter 5 for interrupters and slaves is guaranteed when there is an interchange of the DTB mastership.
4	**Rule 4.18** The interrupt handler shall not drive AS* low until IACK* has been low, and LWORD* and A01-A03 have been valid for this minimum time.
5	**Rule 4.19** When using the DTB for two consecutive cycles, the interrupt handler shall not drive AS* low until it has been high for this minimum time.
9	**Rule 4.20** The interrupt handler shall not drive DSA* low until both DTACK* and BERR* are high.
10	**Rule 4.21** The interrupt handler shall not drive DSA* low before it has driven AS* low.
11	**Rule 4.22** The interrupt handler shall not drive DSA* low until DS0* and DS1* have been simultaneously high for this minimum time.
12	**Rule 4.23** The interrupt handler shall not drive DSA* low until WRITE* has been high for this minimum time.
13	**Rule 4.24** During double-byte or quad-byte interrupt acknowledge cycles, the interrupt handler shall drive DSB* low within this maximum time after it drives DSA* low.

(*Continued on Page 191*)

Table 46 *(Continued)*
Interrupt Handler, Timing Rules and Observations

Timing Parameters Specified in Table 45	Rules and Observations
	Observation 4.15 Timing parameter 13 does not apply to single-byte interrupt acknowledge cycles.
14	**Rule 4.25** During all interrupt acknowledge cycles, the interrupt handler shall hold the 3-bit interrupt acknowledge code valid on A01-A03, and maintain the appropriate level on LWORD* until it detects a falling edge on DTACK* or BERR*.
16	**Rule 4.26** During all interrupt acknowledge cycles, the interrupt handler shall maintain IACK* low until it detects a falling edge on DTACK* or BERR*.
18	**Rule 4.27** The interrupt handler shall hold AS* low until it detects DTACK* or BERR* low.
19	**Rule 4.28** The interrupt handler shall hold AS* low for this minimum time.
20	**Rule 4.29** Once an interrupt handler has driven DSA* low, it shall maintain it low until it detects DTACK* or BERR* low.
21	**Rule 4.30** Once an interrupt handler has driven DSB* low, it shall maintain it low until it detects DTACK* or BERR* low.
23	**Rule 4.31** Once an interrupt handler has driven DSA* low, it shall maintain a high on WRITE* until this minimum time after it drives DSB* high.
24A	**Rule 4.32** If the interrupt handler drives or releases AS* high after its requester releases BBSY*, then it shall release IACK*, A01-A03, LWORD*, WRITE*, DS0*, and DS1* before allowing AS* to rise above the low level.
24B	**Rule 4.33** If the interrupt handler drives or releases AS* high before its requester releases BBSY*, then it shall release AS*, IACK*, A01-A03, LWORD*, WRITE*, DS0*, and DS1* before changing its DEVICE WANTS BUS signal from true to false.
25	**Rule 4.34** If the interrupt handler drives or releases AS* high after its requester releases BBSY*, then it shall release AS* within this time after allowing it to rise above the low level.
26	**Observation 4.16** Timing parameter 26 guarantees that the data bus will not be driven until the interrupt handler drives DSA* low.
27	**Observation 4.17** The interrupt handler is guaranteed that the data bus will be valid within this time after DTACK* goes low. This time does not apply to cycles where the interrupter drives BERR* low instead of DTACK*.

(*Continued on Page 192*)

Table 46 *(Continued)*
Interrupt Handler, Timing Rules and Observations

Timing Parameters Specified in Table 45	Rules and Observations
28	**Observation 4.18** The interrupt handler is guaranteed that neither DTACK* nor BERR* will go low until this minimum time after it drives DSA* low. The bus timer guarantees the interrupt handler that if DTACK* has not gone low after its time-out period has elapsed, and within twice its time-out period, then the bus timer will drive BERR* low.
29	**Observation 4.19** The interrupt handler is guaranteed that the data bus remains valid until it drives DSA* high.
30	**Observation 4.20** This guarantees that neither DTACK* nor BERR* goes high until the interrupt handler drives both DS0* and DS1* high.
31	**Observation 4.21** The interrupt handler is guaranteed that the data bus has been released by the time DTACK* and BERR* are high.

Table 47
Interrupter, Timing Rules and Observations

Timing Parameters Specified in Table 45	Rules and Observations
4	**Observation 4.22** Interrupters are guaranteed that IACK*, LWORD*, and A01-A03 have been valid for this minimum time when they detect a falling edge on AS*.
5	**Observation 4.23** Interrupters are guaranteed this minimum high time on AS* between DTB cycles.
6	**Observation 4.24** The responding interrupter is guaranteed that none of D00-D31 will be driven by any other module until the responding interrupter releases DTACK* and BERR* high.
7	**Observation 4.25** The responding interrupter is guaranteed that the D00-D31 are released by all other modules by the time DSA* goes low.
9	**Observation 4.26** The responding interrupter is guaranteed that neither DS0* nor DS1* will go low until DTACK* and BERR* from the the previous cycle have gone high.
11	**Observation 4.27** Interrupters are guaranteed this minimum time during which both DS0* and DS1* are simultaneously high between cycles.
12	**Observation 4.28** Interrupters are guaranteed that WRITE* has been high for this minimum time when they detect a falling edge on DSA*.
13	**Observation 4.29** If the interrupt handler will drive both DS0* and DS1* low, then the responding interrupter is guaranteed that DSB* will go low within this maximum time after DSA*. And therefore: if DSB* does not go low within this maximum time, then the responding interrupter assumes that it is to respond with a single-byte status/ID.
14	**Observation 4.30** The responding interrupter is guaranteed that LWORD* and A01-A03 will remain valid until it drives DTACK* or BERR* low, provided it does so within the bus time-out period.
16	**Observation 4.31** The responding interrupter is guaranteed that IACK* will remain low until it drives DTACK* or BERR* low, provided it does so within the bus time-out period.
18	**Observation 4.32** The responding interrupter is guaranteed that AS* will remain low until it drives DTACK* or BERR* low, provided that it does so within the bus time-out period.
19	**Observation 4.33** Interrupters are guaranteed that AS* will remain low for this minimum time.

(*Continued on Page 194*)

Table 47 (*Continued*)
Interrupter, Timing Rules and Observations

Timing Parameters Specified in Table 45	Rules and Observations
20	**Observation 4.34** The responding interrupter is guaranteed that once DSA* goes low, it will remain low until it has driven DTACK* or BERR* low, provided that the responding interrupter does so within the bus time-out period.
21	**Observation 4.35** The responding interrupter is guaranteed that once DSB* goes low, it will remain low until it has driven DTACK* or BERR* low, provided that the responding interrupter does so within the bus time-out period.
23	**Observation 4.36** Interrupters are guaranteed that WRITE* remains high until both DS0* and DS1* are high.
26	**Rule 4.35** The responding interrupter shall not drive any of D00-D31 until DSA* goes low.
27	**Rule 4.36** The responding interrupter shall not drive DTACK* low before it drives the data lines with a valid status/ID.
	Observation 4.37 This time does not apply to cycles where the responding interrupter drives BERR* low instead of DTACK*.
28	**Rule 4.37** The responding interrupter shall wait this minimum time after DSA* goes low before driving DTACK* or BERR* low.
29	**Rule 4.38** Once the responding interrupter has driven DTACK* low, it shall not change D00-D31 until DSA* goes high.
30	**Rule 4.39** Once the responding interrupter has driven DTACK* or BERR* to low, it shall not release it until it detects both DS0* and DS1* high.
31	**Rule 4.40** The responding interrupter shall release all of D00-D31 before releasing DTACK* and BERR* to high.
32	**Observation 4.38** The responding interrupter is guaranteed that IACK*, LWORD*, and A01-A03 have been valid for this minimum time when it detects a falling edge on DSA*. This time is derived from timing parameters 4, and 10.
34	**Observation 4.39** Interrupters are guaranteed that AS* has been low for this minimum time, when they detect a falling edge on IACKIN*.
35	**Rule 4.41** A participating interrupter shall drive IACKOUT* high within this maximum time after the rising edge on AS*.
36	**Rule 4.42** The responding interrupter shall not drive any of D00-D31 until IACKIN* goes low.

(*Continued on Page 195*)

Table 47 *(Continued)*
Interrupter, Timing Rules and Observations

Timing Parameters Specified in Table 45	Rules and Observations
37	**Rule 4.43** IF a participating interrupter drives any of D00-D31, then it shall release them before driving IACKOUT* low.
38A	**Rule 4.44** A participating interrupter shall not drive IACKOUT* low until it detects IACKIN* low.
38B	**Rule 4.45** The responding interrupter shall not drive DTACK* low until it detects IACKIN* low.
39	**Observation 4.40** This time guarantees that each interrupter's IACKIN* will go high within this time after the rising edge on AS*. This time is derived from timing parameter 35, where the IACK daisy-chain driver and participating interrupters are required to drive IACKOUT* high within a maximum time.
40	**Observation 4.41** Interrupters are guaranteed that IACKIN* will stay high for this minimum time between consecutive DTB cycles.
41	**Observation 4.42** This time guarantees that A01-A03 and LWORD* remain valid until this time after the participating interrupter drives IACKOUT* low, provided it does so within the bus time-out period.
43	**Observation 4.43** This time guarantees that AS* remains low for this minimum time after the participating interrupter drives IACKOUT* low, provided it does so within the bus time-out period.

Table 48
IACK Daisy-Chain Driver, Timing Rules and Observations

Timing Parameters Specified in Table 45	Rules and Observations
	Observation 4.44 Since the backplane connects IACK* to the slot 1 IACKIN*, these two signals are equivalent. And therefore, all rules and observations that apply to one, are also applicable to the other.
5	**Observation 4.45** The IACK daisy-chain driver is guaranteed this minimum high time on AS* between DTB cycles.
19	**Observation 4.46** The IACK daisy-chain driver is guaranteed that AS* will remain low for this minimum time. This time is derived from timing parameters 8, 16, and 27 of the interrupter.
32	**Observation 4.47** The IACK daisy-chain driver is guaranteed that IACK* (and the slot 1 IACKIN*) has been valid for this minimum time when it detects a falling edge on DSA*.
34	**Rule 4.46** If IACKIN* is low when the IACK daisy-chain driver detects a falling edge on DSA*, then it shall drive IACKOUT* low, but it shall not do so until this time after the falling edge on DSA*.
	Observation 4.48 The IACK daisy-chain driver does not drive IACKOUT* low every time DSA* goes low. It only does so when IACK* is also low, indicating that an interrupt acknowledge cycle is in progress.
35	**Rule 4.47** If the IACK daisy-chain driver drives IACKOUT* low, then it shall drive IACKOUT* high within this time after the rising edge of AS*.
40	**Rule 4.48** The IACK daisy-chain driver shall not drive IACKOUT* low until it has been high for this minimum time.
42	**Observation 4.49** If the IACK daisy-chain driver drives IACKOUT* low within the bus time-out period, then this time guarantees that IACK* (and the slot 1 IACKIN*) remains valid for this minimum time.

5. Utility Bus

5.1 Introduction. This section defines the signal lines and modules that provide utility functions such as periodic timing, initialization and diagnostic for the system (see Fig 62).

5.2 Utility Bus Signal Lines. The utility bus signal lines are listed below:

SYSCLK	System Clock
SERCLK	Serial Clock
SERDAT*	Serial Data
ACFAIL*	AC Fail
SYSRESET*	System Reset
SYSFAIL*	System Failure

5.3 Utility Bus Modules

5.3.1 The System Clock Driver. The system clock is an independent, non-gated, fixed frequency, 16 MHz, 50% (nominal) duty cycle signal. The system clock driver is located on the system controller located in board slot one (see Section 1). It provides a known time base that is useful for counting off time delays. Figure 63 shows the system clock driver timing diagram. For additional information see 6.5.3.

> **Observation 5.1** SYSCLK has no fixed phase relationships with other timings.

5.3.2 The Serial Clock Driver. The serial clock driver, which is located in 6.5.3, provides a fixed frequency, special waveform signal. Its waveform is specified in the IEEE P1132 specification*. For the convenience of designers, the timing parameters in effect at the time that this standard is published are provided in Appendix C. For additional information see 6.5.3.

*At the time of publication of this standard IEEE P1132 is under preparation.

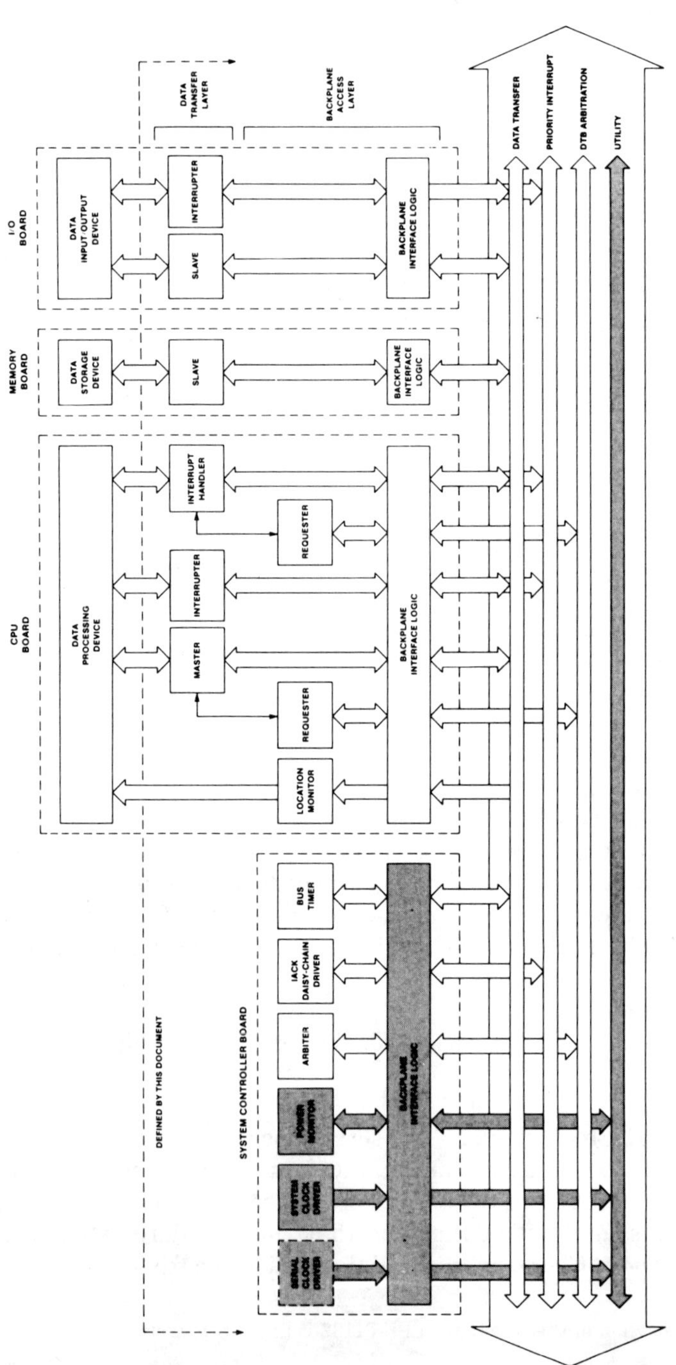

Fig 62
Utility Bus Block Diagram

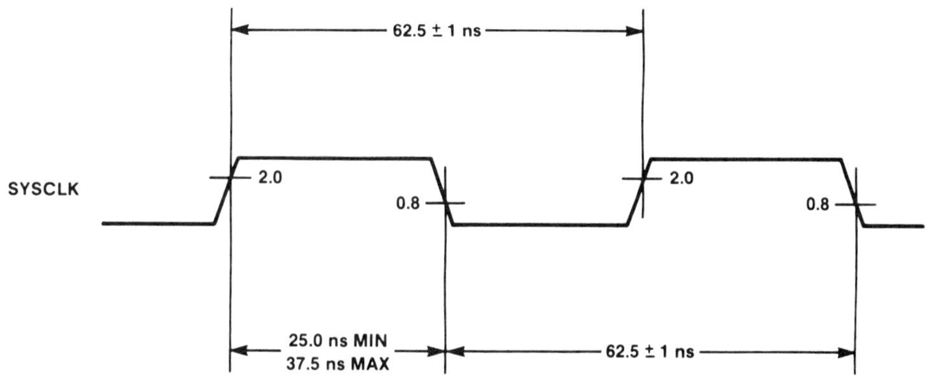

Fig 63
System Clock Driver Timing Diagram

5.3.3 The Power Monitor. Figure 64 is the block diagram for the power monitor module. This module detects power failures and signals the system in time to effect orderly shutdown. When power is then reapplied to the system the power monitor ensures that all other modules are initialized.

The power monitor might also monitor a manually operated push button and initialize the system whenever that button is depressed by the operator.

The ACFAIL* and SYSRESET* transitions, and the point at which the system dc voltages violate the power specifications, have certain timing relationships. These relationships are shown in Figs 65 and 66.

Permission 5.1 Systems may be built with or without a power monitor module.

Rule 5.1 Power monitors shall comply with the timing specifications given in Figs 65 and 66.

Permission 5.2 The SYSRESET* line may be driven low by any board to initialize the system from a manual push button. Where a board drives SYSRESET*, but does not drive ACFAIL*, the timing in Figs 65 and 66 does not apply.

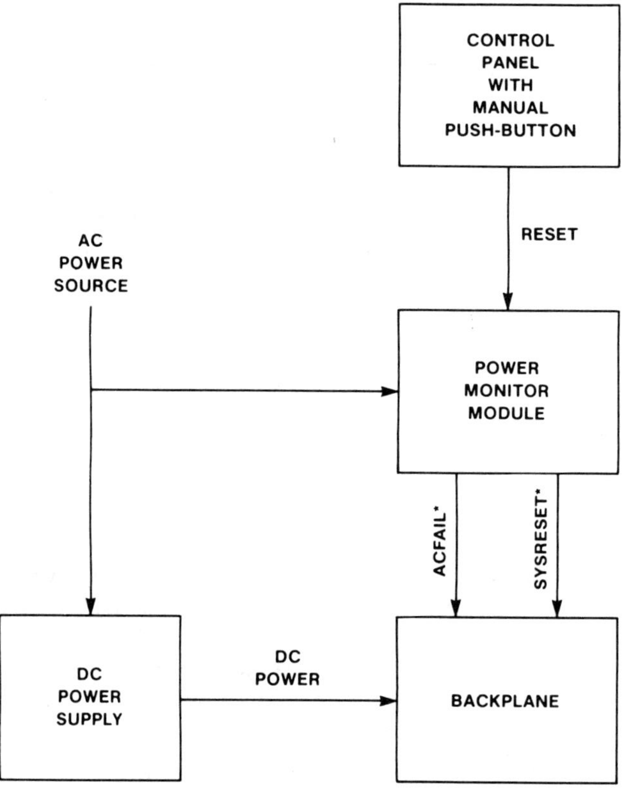

Fig 64
Power Monitor: Block Diagram

Rule 5.2 Whenever any board drives SYSRESET* low, it shall hold it low for a minimum period of 200 ms.

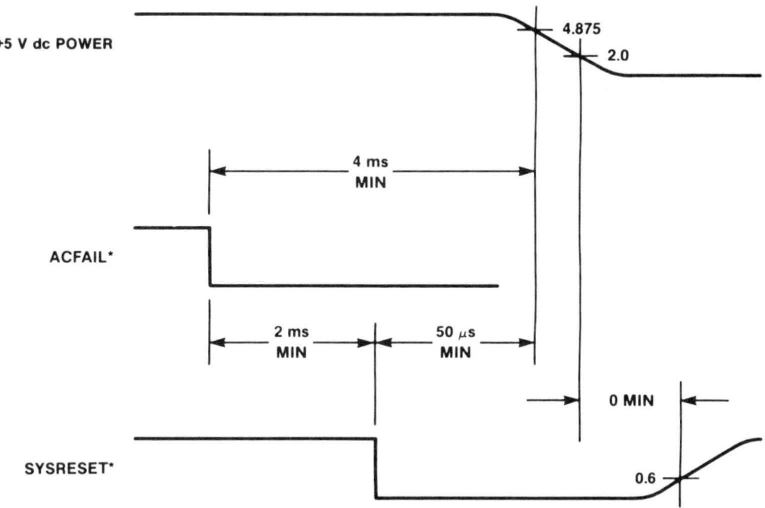

Fig 65
Power Monitor: Power Failure Timing

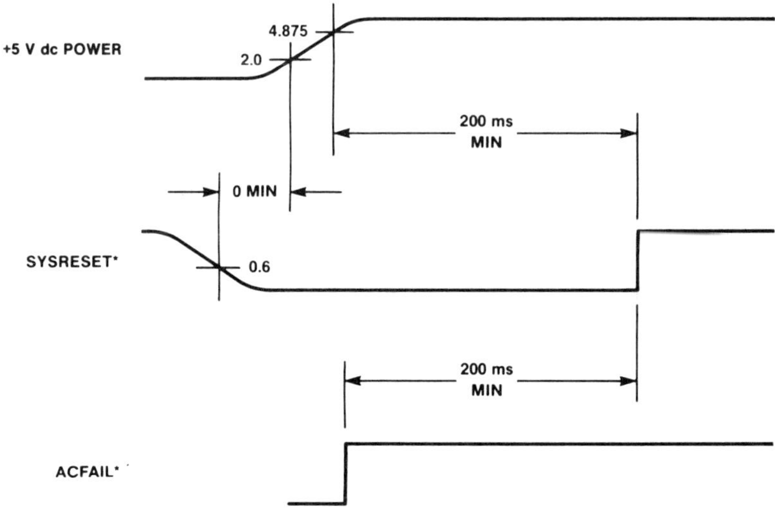

Fig 66
Power Monitor: System Restart Timing

5.4 System Initialization and Diagnostics. The following information provides protocols that allow the system to be shut down and powered up in an orderly manner. Two signal lines are used in the power-down and power-up sequence: ACFAIL* and SYSRESET*. Another signal line, SYSFAIL*, is used during the power-up sequence. The following information specifies the behavior of the various functional modules during the power-down sequence:

> **Recommendation 5.1** Design masters so that they will not request the bus for any purpose except power-fail activity, after ACFAIL* has been low for 200 μs.

> **Recommendation 5.2** If masters and interrupt handlers have a bus request pending prior to detecting ACFAIL* low, then they should limit their subsequent nonpower-fail activity to 200 μs.

> **Observation 5.2** Bus accesses required to save and restore system data to global memory depend upon the application, and are not specified here. The operating system has to ensure that data saved during the shutdown process is restored prior to system operation. In the case of a multiprocessing system, this might require some interprocessor communication.

SYSRESET* is an open-collector line driven by the power-monitor module, or by any board in response to a push-button switch closure.

> **Observation 5.3** Special circuitry is needed where push-button reset switches are used, to ensure that switch bounce does not cause the board to violate the 200 ms minimum SYSRESET* low time.

Rule 5.3 The system clock driver shall continue to provide the specified SYSCLK waveform regardless of the state of the SYSRESET* line.

> **Permission 5.4** When SYSRESET* goes low, any board that requires more than 200 ms to complete its initialization may turn on its SYSRESET* driver low to maintain SYSRESET* low for the required period.

Rule 5.4 If the +5 V dc power source is within its specified range when SYSRESET* goes low, then functional modules shall satisfy the timing rules given in Table 49 within the specified time after SYSRESET* goes low.

Rule 5.5 If the SYSRESET* is low when the +5 V dc enters its specified range, utility bus then functional modules shall satisfy the timing rules given in Table 49 within the specified time after the power source enters its specified range.

Rule 5.6 After satisfying the rules in Table 49, functional modules shall not change the state of their drivers until SYSRESET* goes high, unless the +5 V dc power source exits its specified range.

Table 49
Module Drive During Power-Up and Power-Down Sequences

Module	Shall Not	After
Masters and Interrupt Handlers	Drive AS*, DS0*, or DS1* from high to low	5 μs
Masters and Interrupt Handlers	Drive IACK*, LWORD*, AS*, DS0*, DS1*, AM0-AM5, A01-A31, WRITE*, or D00-D31	20 μs
Slaves and Interrupters	Drive D00-D31, DTACK*, or BERR*	30 μs
Interrupters	Drive IRQ1*-IRQ7*	30 μs
Bus Timer	Drive BERR*	30 μs
Arbiter	Drive BG0IN*-BG3IN* from high to low	5 μs
Arbiter	Drive BG0IN*-BG3IN* low	30 μs
Requesters	Drive BBSY*	30 μs

Rule 5.7 If the +5 V dc power source is within its specified range when SYSRESET* goes low, and a master or interrupt handler is driving AS*, DS0*, or DS1* low, then it shall maintain these strobes low long enough to satisfy the minimum low times given in Sections 2 and 4.

SYSFAIL* is an open collector line that is held low when the system is powered-up and remains low until system self-tests are complete (see Fig 67). The following information applies:

Suggestion 5.1 On intelligent master boards, include a locally accessible control register bit that is initialized to drive SYSFAIL* low when power is first applied. This allows the board's local intelligence to do a self-test and release SYSFAIL* only if the self-test passes.

Suggestion 5.2 Design nonintelligent boards with a globally accessible control register bit that is initialized to drive SYSFAIL* low. This allows an intelligent board to run a test on the nonintelligent board and then write to the global control register bit releasing the board's SYSFAIL* driver.

Suggestion 5.3 Where a SYSFAIL* control register bit is included on the board, provide a status LED on the board's front panel to indicate the status of the control register bit. Then, if a system failure is indicated by the SYSFAIL* signal line, a visual inspection will help determine which board has failed.

Rule 5.8 If a board is designed to drive SYSFAIL*, then it shall drive SYSFAIL* low within 50 ms after SYSRESET* goes low, as shown in Fig 67.

Permission 5.4 A board may also drive SYSFAIL* low at any time during normal operation to indicate that it has detected some kind of failure.

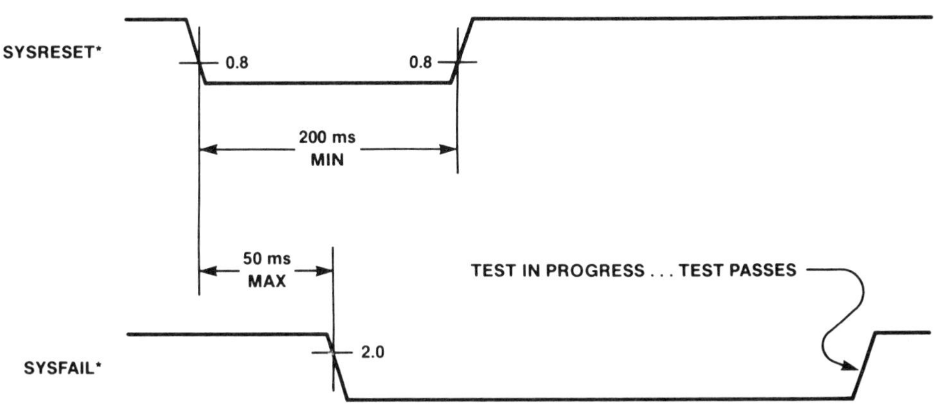

Fig 67
SYSRESET* and SYSFAIL* Timing Diagram

5.5 Power Pins. Figure 68 gives the current rating for the power pins at various temperatures.

> **Observation 5.4** Some connector pins have a slightly higher contact resistance than others when plugged into the backplane. This produces imbalanced current flow in pins that are paralleled. Suppose that two pins are paralleled and are carrying a total current of 2 A. If the contact resistance on one is 1 mΩ and the other is 2 mΩ, then one pin will be carrying only 0.67 A while the other carries 1.33 A.

> **Rule 5.9** Each connector pin shall be capable of carrying at least the currents shown by the solid line in Fig 68.

> **Observation 5.5** If one or more power pins fail completely, all of the load current flows through the remaining pins. For example, if half of the pins fail, the remaining pins carry twice the normal current. Depending upon the load current, this might cause damage to these remaining good pins.

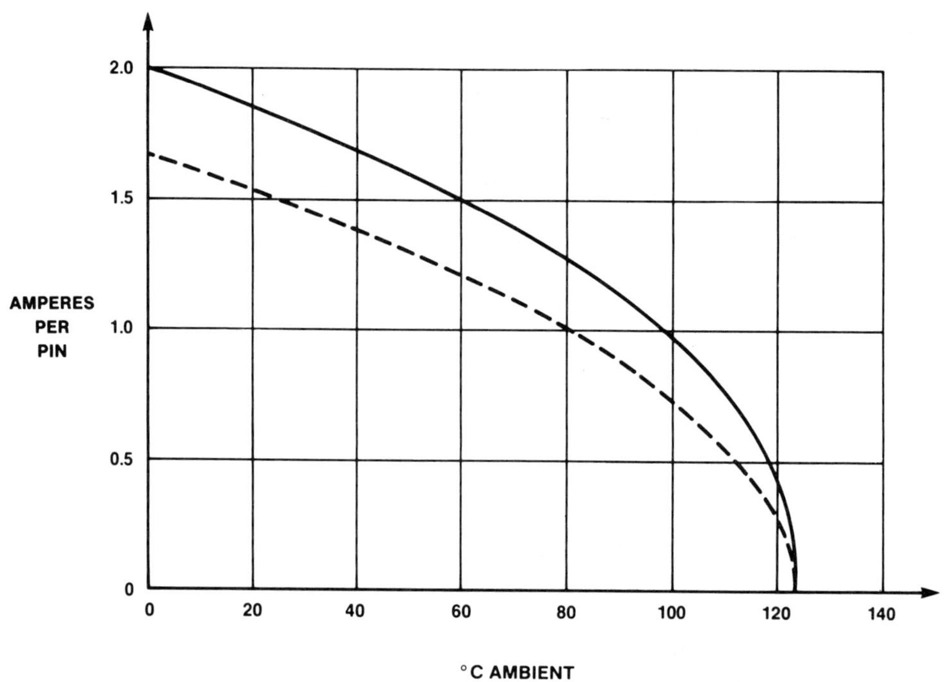

NOTES: (1) The solid line shows the current that can be drawn per +5 V dc power pin where each pin is connected to a separate power grid.

(2) The broken line shows the current that can be drawn per +5 V dc power pin where two or more pins are connected to a common on-board power grid.

Fig 68
Current Rating for Power Pins

Suggestion 5.4 When designing a board with a high current load, divide the board's area into zones that are each powered by a separate power grid. Don't connect these grids to each other on the board. Instead, connect each to its own power pin.

Observation 5.6 If a double height board that draws more power than its P1 connector can provide is plugged into a subrack that contains only a J1 backplane, then its P1 power pins will overheat, and might be damaged.

5.6 Reserved Line. One signal line is labeled as RESERVED.

Observation 5.7 As defined in Section 6, Table 52, the reserved line is terminated and bused.

Rule 5.10 The reserved line is set aside for future use and shall not be used in any board designs.

6. Electrical Specifications

6.1 Introduction. The transmission of data between boards such as processors, memories and I/O devices takes place over one or two backplanes, depending on the design. The rules in this section ensure proper timing, minimal noise, and minimal crosstalk problems on the backplane signal lines. The design of backplanes is governed by the following rules:

Rule 6.1 Backplanes shall not have any signal conductors longer than 19.68 in (500 mm).

Rule 6.2 Backplanes shall not have more than 21 slots.

Rule 6.3 For those lines requiring termination (see 6.7) the backplane shall provide some means for terminating them at both ends of the signal line.

Rule 6.4 The backplane shall provide power conductors for distribution of +5 V, +5 STDBY, +12 V, and -12 V to all of the power pins specified in 7.6.

Rule 6.5 The backplane shall provide ground connections to all of the ground pins specified in 7.6.

Permission 6.1 Signal lines are normally driven by bipolar drivers, but any technology that complies with this specification may be used.

6.2 Power Distribution. Power in the system is distributed on the backplane(s) as regulated direct-current voltages. The available voltages are:

+5 V dc	This is the main power source for most systems. Most of the system circuitry, including TTL logic, MOS microprocessors, and memories, requires this voltage.
± 12 V dc	These are often used for powering RS232C drivers. They are also sometimes used for powering MOS and analog devices. In some cases -5 V dc bias voltage or -5.2 V dc ECL voltages are also derived from the -12 V dc source using on-board regulators. These supplies normally don't supply as much power to the system as the +5 V dc source does.
+5 V dc STDBY	This is used to sustain memory, time-of-day clocks, etc, when the +5 V dc power is lost.

6.2.1 DC Voltage Specifications. Table 50 summarizes the dc voltage specifications. The listed specifications are the maximum allowed variance as measured at the connector pins of any card plugged into the backplane.

Recommendation 6.1 Design and connect backplanes so that the power supply sense point is located somewhere near the center of the backplane, and as close as possible to the point where power is introduced into the backplane.

Observation 6.1 Placing the power supply sense point near the power input point prevents boards near the power input point from receiving too high a voltage.

Observation 6.2 The nonsymmetric variation given in Table 50 ensures that the dc power remains within the tolerance required by most IC despite the typical voltage drops that occur in the power distribution network.

Table 50
Bus Voltage Specification

Mnemonic	Description	Allowed Variation (see Observations)	Ripple/Noise Below 10 MHz (Peak-to-Peak)
+5 V	+5 V dc	+0.25 V/-0.125 V	50 mV
+12 V	+12 V dc power	+0.60 V/-0.36 V	50 mV
-12 V	-12 V dc power	-0.60 V/+0.36 V	50 mV
+5 V STDBY	+5 V dc standby	+0.25 V/-0.125 V	50 mV
GND	Ground	Reference	

Observation 6.3 The power consumed by some systems fluctuates over a wide range during normal system operation. For example, dynamic memory refreshing might cause significant fluctuations if large amounts of memory are refreshed at one time. In this case the response time of the voltage distribution system becomes important.

Recommendation 6.2 Use bypass capacitors on boards to minimize the effects of power transients.

6.2.2 Pin and Socket Connector Electrical Ratings

Rule 6.6 The 96-pin connector used shall provide

Voltage rating:	$\geq$100 V dc, isolation pin to pin
Contact resistance:	$\leq$50 mΩ, at rated current
Insulation resistance:	$\geq$100 MΩ, pin to pin

Observation 6.17 Connector molding materials vary in their dielectric permitivity, and thus, in their susceptibility to crosstalk.

Suggestion 6.9 Use connectors that have molding material that minimizes crosstalk.

6.3 Electrical Signal Characteristics

Rule 6.7 Boards shall not drive any backplane signal line to a higher steady-state voltage than the highest voltage on any of its +5 V power pins, or to a lower steady-state voltage than the lowest voltage on any of its GND pins.

Rule 6.8 Boards shall use drivers and receivers that meet the following characteristics:

Steady-state driver low output level	≤0.6 V
Steady-state receiver low input level	≤0.8 V
Steady-state driver high output level	≥2.4 V
Steady-state receiver high input level	≥2.0 V

Figure 69 gives a simple graphic representation of these levels.

Fig 69
Signal Levels

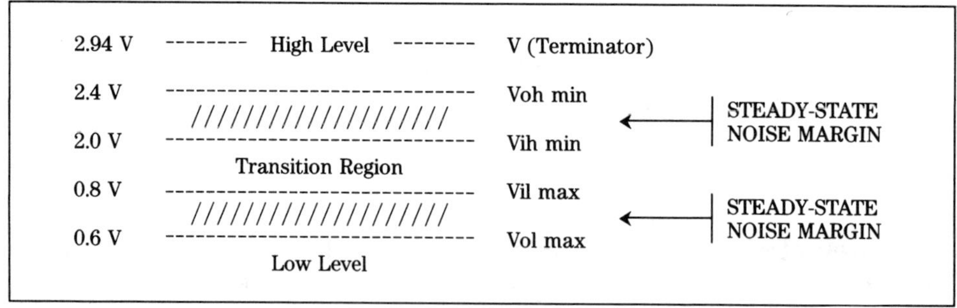

Boards drive the backplane lines with three-state, open collector, and totem-pole drivers. Section 6.4 specifies the drive and loading requirements for the various signal lines. Section 6.7 provides a summary, showing which types of drivers are used to drive each signal line.

Rule 6.9 When making voltage threshold measurements to verify compliance with timing specifications, the ground reference shall be taken from the board's ground pin nearest the signal pin being measured, and the signal voltage shall be measured on the board's connector pin.

6.4 Bus Driving and Receiving Requirements. This section defines the driver and receiver specifications for all signal lines. Table 51 lists all of the signals and shows which of subsections 6.4.1 through 6.4.2.5 discusses it.

Table 51
Bus Driving and
Receiving Requirements

Signal Name	Subsection
A01-A31	6.4.2.2
ACFAIL*	6.4.2.5
AM0-AM5	6.4.2.2
AS*	6.4.2.1
BBSY*	6.4.2.5
BCLR*	6.4.2.3
BERR*	6.4.2.5
BG0OUT*-BG3OUT*	6.4.2.4
BR0*-BR3*	6.4.2.5
D00-D31	6.4.2.2
DS0*	6.4.2.1
DS1*	6.4.2.1
DTACK*	6.4.2.5
IACK*	6.4.2.2 and 6.4.2.5
IACKOUT*	6.4.2.4
IRQ1*-IRQ7*	6.4.2.5
LWORD*	6.4.2.2
SERCLK	6.4.2.3
SYSCLK	6.4.2.3
SYSFAIL*	6.4.2.5
SYSRESET*	6.4.2.5
WRITE*	6.4.2.2

6.4.1 Bus Driver Definitions

totem-pole. An active driver in both states that sinks current in the low state and sources current in the high state. Totem-pole drivers are used on signals that have only a single driver per line (for example, daisy-chain lines).

three-state. Similar to a totem-pole driver except that it can go to a high impedance state (drivers turned off) in addition to the low and high logic states. Three-state drivers are used for lines that can be driven by several devices at different points on the bus (for example, address or data lines). Only one of these drivers can be active at any one time.

open-collector. Sinks current in the low state but sources no significant current in the high state. Terminating resistors on the backplane ensure that the signal line voltage rises to a high level whenever it is not driven low. Open-collector drivers are used for signal lines that can be driven by several devices simultaneously (for example, interrupt and bus request lines).

6.4.2 Driving and Loading Rules for All Lines

Rule 6.10 All boards shall provide clamping on each signal line that they monitor, to prevent negative excursions below -1.5 V.

Observation 6.4 Standard 74LSxxx and 74Fxxx devices have internal clamping diodes on their inputs that will satisfy the clamping requirement specified in Rule 6.10.

Rule 6.11 Receivers shall guarantee detection of a high logic level above a threshold of 2.0 V, as shown in Fig 69.

Rule 6.12 Receivers shall guarantee detection of a low logic level below a threshold of 0.8 V, as shown in Fig 69.

Permission 6.2 A three-state driver may be used as a totem-pole driver if its output is permanently enabled.

6.4.2.1 Driving and Loading Rules for High-Current Three-State Lines (AS*, DS0*, DS1*)

Rule 6.13 If a board drives AS*, DS0*, or DS1*, then its drivers for these lines shall meet the following specifications:

Low-state sink current	IOL $\geq$64 mA
Low-state voltage	VOL $\leq$0.6 V at IOL = 64 mA
High-state source current	IOH $\geq$3 mA
High-state voltage	VOH $\geq$2.4 V at IOH = 3 mA
Minimum source current with board pin grounded	IOS $\geq$50 mA at 0 V
Maximum source current with board pin grounded	IOS $\leq$225 mA at 0 V

Rule 6.14 When drivers are turned off, boards shall limit their loading of AS*, DS0*, and DS1* to the following values:

Current sourced by board at 0.6 V, including leakage current	IOZL+IIL $\leq$450 uA
Current sunk by board at 2.4 V, including leakage current	IOZH+IIH $\leq$100 uA
Total capacitive load on the signal, including signal trace	CT $\leq$20 pF

Observation 6.5 The source and sink currents specified in Rules 6.13 and 6.14 include both driver and receiver currents sourced and sunk on the board.

Suggestion 6.1
Use 74S241 or 74F241/244 devices to drive the lines AS*, DS0*, and DS1*.
Use 74LS240, 74LS241, or 74LS244 devices to receive the lines AS*, DS0*, and DS1*.

6.4.2.2 Driving and Loading Rules for Standard Three-State Lines (A01-A31, D00-D31, AM0-AM5, IACK*, LWORD*, WRITE*)

Rule 6.15 If a board drives the lines A01-A31, D00-D31, AM0-AM5, IACK*, LWORD*, or WRITE*, then its drivers for these lines shall meet the following specifications:

Low-state sink current	IOL $\geq$48 mA
Low-state voltage	VOL $\leq$0.6 V at IOL = 48 mA
High-state source current	IOH $\geq$3 mA
High-state voltage	VOH $\geq$2.4 V at IOH = 3 mA
Minimum source current with board pin grounded	IOS $\geq$50 mA at 0 V
Maximum source current with board pin grounded	IOS $\leq$225 mA at 0 V

Rule 6.16 When drivers are turned off, boards shall limit their loading of the lines A01-A31, D00-D31, AM0-AM5, IACK*, LWORD*, and WRITE* to the following values:

Current sourced by board at 0.6 V, including leakage current	IOZL+IIL $\leq$700 uA
Current sunk by board at 2.4 V, including leakage current	IOZH+IIH $\leq$150 uA
Total capacitive load on the signal, including signal trace	CT $\leq$20 pF

Observation 6.6 The source and sink currents specified in Rules 6.15 and 6.16 include both driver and receiver currents sourced and sunk on the board.

Suggestion 6.2

Use 74ALS645-1, 74F244, 74AS573, or 74AS580 devices to drive the lines A01-A31, D00-D31, AM0-AM5, IACK*, LWORD*, and WRITE*.

Use 74LS240, 74LS241, or 74LS244 devices to receive the lines A01-A31, D00-D31, AM0-AM5, IACK*, LWORD*, and WRITE*.

Use 74ALS645-1, 74ALS245A-1, 74ALS646-1, or 74ALS648-1 devices to transceive the lines A01-A31, D00-D31, AM0-AM5, IACK*, LWORD*, and WRITE*.

6.4.2.3 Driving and Loading Rules for High-Current Totem-Pole Lines (SERCLK, SYSCLK, BCLR*)

Rule 6.17 Systems shall have only one board driving each of the lines SERCLK, SYSCLK, or BCLR*. Its drivers for these lines shall meet the following specifications:

Low-state sink current	IOL $\geq$64 mA
Low-state voltage	VOL $\leq$0.6 V at IOL = 64 mA
High-state source current	IOH $\geq$3 mA
High-state voltage	VOH $\geq$2.4 V at IOH = 3 mA
Minimum source current with board pin grounded	IOS $\geq$50 mA at 0 V
Maximum source current with board pin grounded	IOS $\leq$225 mA at 0 V

Rule 6.18 All boards shall limit their loading of the lines SERCLK, SYSCLK, and BCLR* to the following values:

Current sourced by board at 0.6 V, including leakage current	IOZL+IIL $\leq$600 uA
Current sunk by board at 2.4 V, including leakage current	IOZH+IIH $\leq$50 uA
Total capacitive load on the signal, including signal trace, for system controllers (which have drivers)	CT $\leq$20 pF
Total capacitive load on the signal, including signal trace, for other boards (which have no drivers)	CT $\leq$12 pF

Observation 6.7 The source and sink currents specified in Rules 6.17 and 6.18 include both driver and receiver currents sourced and sunk on the board.

Suggestion 6.3

Use 74S241 or 74F241/244 devices to drive the lines SERCLK, SYSCLK, and BCLR*.

Use 74LS240, 74LS241 or 74LS244 devices to receive the lines SERCLK, SYSCLK, and BCLR*.

6.4.2.4 Driving and Loading Rules for Standard Totem-Pole Lines (BG0OUT*-BG3OUT*/BG0IN*-BG3IN*, IACKOUT*/IACKIN*)

Rule 6.19 If a board drives the lines BG0OUT*-BG3OUT*/BG0IN*-BG3IN*, or IACKOUT*/IACKIN*, then its drivers for these lines shall meet the following specifications:

Low-state sink current	IOL $\geq$8 mA
Low-state voltage	VOL $\leq$0.6 V at IOL = 8 mA
High-state source current	IOH $\geq$400 uA
High-state voltage	VOH $\geq$2.7 V at IOH = 400 uA

Rule 6.20 All boards shall limit their loading of each of the lines BG0OUT*-BG3OUT*/ BG0IN*-BG3IN*, and IACKOUT*/IACKIN* to the following values:

Current sourced by board at 0.6 V, including leakage current	IOZL+IIL $\leq$600 uA
Current sunk by board at 2.4 V, including leakage current	IOZH+IIH $\leq$50 uA
Total capacitive load on the signal, including signal trace	CT $\leq$20 pF

Observation 6.8 The source and sink currents specified in Rules 6.19 and 6.20 include both driver and receiver currents sourced and sunk on the board.

Suggestion 6.4
Use any standard device that meets the specifications above to drive the lines BG0OUT*-BG3OUT*/BG0IN*-BG3IN*, and IACKOUT*/IACKIN*.

Use 74LS240, 74LS241, or 74LS244 devices to receive the lines BG3OUT*-BG3OUT*/BG0IN*-BG3IN*, and IACKOUT*/IACKIN*.

6.4.2.5 Driving and Loading Rules for Open-Collector Lines (BR0*-BR3*, BBSY*, IRQ1*-IRQ7*, DTACK*, BERR*, SYSFAIL*, SYSRESET*, ACFAIL*, and IACK*)

Rule 6.21 If a board drives the lines BR0*-BR3*, BBSY*, IRQ1*-IRQ7*, DTACK*, BERR*, SYSFAIL*, SYSRESET*, ACFAIL*, or IACK*, then its drivers for these lines shall meet the following specifications:

Low-state sink current	IOL $\geq$48 mA
Low-state voltage	VOL $\leq$0.6 V at IOL = 48 mA

Rule 6.22 All boards shall limit their loading of the lines BR0*-BR3*, BBSY*, IRQ1*- IRQ7*, DTACK*, BERR*, SYSFAIL*, SYSRESET*, ACFAIL*, and IACK* to the following values:

Current sourced by board at 0.6 V, including leakage current	IOZL+IIL $\leq$400 uA (DTACK* and BERR*) $\leq$600 uA (all others)
Current sunk by board at 2.4 V, including leakage current	IOZH+IIH $\leq$50 uA
Total capacitive load on signal, including signal trace	CT$\leq$20 pF

Observation 6.9 The sink current specified in Rules 6.21 and 6.22 includes both driver and receiver currents sourced and sunk on the board.

Suggestion 6.5
Use 74S38 or 74F38 devices to drive the lines BR0*-BR3*, BBSY*, IRQ1*IRQ7*, DTACK*, BERR*, SYSFAIL*, ACFAIL*, and IACK*.

Use 74LS240, 74LS241, or 74LS244 devices to receive the lines BR0*-BR3*, BBSY*, IRQ1*-IRQ7*, DTACK*, BERR*, SYSFAIL*, SYSRESET*, ACFAIL*, and IACK*.

Suggestion 6.6 Since most TTL drivers do not work reliably when the +5 V dc power source is out of its specified range, drive SYSRESET* on a power-monitor module with a driver built from a discrete high-gain small-signal transistor.

6.5 Backplane Signal Line Interconnections. To accommodate high performance systems, the design of the bus interface takes into account transmission line effects on the backplane. The address and data setup times specified in Sections 2 and 4 take into account the fact that most drivers do not reliably drive backplane signal lines from the low to the high level until there is a reflection from the end of the bus. Although these reflections serve a useful purpose, they cannot be excessive or ringing will result. The following subsections specify the backplane characteristics that achieve the desired result.

6.5.1 Termination Networks

Rule 6.23 Termination networks shall be used on each end of all signal lines except the daisy-chain lines.

Observation 6.10 The terminations serve four purposes:

(1) They reduce reflections from the ends of the backplanes

(2) They provide a high state pull-up for open-collector drivers

(3) They restore the signal lines to the high level when three-state devices are disabled

(4) They provide a standing current for the driver sink transistor to switch off, causing the signal line to rise more swiftly on positive transitions

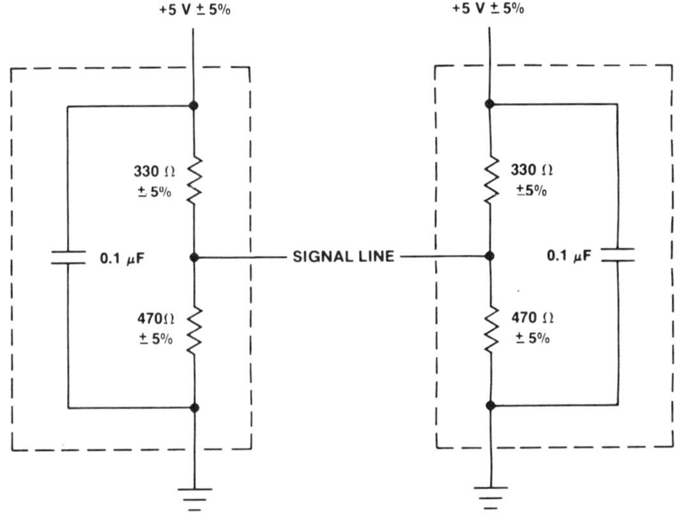

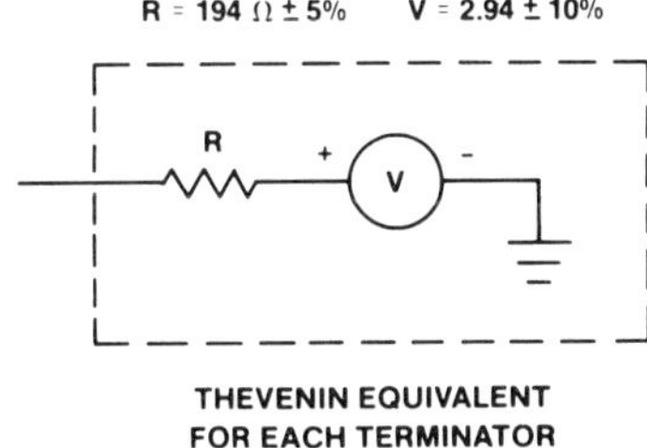

Fig 70
Standard Bus Termination

The Thevenin equivalent of the termination is shown in Fig 70. The voltage divider also shown provides this termination value.

Observation 6.11 If a maximum tolerance of ±5% is maintained on the resistor values and source voltage used in the resistor network shown in Fig 70, then the circuit shown will meet the tolerances shown for the Thevenin equivalent.

Observation 6.12 The resistor network shown in Fig 70 presents its Thevenin equivalent impedance only when its +5 V source is adequately decoupled to ground by a bypass capacitor.

Recommendation 6.3 Provide a bypass capacitor with a value in the range of 0.01 μF to 0.1 μF as close as possible to the Vcc pin of each resistor termination package.

Permission 6.3 Any resistor network and voltage source may be used to provide the termination, as long as they provide the Thevenin equivalent shown in Fig 70.

6.5.2 Characteristic Impedance. Each signal line in the backplane has an associated characteristic impedance Zo. This characteristic impedance is important because discontinuities in Zo (due to capacitive effects and loads on the bus) and mismatches between Zo and the terminations can cause distortions of signal waveforms.

Figure 71 shows a microstrip signal line cross section, which is the normal configuration for a multilayer backplane signal line. The Zo is a function of the width and thickness of the line, the thickness of the dielectric, and its relative dielectric constant. Figure 72 shows characteristic impedance versus microstrip line width for common thickness of fiberglass-epoxy board.

Fig 71
Backplane Microstrip Signal Line Cross Section

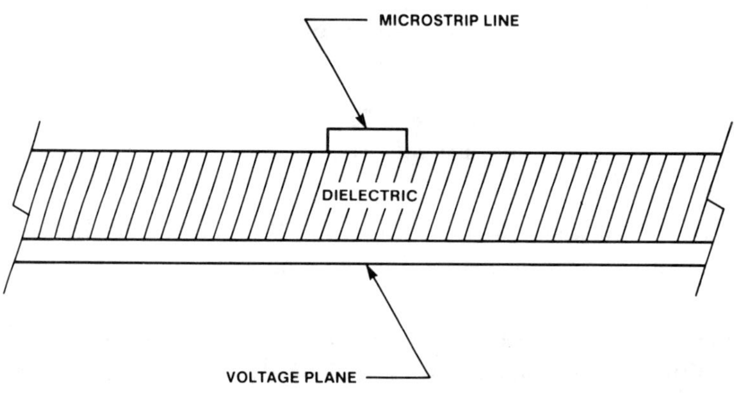

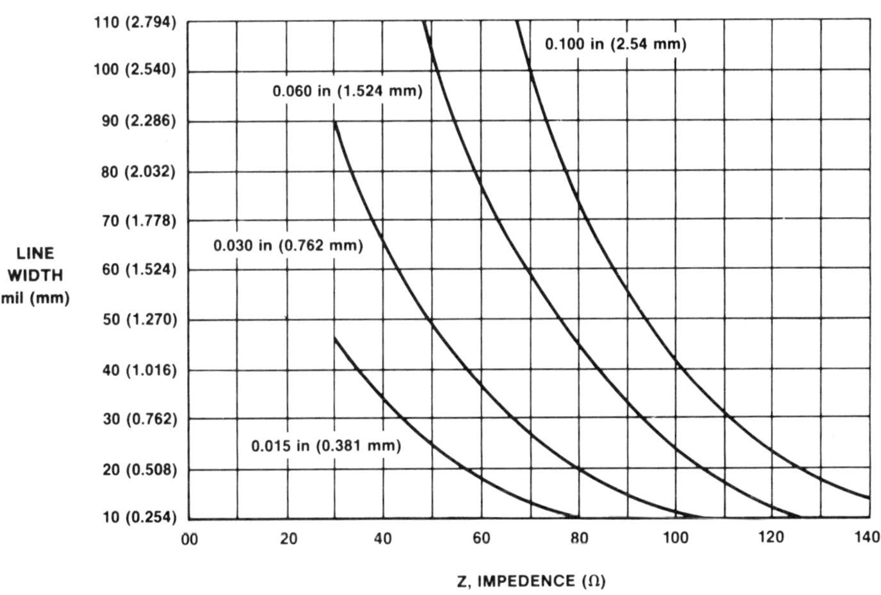

Fig 72
Zo Versus Line Width

The terminations on the backplane signal lines reduce distortion of their signal waveforms. Although a perfect impedance match (which totally eliminates distortions due to reflections) is not maintained between the termination networks and the signal lines, it is important not to allow too great a mismatch, as might be the case if a signal line's Zo value is too low.

> **Recommendation 6.4** When designing a backplane, choose a signal line width and board thickness that gives a Zo (as calculated from Fig 72) as close as possible to 100 Ω.

The actual characteristic impedance of a backplane signal line is called the effective characteristic impedance Zo′, and will be lower than Zo, due to the capacitance of plated-through holes and connector pins. This additional capacitance makes Zo′ go below 100 Ω. Although plated-through holes are necessary to accommodate connectors, other holes should be kept to a minimum.

The backplane signal line impedance (without any boards plugged into the backplane) can be calculated using the following equation:

$$Zo' = \frac{Zo}{\sqrt{1 + Cd/Co}}$$

where

- Zo = impedance of the microstrip line, ignoring the loading effects of plug-in pcb, connectors, and plated-through holes (see Fig 72)
- Cd = distributed capacitance, per unit of distance, of the plated-through holes, and backplane connectors
- Co = intrinsic line capacitance, per unit of distance, of the microstrip line, ignoring the loading effects of plug-in pcb, connectors, and plated-through holes (see Fig 73)
- Zo′ = backplane signal line impedance, including the loading effects of connectors, and plated-through holes but excluding the loading effects of plug-in pcb

Observation 6.13 Typical Zo′ values for a backplane, with no boards inserted, ranges from 50 Ω to 60 Ω. If this impedance is 50 Ω, or higher, it will provide satisfactory operation.

6.5.3 Additional Information

Rule 6.24 Circuit traces from the 96-pin connectors to the on-board circuitry shall not have a length of greater than 2 in (50.8 mm).

Observation 6.14 If the trace from the 96-pin connector to on-board circuitry branches, then the length of each branch is added to get the total length of 2 in (50.8 mm).

Rule 6.25 There shall not be more than one driver driving the SYSCLK SERCLK lines.

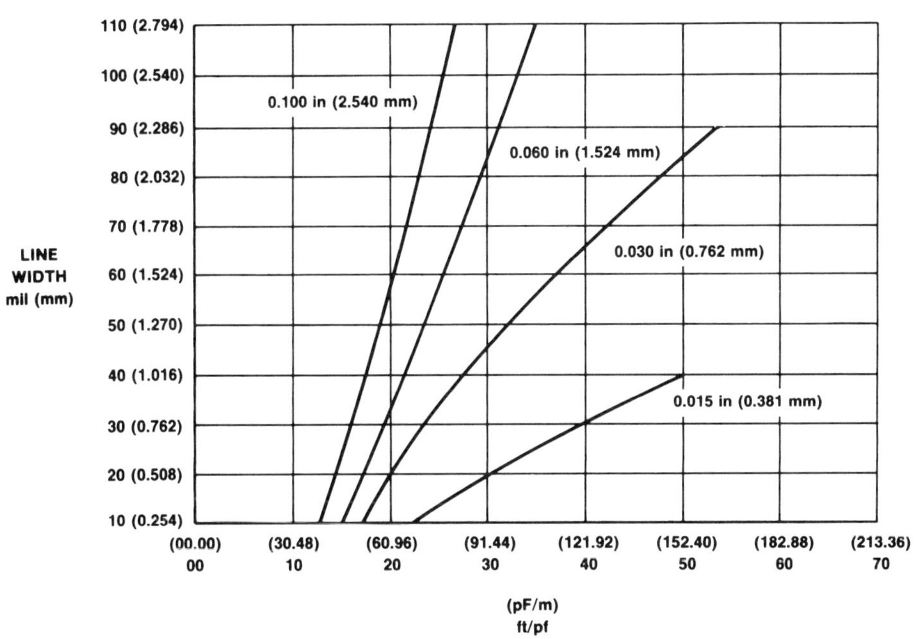

Fig 73
Co Versus Line Width

Rule 6.26 If the system-clock-driver or the serial-clock-driver modules are provided, then they shall be installed in slot 1 of the backplane.

Observation 6.15 Locating the system-clock-driver and the serial-clock-driver on the board in slot 1 minimizes the distortion of their waveforms from the reflections off the ends of the backplane.

Suggestion 6.7 If actual capacitance loading values cannot be obtained from manufacturer specifications sheets, the following values can be used to estimate the total capacitive loading of a board:

The typical capacitance of a receiver	3 pF-5 pF
The typical capacitance of a driver	10 pF-12 pF
The typical capacitance of a transceiver	15 pF-18 pF
The typical capacitance of a 2 in (50.8 mm) PC trace	2 pF-3 pF

Observation 6.16 Circuit traces that run parallel to each other, such as in a backplane, sometimes induce signal transitions in each other. This phenomenon is commonly known as crosstalk. When designing backplanes, the spacings of lines and their position relative to ground and power planes have a large effect on the amount of crosstalk observed.

Suggestion 6.8 Propagation delays through bus drivers depend on how heavily they are loaded, and signal lines typically represent heavy loads. This has to be taken into account when calculating worst case timing. If the manufacturer's data sheet for the driver gives a propagation delay for a 300 pF load, use that to do the worst case calculations. If the only propagation delay values are for a 30 pF load, add 10 ns to the propagation delay and 15 ns to the turn-on delay.

6.6 User-Defined Signals

Recommendation 6.5 If a board has a 96-pin connector in its P2 location, do not allow any of the P2 pins to be driven to a voltage greater than ±15 V. This reduces the likelihood of serious damage to the system in the event that a signal trace from one of these pins is accidentally shorted to some other signal line.

6.7 Signal Line Drivers and Terminations. This section summarizes the types of drivers that must be used for each of the signal lines.

To simplify Table 52, an abbreviated notation is used to describe the various types of drivers. The notations used are shown below:

Totem-pole (high current)	— TP HC
Totem-pole (standard)	— TP STD
Three-state (high current)	— 3 HC
Three-state (standard)	— 3 STD
Open-collector	— OC

For detailed specifications, see 6.4.

Table 52
Bus Driver Summary

Signal Mnemonic	Signal Name	Driver Type	Bused and Terminated?
A01-A31 (31 lines)	Address bus	3 STD	Yes
ACFAIL*	AC power failure	OC	Yes
AM0-AM5 (6 lines)	Address modifier	3 STD	Yes
AS*	Address strobe	3 HC	Yes
BBSY*	Bus busy	OC	Yes
BCLR*	Bus clear	TP HC	Yes
BERR*	Bus error	OC	Yes
BG0IN*-BG3IN* BG0OUT*-BG3OUT* (Daisy-chain)	Bus grant daisy-chain	TP STD	No
BR0*-BR3* (4 lines)	Bus request	OC	Yes
D00-D31 (32 lines)	Data bus	3 STD	Yes
DS0*-DS1* (2 lines)	Data strobes	3 HC	Yes
DTACK*	Data transfer acknowledge	OC	Yes
IACK*	Interrupt acknowledge	3 STD or OC	Yes
IACKIN*/IACKOUT* (Daisy-chain)	Interrupt acknowledge Daisy-chain	TP STD	No
IRQ1*-IRQ7* (7 lines)	Interrupt request	OC	Yes
LWORD*	Longword	3 STD	Yes
RESERVED	Reserved	—	Yes

(*Continued on Page 228*)

Table 52 (*Continued*)
Bus Driver Summary

Signal Mnemonic	Signal Name	Driver Type	Bused and Terminated?
SERCLK	Serial clock	TP HC	Yes
SERDAT*	Serial data	OC	Yes
SYSCLK	System clock	TP HC	Yes
SYSFAIL*	System failure	OC	Yes
SYSRESET*	System reset	OC	Yes
WRITE*	Write	3 STD	Yes

7. Mechanical Specifications

7.1 Introduction. Information is provided in this section to ensure that the system's board assemblies, backplanes, subracks, and associated mechanical accessories are dimensionally compatible.

The mechanical dimensions given in this section conform to IEC Publications 297-1, 297-3, 297-3A and 603-2. The electrical characteristics for connectors, as specified in Sections 5 and 6 supersede Publication 603-2 where they differ.

IEC Publication 603-2 describes a family of connector types, which are identified by labels of the form:

603-2-IEC-xxxxxx-xxx

All of the P1/J1 and P2/J2 connectors used on boards and backplanes are members of this family. In this section, the label 603-2-IEC-xxxxxx-xxx is used when referring to all of these connector types as a group. The label 603-2-IEC-C096Mx-xxx is used when referring to the 96-pin male connector types within this family, which are used on boards. 603-2-IEC-C096Fx-xxx is used when referring to the 96-pin female connector types, which are used on backplanes.

Figure 74 is a front view of a 19 in wide subrack that shows how single-height and double-height boards can be mixed in a single subrack. Boards are inserted into the subrack from the front, in a vertical plane with the component face of the board on the right.

Permission 7.1 A system may be composed of single-height boards, double-height boards, or a mixture of both.

Rule 7.1 Single-height subracks shall have a single J1 backplane.

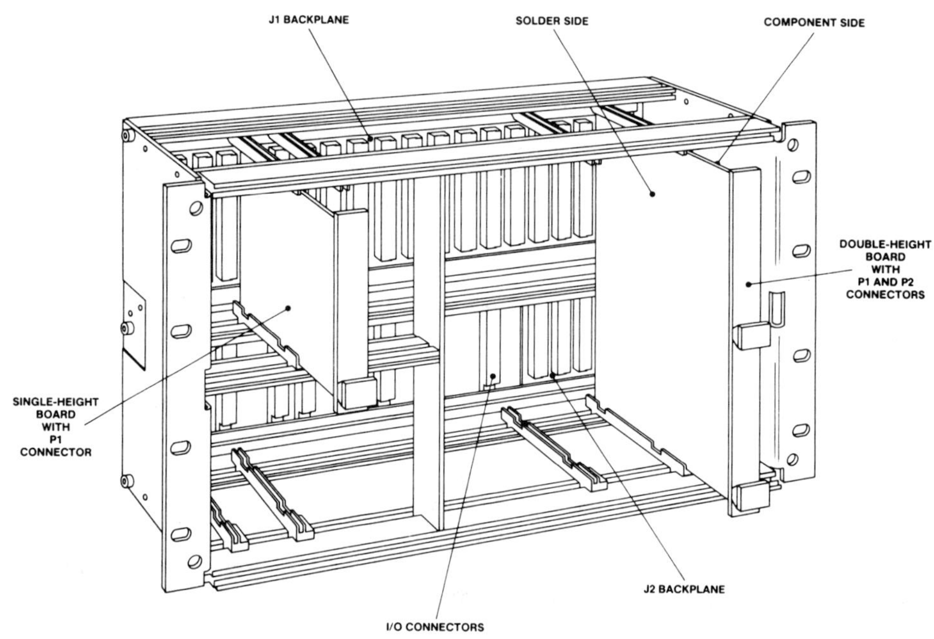

Fig 74
Subrack with Mixed Board Sizes

Rule 7.2 Double-height subracks shall have either (1), (2), or (3).

(1) A J1 backplane mounted in the upper portion of the subrack.

(2) A J1 and a J2 backplane, with the J1 backplane mounted in the upper portion and the J2 backplane mounted in the lower portion.

(3) A double-height J1/J2 backplane that provides both J1 and J2 connectors.

Rule 7.3 Backplanes shall not have more than 21 slots.

Permission 7.2 When using backplanes of fewer than 21 slots, the subrack may be less than the standard 19 in (482.6 mm) rack size.

Rule 7.4 Except for the rack width, which varies depending on the number of slots it supports, all subrack dimensions shall agree with those given in this section to ensure mechanical compatibility between the boards and the subrack.

7.2 Boards

Recommendation 7.1 Make boards 0.063 in ±0.008 in (1.6 mm ±0.2 mm) thick.

Observation 7.1 The thickness of boards is important because the subrack's guide rails are designed to accommodate boards of this thickness. Thicker boards might not fit into the guides and thinner boards might not be guided properly into the backplane's J1 and J2 connectors.

Observation 7.2 The dimensions of the 603-2-IEC-xxxxxx-xxx connectors provide a certain distance between the connector's mounting face and the center line of each of the connector's pins. This ensures that the P1 and P2 connector pin centers will align properly with the J1 and J2 connectors of the backplane.

Permission 7.3 Boards may be designed with board thicknesses greater than 0.063 in (1.6 mm) if

(1) The thickness of the top and bottom edges of the board, which fit into the guide rails, is reduced to 0.063 in (1.6 mm) for distance of 0.098 in (2.5 mm) from the top and bottom edges of the board (see Figs 75 and 76) and,

(2) The mounting surface provided by the board for the IEC 602-3 connector(s) is 0.160 in (4.07 mm) from the interboard separation plane (see Fig 78).

Rule 7.32 Boards shall be 0.063 in ±0.008 in (1.6 mm ±0.2 mm) thick in the guide area.

Two board sizes are defined: single-height and double-height (see Figs 75 and 76).

Fig 75
Single-Height Board: Basic Dimensions

NOTES: (1) All dimensions are shown in inches. Millimeter dimensions are shown in parentheses.
(2) These grids are provided to help the board designer to align components with the front panel grid.

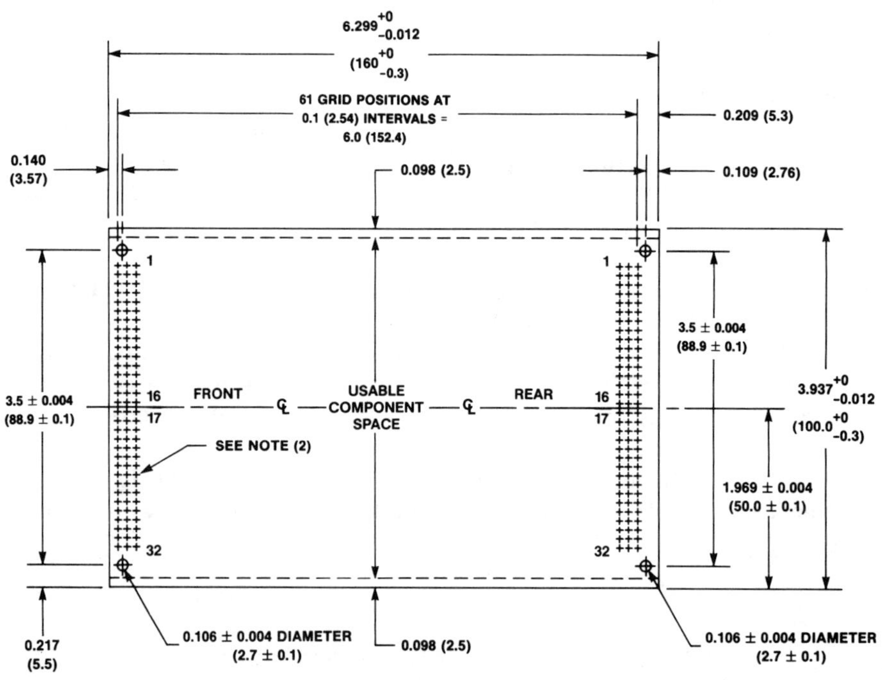

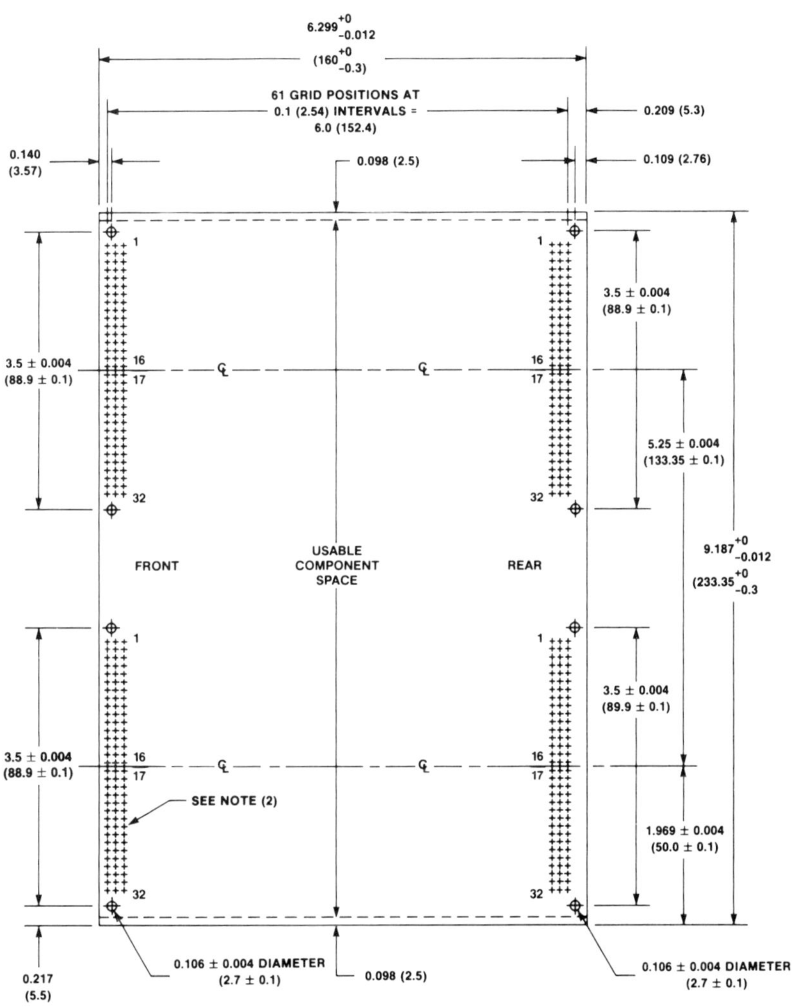

NOTES: (1) All dimensions are shown in inches. Millimeter dimensions are shown in parentheses.
(2) These grids are provided to help the board designer to align components with the front panel grid.

Fig 76
Double-Height Board: Basic Dimensions

7.2.1 Single-Height Boards

Observation 7.3 A single-height board is 3.937 in (100 mm) high and 6.299 in (160 mm) deep with an area of approximately 24.8 in^2 (160.0 cm^2).

Rule 7.5 All single-height boards shall be designed to the dimensions given in Fig 75.

Rule 7.6 The hole pattern for the 96-pin, 603-2-IEC-C096Mx-xxx P1 connector shall be as shown in Fig 75.

Suggestion 7.1 Use the pcb layout grid shown in Fig 75.

Observation 7.4 Modular front panel hardware is available from several manufacturers, which when mounted on the grid shown in Fig 75, properly aligns with the front panel grid shown in Fig 80.

Permission 7.4 Components, other than the 603-2-IEC-C096Mx-xxx connector, may be placed in such a way that they do not align with the grid pattern.

7.2.2 Double-Height Boards

Observation 7.5 A double-height board is 9.187 in (233.35 mm) high and 6.299 in (160 mm) deep with an area of approximately 57.9 in^2 (373.4 cm^2).

Rule 7.7 Double-height boards shall be designed according to the dimensions given in Fig 76.

Rule 7.8 The hole pattern for the 96-pin 603-2-IEC-C096Mx-xxx P1 connector shall be as shown in Fig 76.

Rule 7.9 If a 96-pin 603-2-IEC-C096Mx-xxx connector is used for P2, then its hole pattern shall be as shown in Fig 76.

Observation 7.6 As in the case of the single-height boards in 7.2.1, the grid shown in Fig 76 properly aligns modular front panel components with the front panel grid shown in Fig 81.

Permission 7.5 Components, other than the 603-2-IEC-xxxxxx-xxx connectors, may be placed in such a way that they do not align with the grid pattern.

Observation 7.7 There is a discontinuity of 0.05 in (1.27 mm) between the 0.10 in (2.54 mm) grid patterns for the upper and lower half of the board.

7.2.3 Board Connectors. The single-height board has only one connector on its back edge. It is called the P1 connector. A double-height board has either one or two connectors on its back edge. If it has one connector, that connector is called the P1 connector and is located on the upper half of the back edge. If it has two connectors the upper one is called the P1 connector and the lower one is called the P2 connector.

Rule 7.10 The P1 and P2 connectors of boards shall meet or exceed the mechanical specifications of a 603-2-IEC-C096Mx-xxx class 2 connector, and shall be mounted as shown in Fig 77.

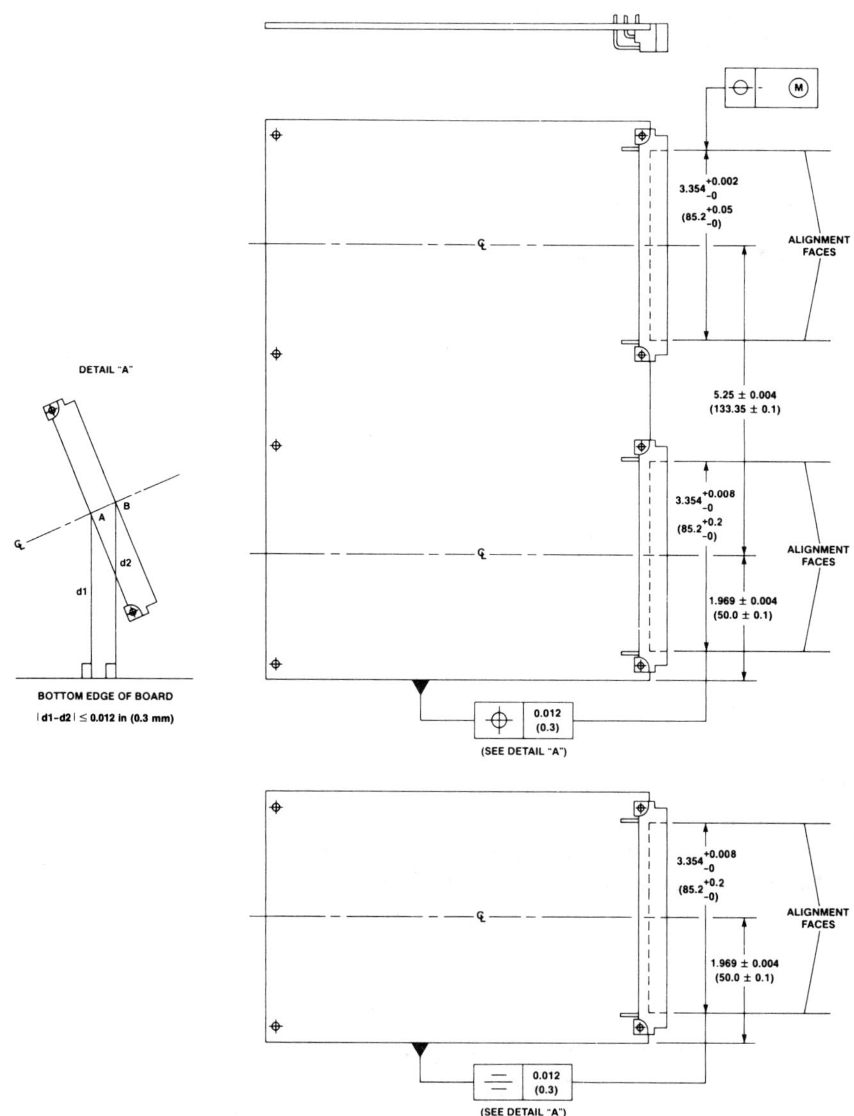

NOTE: All dimensions are shown in inches. Millimeter dimensions are shown in parentheses.

Fig 77
Connector Position on Single-Height and Double-Height Boards

Observation 7.8 603-2-IEC class 2 connectors have a minimum mechanical endurance of 400 insertion/extraction cycles.

Observation 7.9 The symmetry symbol in the box below each board outline in Fig 77 sets an upper limit on how much the connector's center line can be tilted with respect to the board's lower edge. This limit is described in Rule 7.11.

Rule 7.11 The perpendicular distance (d1) from the board's lower edge to the point A in Fig 77 shall not differ its perpendicular distance (d2) to point B by more than 0.012 in (0.3 mm).

Rule 7.12 If a board is designed to use the center row of P2 for address or data bus expansion, or the board requires more power than the P1 connector can provide, then a 96-pin 603-2-IEC-C096 Mx-xxx mechanically compatible P2 connector shall be provided and it shall be mounted as shown in Fig 77.

Permission 7.6 Where neither address nor data bus expansion is required, and where the board does not require more power than the P1 connector can provide, any 603-2-IEC-xxxxxx-xxx connector may be used for P2 on a double-height board or the board may be designed without a P2 connector.

Permission 7.7 On double-height boards, the two outside rows of pins on the P2 connector may be used to provide user-defined connections (see 7.6.2).

Permission 7.8 I/O cables may be connected to the front edge of a board. No connectors are prescribed for these cable connections.

Suggestion 7.2 Where possible, avoid the use of cable connections to the front edge of boards. This makes it much easier to install and remove boards from the subrack during maintenance.

7.2.4 Board Assemblies. The board assembly typically consists of a pcb, with either one or two 603-2-IEC-xxxxxx-xxx connectors affixed to the board's back edge, electronic components, and an optional front panel with handles. For more detail on the front panels see 7.3.

> **Rule 7.13** Solder filets, tracking, and components on boards shall not be closer than 0.098 in (2.5 mm) from the top and bottom edges of the board to guarantee clearance between them and the board guides. Figures 75 and 76 show these dimensions.

Figure 78 shows a cross-sectional view of a pcb, its front panel, its connector and the backplane. The dimensions given are nominal values and are based upon the dimensions given in the other drawings in this section.

7.2.5 Board Widths. Boards designed to occupy a single slot of the subrack are called single-width boards.

Permission 7.9 Boards may be designed to occupy more than one slot.

7.2.6 Board Warpage, Lead Length, and Component Height. During the manufacturing process boards sometimes become warped.

> **Rule 7.14** The sum of warpage and component lead length shall be $\leqq$0.097 in ($\leqq$2.47 mm) from where the solder side of an ideal (unwarped) board would be, and the sum of component height and warpage (in the other direction) shall be $\leqq$0.54 in ($\leqq$13.71 mm) plus an integral multiple N of 0.8 in (20.32 mm), from where the component side of an ideal (unwarped) board would be (where N = number of slots the board occupies -1).

Observation 7.10 During insertion into the subrack, the component leads of a board might contact the right edge of the front panel to its left. For this reason, the board should be inserted carefully to avoid bending the component leads.

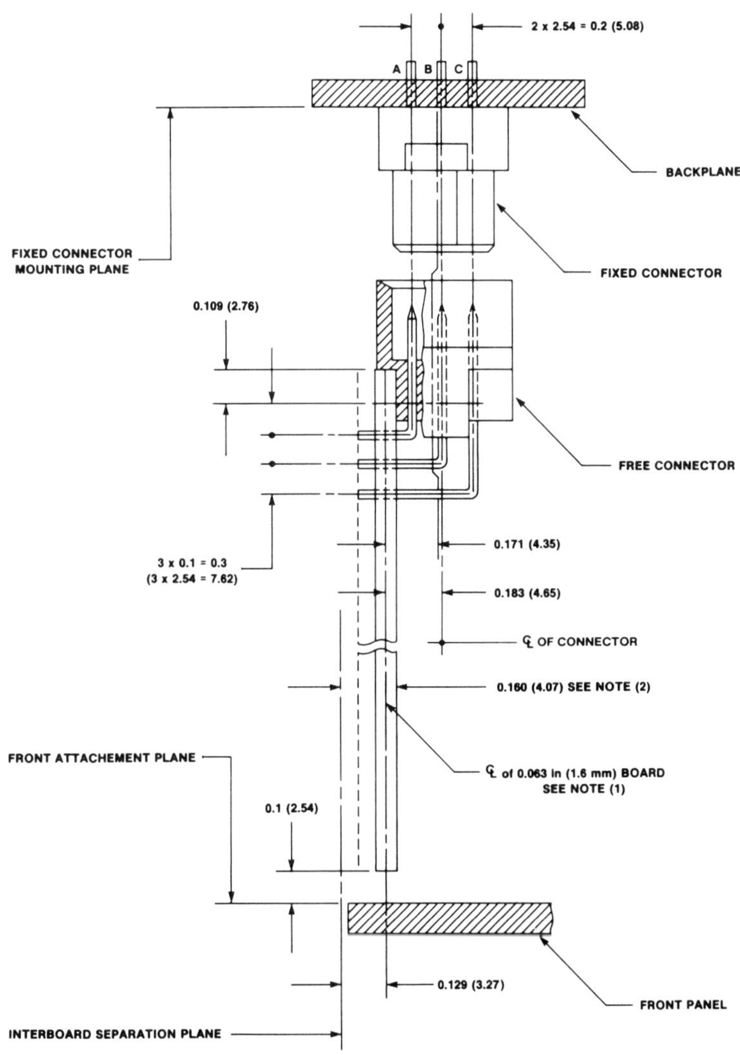

NOTES: (1) For additional information regarding the allowed thickness of boards, see 7.2.
(2) This 0.160 in (4.07 mm) dimension is the same regardless of the thickness of the board.

Fig 78
Cross-Sectional View of Board, Connector, Backplane, and Front Panel

Suggestion 7.3 Where possible, trim the component lead lengths to 0.06 in (1.52 mm). This makes installation and removal of boards more convenient. Since the maximum allowable warpage is affected by the length of these component leads, trimming them allows boards with larger warpage to meet the specifications.

Observation 7.11 The dimensions given in Suggestion 7.3 ensure that there will be a clearance of at least 0.1 in (2.54 mm) between components of each board and the component leads of the board to its right. This space allows adequate air flow and prevents additional warpage and vibration from causing interboard contact.

Rule 7.15 All boards shall be measured, after they are assembled, to ensure that the combination of board warpage, component lead length, and component height do not exceed the specified limits when the board is inserted into a subrack. To properly make these measurements, the board shall be placed in a subrack (or a similar test fixture) while the measurements are taken.

Figure 79 shows a board (single- or double-height) in a subrack, and shows how the combination of board warpage, component lead length, and component height are to be measured. The interboard separation planes defined in that figure provide the reference from which the measurements are made.

Observation 7.12 A special test fixture, which simulates a subrack, is helpful in speeding up the measurements shown in Fig 79.

Suggestion 7.12 Trim component lead lengths to no more than 0.06 in (1.52 mm).

Rule 7.34 Component leads and components mounted on the solder side of the board shall not protrude through the interboard separation plane after it has been completely seated in the backplane.

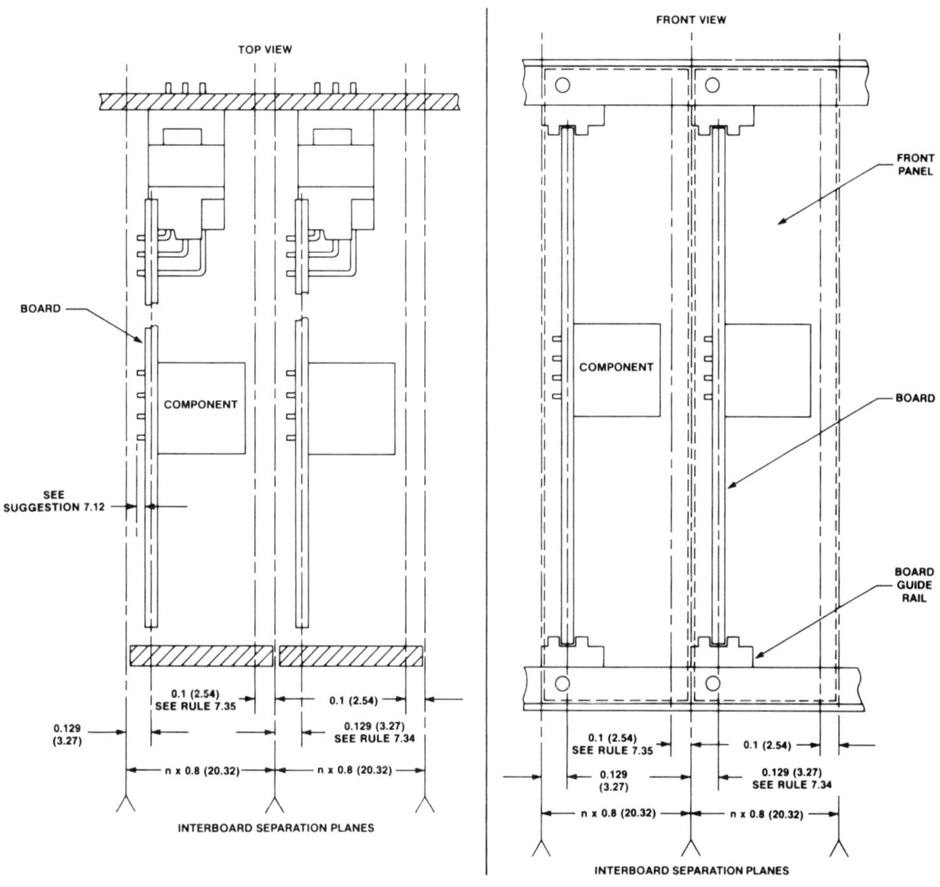

NOTE: All dimensions are shown in inches. Millimeter dimensions are shown in parentheses.

Fig 79
Component Height, Lead Length, and Board Warpage

Rule 7.35 Components mounted on the component side of the board shall not be any closer than 0.1 in (2.54 mm) to the interboard separation plane after it has been completely seated in the backplane.

7.3 Front Panels. This section provides the mechanical specifications for the single- and double-height board front panels and associated hardware.

Permission 7.10 Boards may be manufactured with or without front panels.

Recommendation 7.2 Use front panels and associated hardware to prevent boards from vibrating out of the subrack, and to guide airflow through the subrack.

Rule 7.16 If front panels are used, then screws shall be provided on those panels to secure the top and bottom of the panels to the subrack, and their screw threads shall be M2.5 × 0.45 pitch (see Fig 80).

Figure 80 shows a single-height, single-width front panel. Figure 81 shows a double-height, single-width front panel. The grid format on the rear face of these front panels are aligned with the board grids in Figs 75 and 76, respectively.

Suggestion 7.4 Install front panel components such as light emitting diodes (LED) and switches so that their centers are aligned with a front panel grid point.

Recommendation 7.11 Locate the mounting hole 0.3 in (7.62 mm) from the interboard separation plane.

Permission 7.20 The mounting hole may be located 0.5 in (12.7 mm) from the interboard separation plane.

7.3.1 Handles

Permission 7.11 Boards front panels may be designed with or without handles.

Recommendation 7.3 Provide handles to make boards easier to remove from the subrack.

Observation 7.13 The handles available from various manufacturers vary somewhat in overall shape.

Fig 80
Single-Height, Single-Width Front Panel

NOTES: (1) All dimensions are shown in inches. Millimeter dimensions are shown in parentheses.
(2) Dimensions given for height and depth of handles are suggestions only.

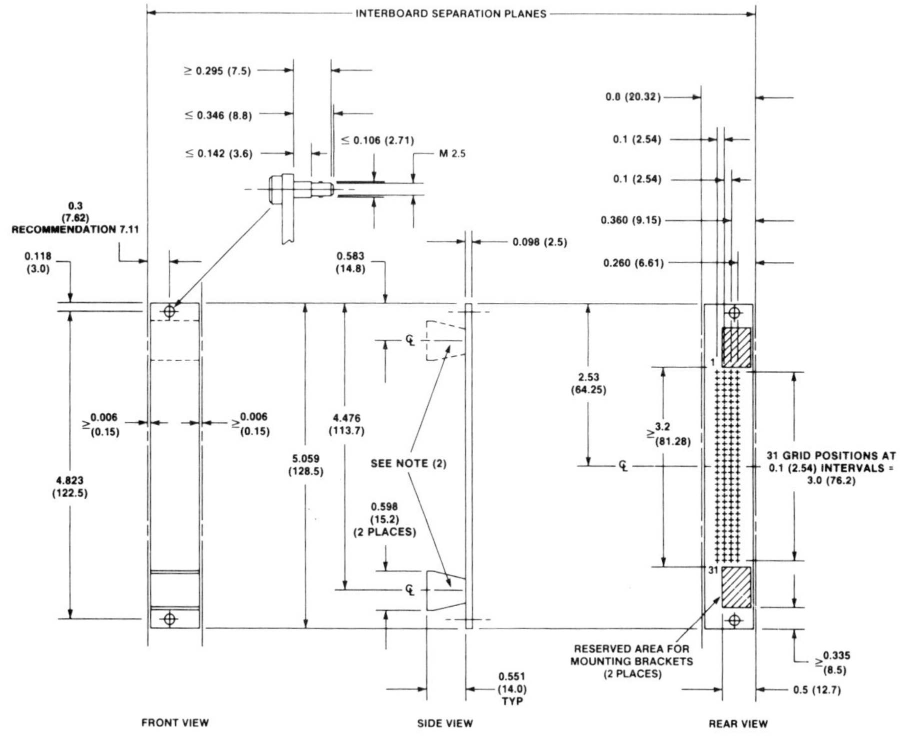

Suggestion 7.5 Choose handles whose depth and height conform to the dimensions shown in Figs 80 and 81.

Fig 81
Double-Height, Single-Width Front Panel

NOTES: (1) All dimensions are shown in inches. Millimeter dimensions are shown in parentheses.
(2) Dimensions given for height and depth of handles are suggestions only.

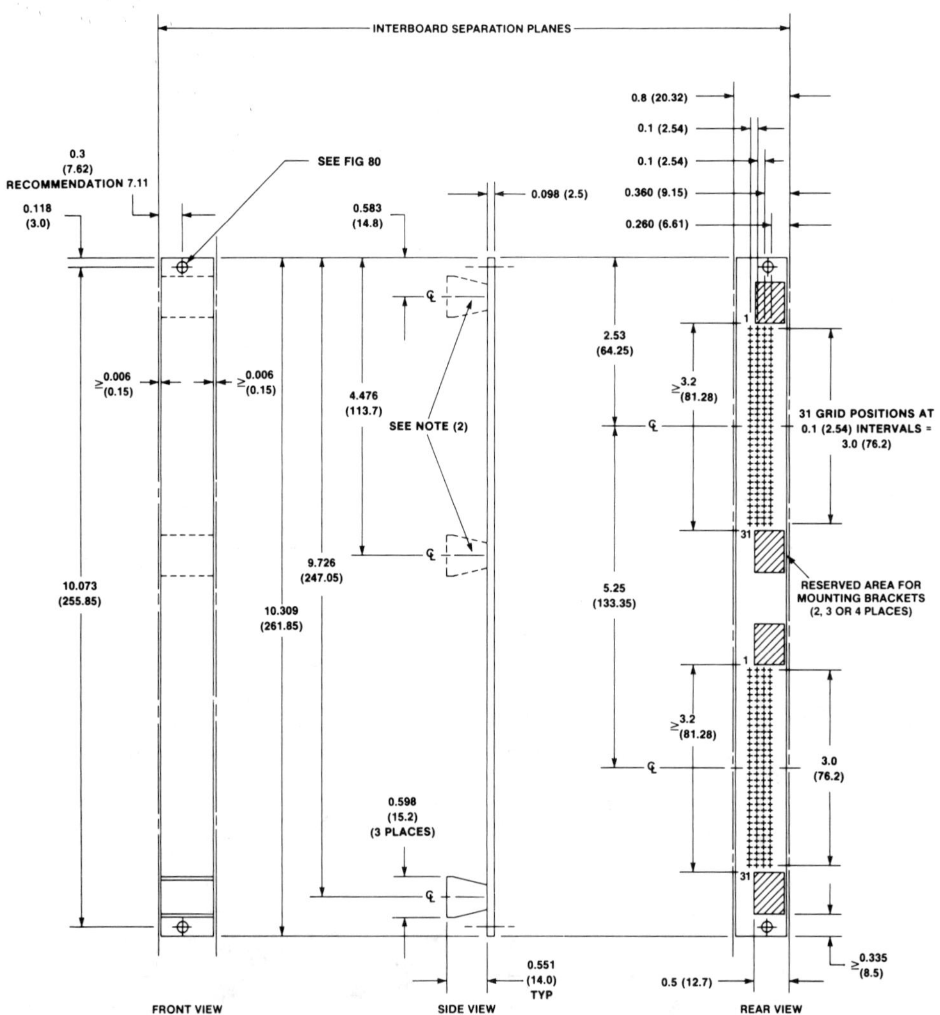

Recommendation 7.4 When mounting handles on board front panels, choose one or more of the locations shown in Figs 80 and 81, and Figs 84 and 85.

Permission 7.12 On single-height boards, handles may be installed in any of the following combinations:

(1) Top only
(2) Bottom only
(3) Top and bottom

Permission 7.13 On double-height boards handles may be installed in any of the following combinations:

(1) Top only
(2) Middle only
(3) Bottom only
(4) Top and middle
(5) Bottom and middle
(6) Top and bottom

Observation 7.14 When double- and single-height boards share the same subrack, handles in the center of the double-height front panels align with the handles of single-height boards, forming an unbroken line and giving a more consistent appearance.

Observation 7.15 Removal of double-height boards that have both a P1 and a 96-pin P2 connector requires up to 40.5 lbf (180 N) of extraction force. Placing handles at the top and bottom of double-height boards makes removal of these boards easiest.

7.3.2 Front Panel Mounting

Recommendation 7.5 If front panels are used, then keep the reserved areas shown in Figs 82 and 83 free of components to allow for installation of front panel mounting brackets. Locate the holes used to mount these brackets as shown in Figs 75 and 76.

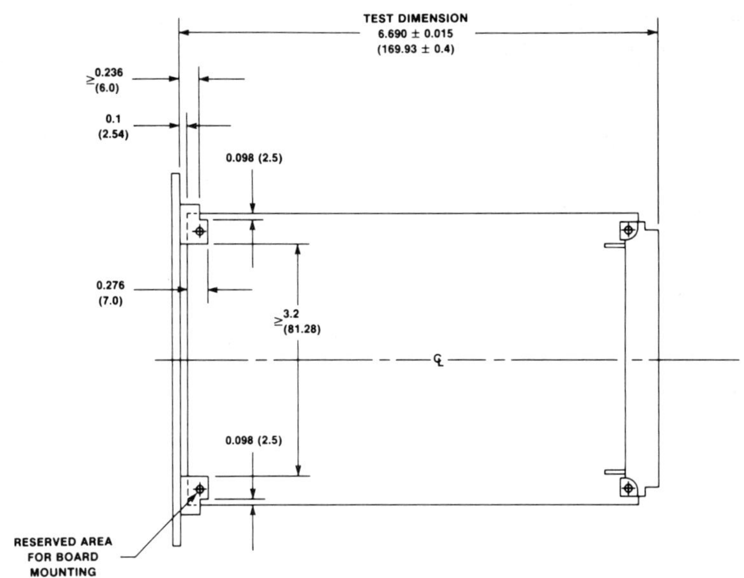

NOTE: All dimensions are shown in inches. Millimeter dimensions are shown in parentheses.

Fig 82
Front Panel Mounting Brackets and Dimension of Single-Height Boards

Recommendation 7.6 If front panels are used on double-height boards, then provide at least one center mounting bracket at one of the two locations shown in Fig 83.

Rule 7.17 If front panels are used, then the test dimension shown in Figs 82 and 83, from the rear face of the front panel to the rear face of the connector, shall be maintained.

Observation 7.16 The test dimensions from the rear face of the front panel to the front face of the backplane guarantee that the P1 and P2 connectors will be fully engaged and that the front panel fasteners will be able to secure the board into the subrack.

7.3.3 Front Panel Dimensions. All dimensioning of the front panel is done from a datum point 0.006 in (0.15 mm) to the left of its top left corner as viewed from the front.

Fig 83
Front Panel Mounting Brackets and Dimension of Double-Height Boards

NOTE: All dimensions are shown in inches. Millimeter dimensions are shown in parentheses.

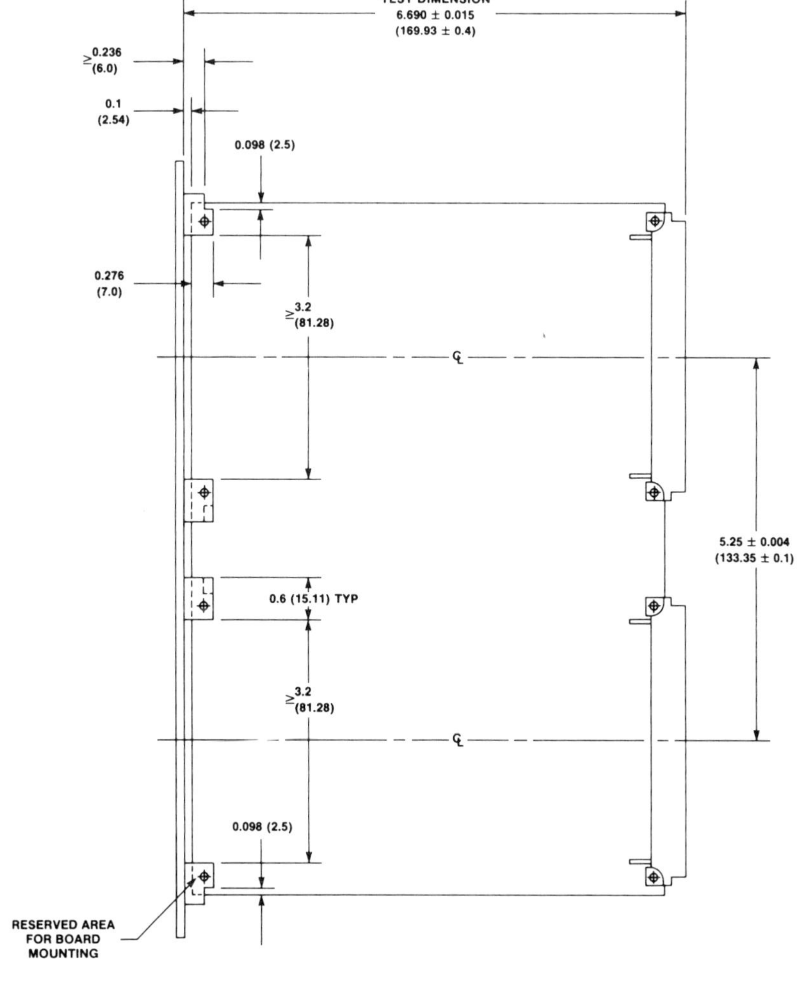

Rule 7.18 Single-width front panels shall be designed to the dimensions shown in Figs 80 and 81.

Recommendation 7.7 Make front panels 0.098 in (2.5 mm) nominal thickness.

Observation 7.17 The 0.788 in (20.02 mm) width of the single slot front panels is 0.012 in (0.30 mm) narrower than the 0.8 in (20.32 mm) slot spacing. This prevents mechanical interference between adjacent front panels due to tolerances in the board assemblies and subracks.

Rule 7.19 If a board occupies more than one slot and has a front panel, then the width of the front panel shall be 0.78 in (20.02 mm) plus an integral multiple n-1 of 0.8 in (20.32 mm), where n is the number of slots that the board occupies.

Rule 7.20 Single-slot front panels shall be equipped with one fastener at the top and another at the bottom, located as shown in Figs 80 and 81.

7.3.4 Filler Panels. Filler panels are sometimes used where the backplane positioning leaves a gap on the left or right end of the subrack's front panel or where there are empty slots. These filler panels require no mounting brackets because they are not attached to printed circuit boards. They are secured to the subrack by screws or quarter-turn fasteners on their top and bottom ends as the front panels of boards.

Rule 7.21 Filler panels shall be designed to conform to the dimensions given in Figs 84 and 85.

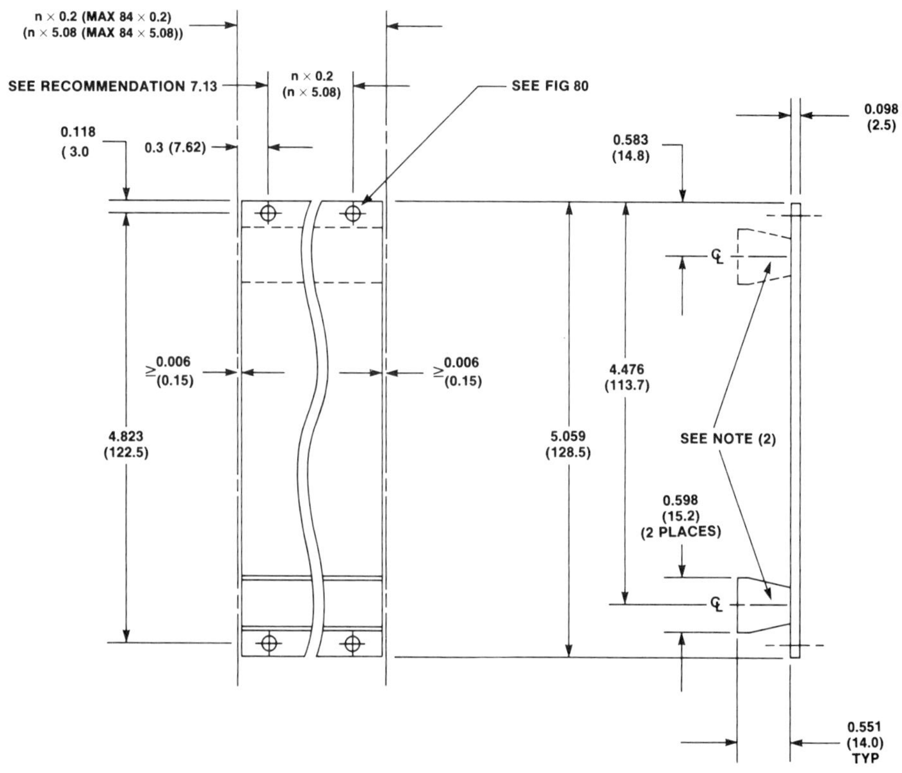

NOTES: (1) All dimensions are shown in inches. Millimeter dimensions are shown in parentheses.
(2) Dimensions given for height and depth of handles are suggestions only.

Fig 84
Single-Height Filler Panel

Rule 7.22 Single-slot filler panels shall be equipped with one fastener at the top and another at the bottom, located as shown in Figs 84 and 85.

Recommendation 7.8 Use filler panels on systems to maintain proper air flow within the subrack and to improve the appearance of the assembled system.

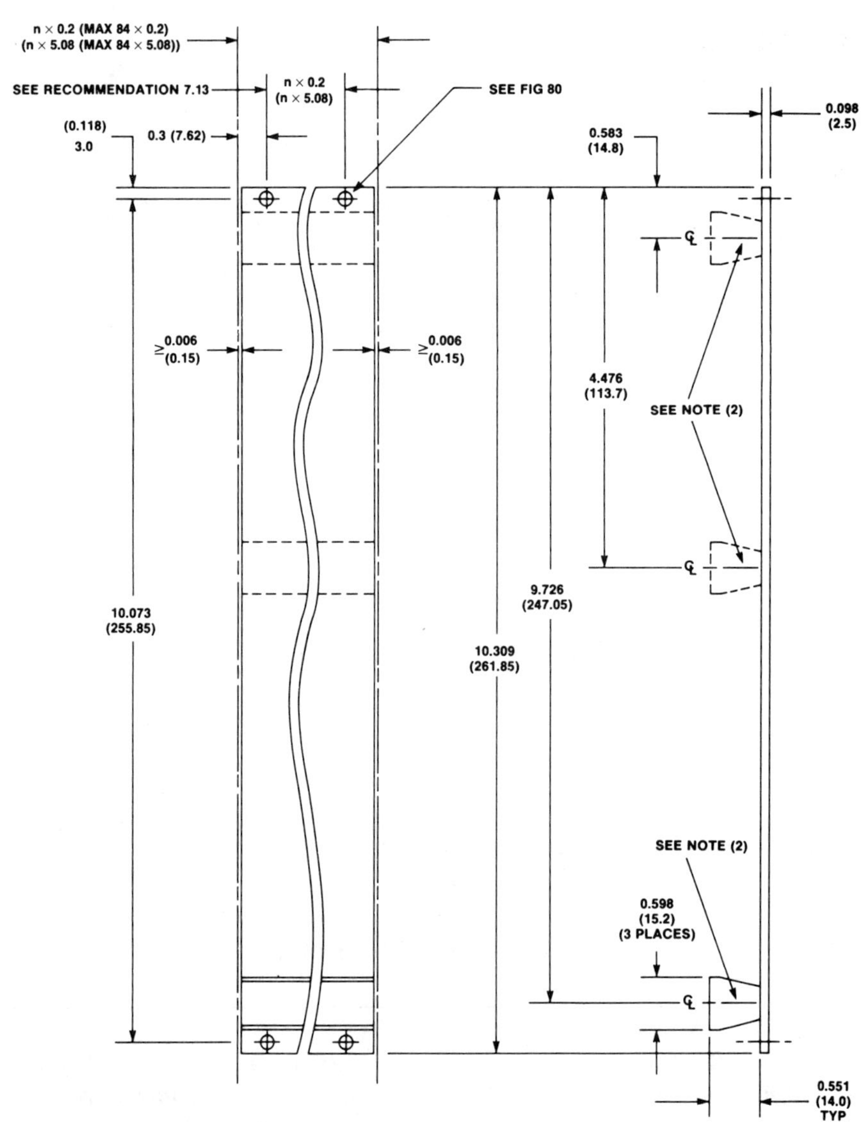

NOTES: (1) All dimensions are shown in inches. Millimeter dimensions are shown in parentheses.
(2) Dimensions given for height and depth of handles are suggestions only.

Fig 85
Double-Height Filler Panel

Suggestion 7.6 Equip filler panels with handles. This will give a more consistent appearance when they are installed in the same subrack with boards that have front panels and handles.

Suggestion 7.7 Provide additional mounting holes on filler panels wider than 4.0 in (101.60 mm) to provide better attachment to the subrack.

Recommendation 7.13 Where a panel is more than 2.0 in (50.8 mm) wide use at least four mounting holes; two at the top and two at the bottom.

7.3.5 Board Ejectors and Injectors

Observation 7.18 Several vendors offer different types of board ejectors/injectors that make insertion and removal of boards easier.

Observation 7.19 The insertion force for a single 603-2-IEC-C096 Mx-xxx connector might be 20.23 lbf (90 N).

Permission 7.14 Boards may be equipped with any type of ejectors, injectors, or retainers as long as they do not make the products they are used on incompatible with boards or subracks designed to this specification.

7.4 Backplanes. The primary backplane is designated as the J1 backplane. In some cases this is the only backplane in the system. When a double-height subrack is used, this backplane is mounted in the upper portion of that subrack. When the expanded system is used, a second backplane, designated the J2 backplane, is installed below the J1 backplane in the lower portion of the subrack. This J2 backplane buses only the center row (row b) of the P2 connector pins, allowing the two outer rows (rows a and c) to be used to implement any other user-defined functions. The term J1/J2 is used to describe a combined backplane that provides both the P1 and the P2 connectors on the same pcb.

Board slots are designated 1, 2, 3, ... 21, with the slot numbering starting at the left end of the subrack, as viewed from the front. The daisy-chain propagation starts at slot 1 and goes to slot 21.

Rule 7.23 J1 backplanes shall bus all signals in all slots except for the daisy-chained signals (see 7.6.1).

Rule 7.24 When either a J2 or a J1/J2 backplane are used to provide for 32-bit wide address and data transfers, it shall bus all pins of the center row (row b) of those slots for which it has connectors (see 7.6.2).

Rule 7.25 The 96-pin 603-2-IEC-C096Fx-xxx connectors shall be used on all J1 backplanes and on all J2 expansion backplanes.

Rule 7.26 All J1 backplanes shall have some provision for jumpering the interrupt acknowledge and bus grant daisy-chains when boards are not plugged into a slot.

Suggestion 7.8 To provide for the jumpering of the J1 backplane daisy-chains, use 603-2-IEC-C096Fx-xxx connectors that have wire-wrap pins.

Suggestion 7.9 If J1 connectors without wire-wrap pins are used, then place all the jumper pins for daisy-chains next to the J1 connector that they are jumpering.

Recommendation 7.15 To improve system ground integrity in expanded configurations, use a J1/J2 backplane.

Suggestion 7.10 Use 603-2-IEC-C096Fx-xxx connectors with wire-wrap pins for the connectors on J2 backplanes. This allows attachment of ribbon cables and secondary backplanes to those pins.

7.4.1 Backplane Dimensional Requirements. Figure 86 depicts a single-high 21-slot backplane, and Fig 88 depicts a double-high 21-slot backplane.

Permission 7.16 Backplanes may be designed with up to 21 slots.

Recommendation 7.9 When designing a backplane with fewer than 21 slots, make the width
($n \times$ 20.32 mm) -1.44 mm, +0/-0.3 mm
or
($n \times$ 20.32 mm) +0/-0.3 mm
where
n = number of slots
This allows two backplanes to be installed next to each other without wasting a slot position in the subrack.

Recommendation 7.10 Do not design backplanes with widths greater than 16.743 in (425.28 mm +0/-0.3 mm). Backplanes longer than this might not fit into widely available subracks.

Permission 7.17 Backplanes may be designed with or without threaded studs for power cable connections to the backplane.

Permission 7.23 The overall height dimension of a J1 or a J2 backplane may be 5.067 in +0/-0.012 in (128.7 mm +0/-0.3 mm).

Rule 7.27 Except for the width dimension, which varies with the number of slots, J1 and J2 backplanes shall be designed to the dimensions given in Figs 86 and 87.

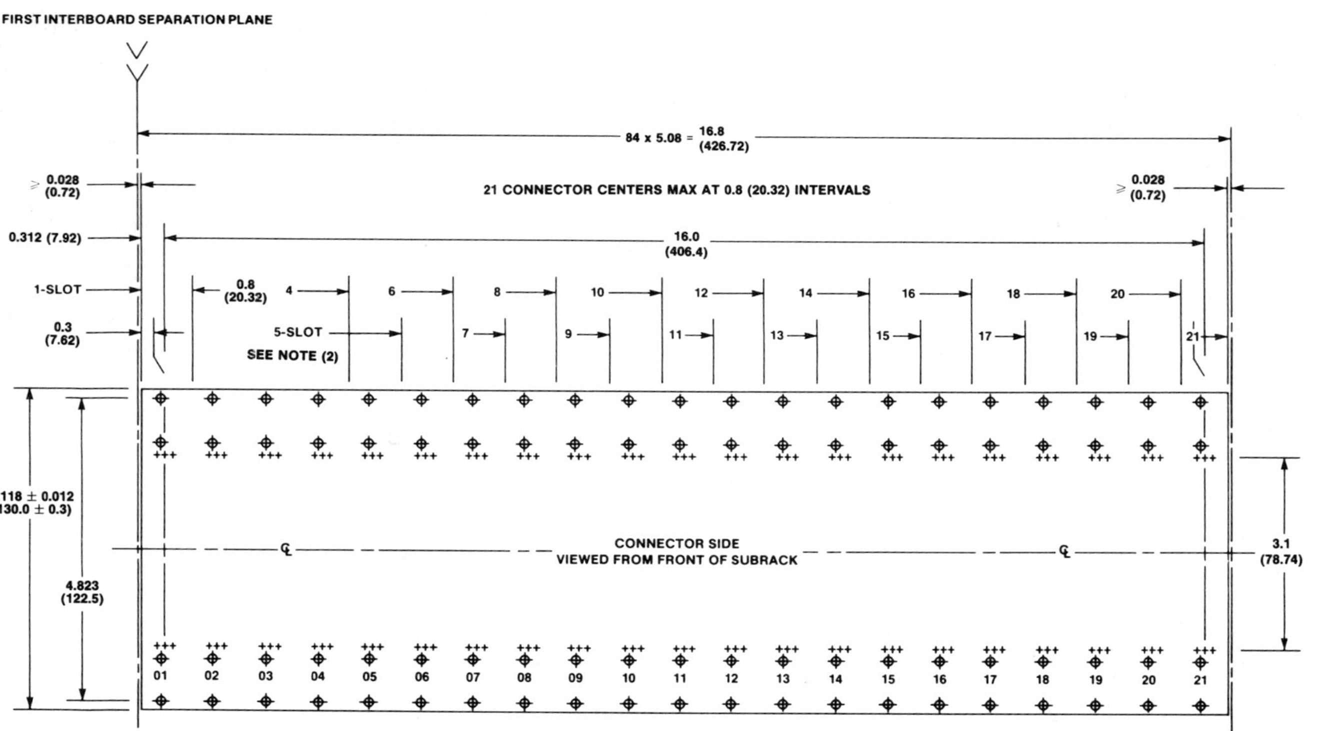

NOTES: (1) All dimensions are shown in inches. Millimeter dimensions are shown in parentheses.
(2) Backplane width varies depending on the number of slots.

Fig 86
Overall Dimensions of a J1 and a J2 Backplane

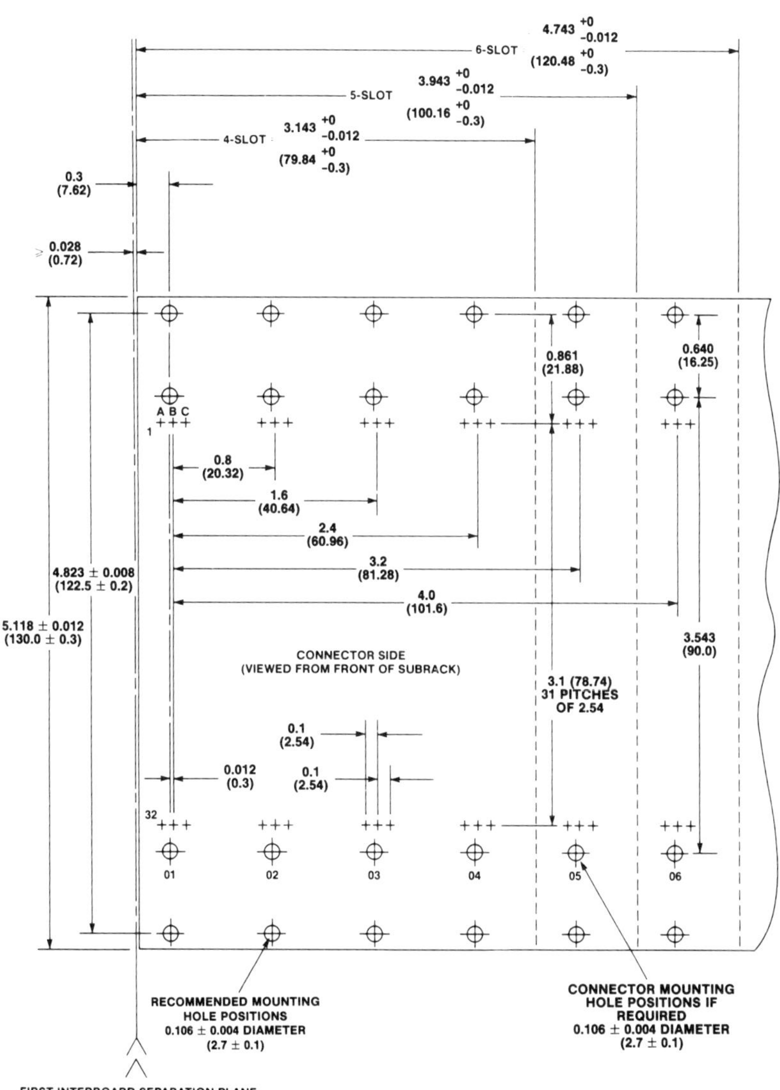

NOTE: All dimensions are shown in inches. Millimeter dimensions are shown in parentheses.

Fig 87
Detailed Dimensions of a J1 and a J2 Backplane

Permission 7.24 The overall height dimension of a J1/J2 backplane may be 10.317 in +0/-0.012 in (262.05 mm +0/-0.3 mm).

Rule 7.37 Except for the width dimension, which varies with the number of slots, J1/J2 backplanes shall be designed to the dimensions given in Figs 88 and 89.

Observation 7.20 The backplane dimensions shown in Figs 87 and 89 repeat every 0.8 in (20.32 mm).

7.4.2 Signal Line Termination Networks

Rule 7.28 Backplanes shall provide for termination networks for all of the signal lines indicated in 6.7.

Observation 7.25 Termination networks that are built onto the backplane provide better signal quality than plug-on terminator boards.

Recommendation 7.15 Include built-in termination networks on backplanes.

Rule 7.29 Backplane signal trace lengths, including any plug-on terminator boards, shall not exceed 20.0 in (508 mm).

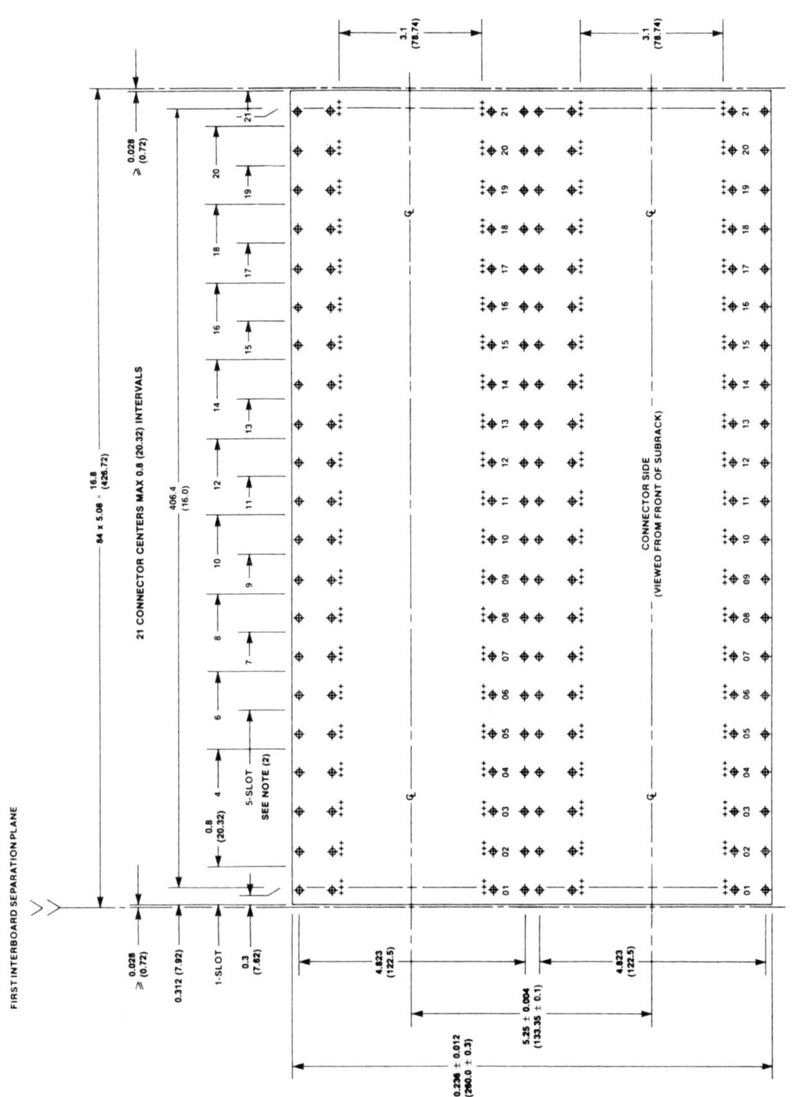

NOTES: (1) All dimensions are shown in inches. Millimeter dimensions are shown in parentheses.
(2) Backplane width varies depending on the number of slots.

Fig 88
Overall Dimensions of a J1/J2 Backplane

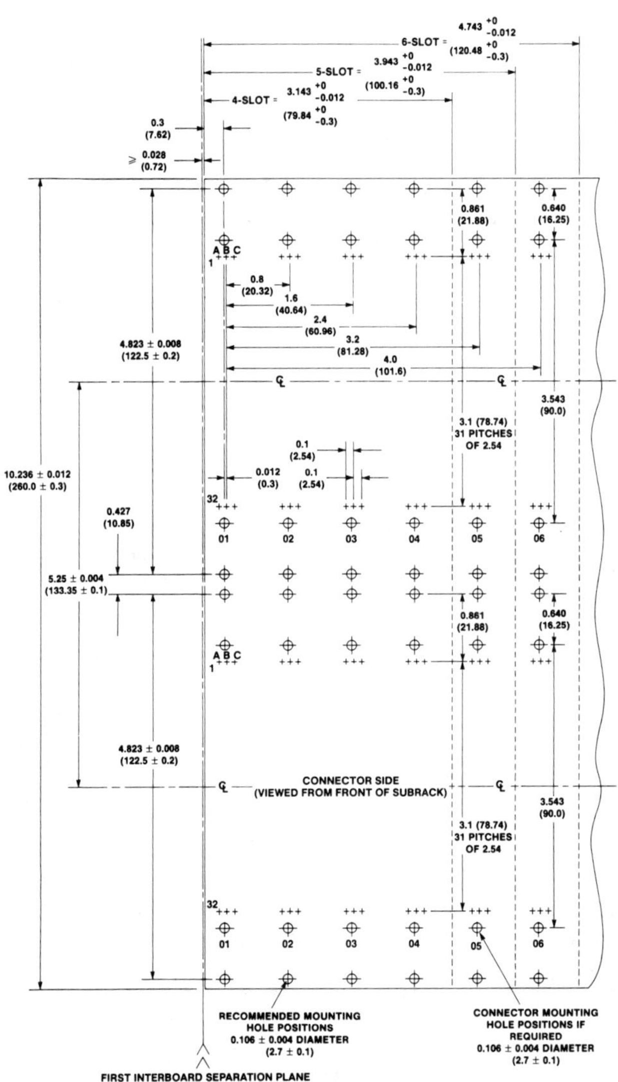

NOTE: All dimensions are shown in inches. Millimeter dimensions are shown in parentheses.

Fig 89
Detailed Dimensions of a J1/J2 Backplane

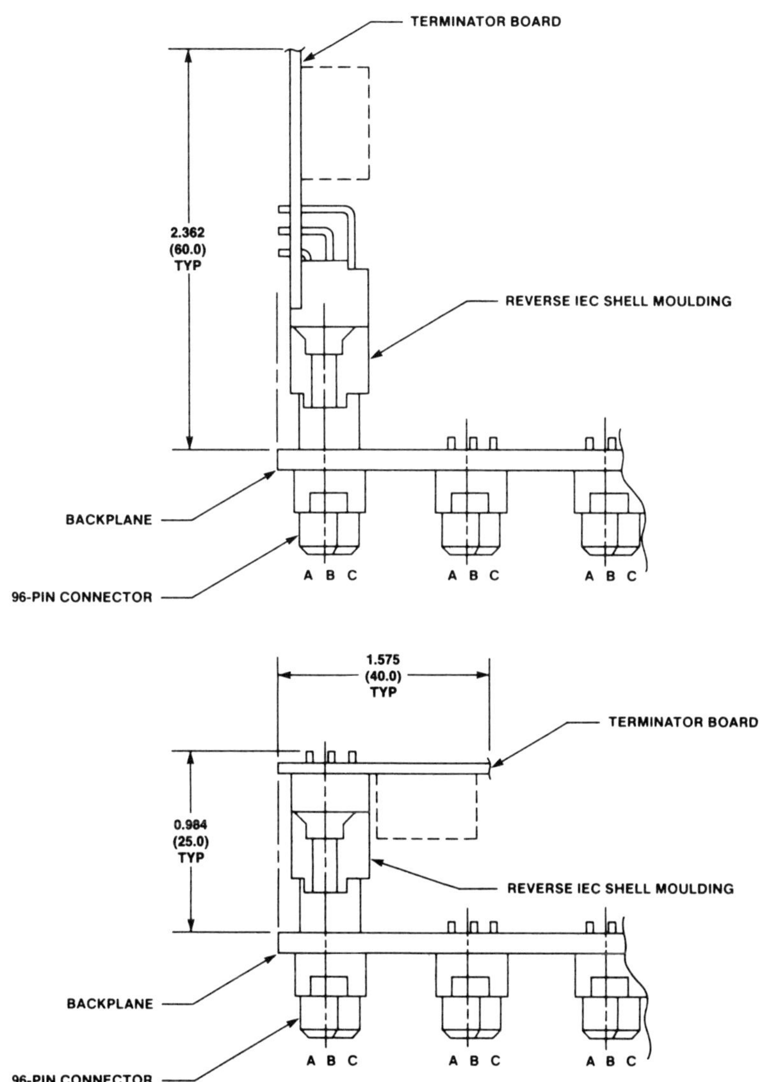

Fig 90
***Off-Board Type* Backplane Termination**
(Viewed From Top of Backplane)

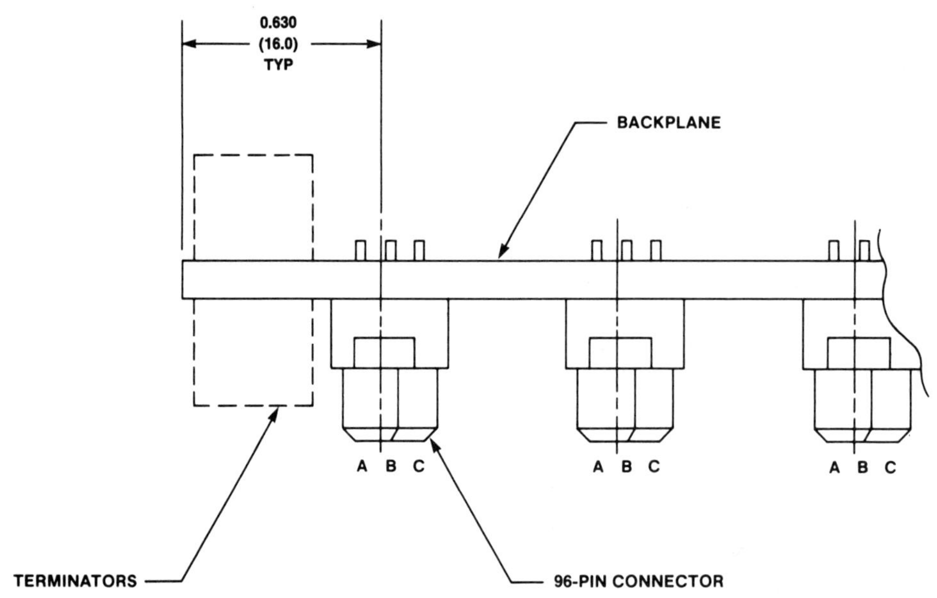

Fig 91
***On-Board Type* Backplane Termination**
(Viewed From Top of Backplane)

7.5 Assembly of Subracks. This section shows how subracks are assembled. All horizontal dimensions are from the left-hand edge of the front opening of the subrack.

7.5.1 Subracks and Slot Widths. Figure 92 shows a typical double-height 21-slot subrack.

Permission 7.19 Double-height subracks may be used to house only double-height boards or they may be subdivided by the installation of a bracket, into two single-height sections, one above the other.

Observation 7.22 The bracket allowed in Permission 7.19 provides two board guides: the lower guide for the board above it and the upper guide for the board below it.

Suggestion 7.11 Where possible, install the leftmost (slot 1) board guides so that their center line is 0.129 in (3.27 mm) from the left end of the rack opening. This provides sufficient clearance for the component leads of the board installed in that slot, and doesn't waste any horizontal space (If this board guide is installed farther to the right there will not be room for 21 slots).

7.5.2 Subrack Dimensions

Rule 7.30 All double-height subracks shall meet all of the dimensional requirements given in Fig 92, except for the width dimension, which varies according to how many slots are in the subrack.

Rule 7.31 All single-height subracks shall meet all of the dimensional requirements given in Fig 92, except for the width dimension, which varies according to how many slots are in the subrack, and the vertical distance between the lower- and upper-board guides, which is 3.94 in +0.015/-0.00 in instead of 9.19 in (100.2 mm, +0.4/-0.0 mm instead of 233.55 mm).

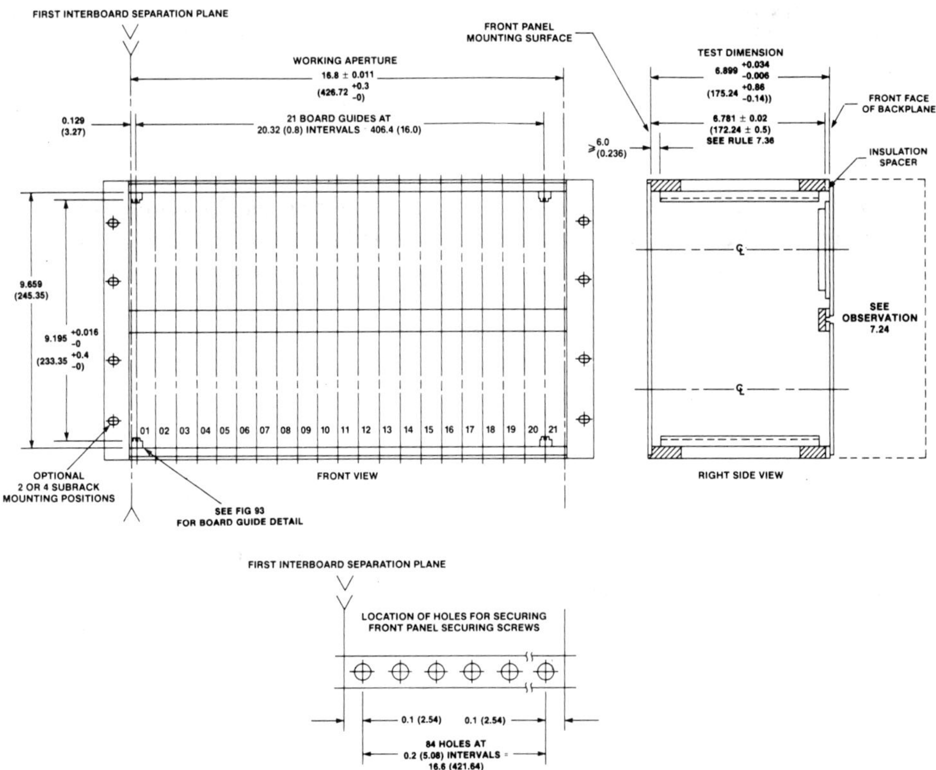

NOTES: (1) All dimensions are shown in inches. Millimeter dimensions are shown in parentheses.
(2) For additional information, see IEC 297-1 and IEC 297-3.

Fig 92
21-Slot Subrack

Observation 7.23 The dimension from the front panel mounting surface to the front face of the backplane is particularly critical, since it guarantees correct connector engagement.

Rule 7.36 The thickness of the insulation spacer (shown in the right side view of Fig 92) shall be chosen to ensure that the face of the backplane is the correct distance from the front panel mounting surface.

Observation 7.24 The thickness of the spacer specified in Fig 92 might vary from one vendor to another.

Permission 7.22 Side plates may be extended to the rear as required.

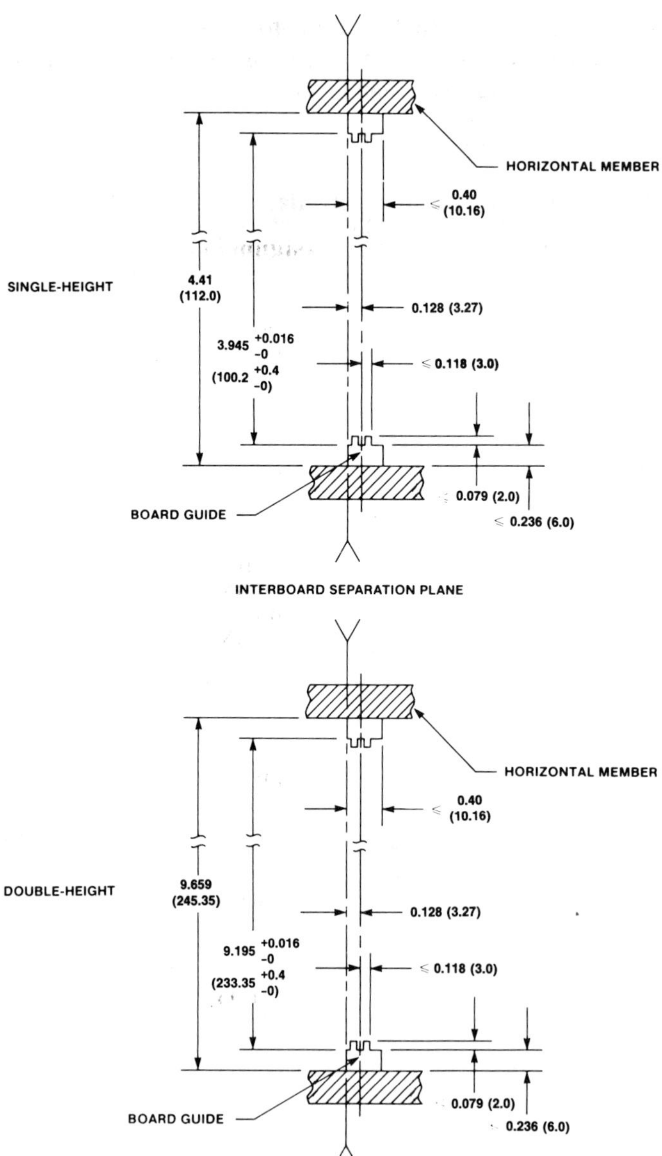

Fig 93
Board Guide Detail

7.6 Backplane Connectors and Board Connectors

7.6.1 Pin Assignments for the J1/P1 Connector. Table 53 provides signal names for the J1/P1 connector pins [The connector consists of three rows of pins labeled rows (a), (b), and (c)].

Table 53
J1/P1 Pin Assignments

Pin Number	(a) Signal Mnemonic	(b) Signal Mnemonic	(c) Signal Mnemonic
1	D00	BBSY*	D08
2	D01	BCLR*	D09
3	D02	ACFAIL*	D10
4	D03	BG0IN*	D11
5	D04	BG0OUT*	D12
6	D05	BG1IN*	D13
7	D06	BG1OUT*	D14
8	D07	BG2IN*	D15
9	GND	BG2OUT*	GND
10	SYSCLK	BG3IN*	SYSFAIL*
11	GND	BG3OUT*	BERR*
12	DS1*	BR0*	SYSRESET*
13	DS0*	BR1*	LWORD*
14	WRITE*	BR2*	AM5
15	GND	BR3*	A23
16	DTACK*	AM0	A22
17	GND	AM1	A21
18	AS*	AM2	A20
19	GND	AM3	A19
20	IACK*	GND	A18
21	IACKIN*	SERCLK (1)	A17
22	IACKOUT*	SERDAT* (1)	A16
23	AM4	GND	A15
24	A07	IRQ7*	A14
25	A06	IRQ6*	A13
26	A05	IRQ5*	A12
27	A04	IRQ4*	A11
28	A03	IRQ3*	A10
29	A02	IRQ2*	A09
30	A01	IRQ1*	A08
31	-12 V	+5 V STDBY	+12 V
32	+5 V	+5 V	+5 V

NOTE: See Appendix C for further information on the use of these signals.

7.6.2 Pin Assignments for the J2/P2 Connector. Table 54 provides signal names for the J2/P2 connector pins [The connector consists of three rows of pins labeled rows (a), (b), and (c)].

Table 54
J2/P2 Pin Assignments

Pin Number	(a) Signal Mnemonic	(b) Signal Mnemonic	(c) Signal Mnemonic
1	User-defined	+5 V	User-defined
2	User-defined	GND	User-defined
3	User-defined	RESERVED	User-defined
4	User-defined	A24	User-defined
5	User-defined	A25	User-defined
6	User-defined	A26	User-defined
7	User-defined	A27	User-defined
8	User-defined	A28	User-defined
9	User-defined	A29	User-defined
10	User-defined	A30	User-defined
11	User-defined	A31	User-defined
12	User-defined	GND	User-defined
13	User-defined	+5 V	User-defined
14	User-defined	D16	User-defined
15	User-defined	D17	User-defined
16	User-defined	D18	User-defined
17	User-defined	D19	User-defined
18	User-defined	D20	User-defined
19	User-defined	D21	User-defined
20	User-defined	D22	User-defined
21	User-defined	D23	User-defined
22	User-defined	GND	User-defined
23	User-defined	D24	User-defined
24	User-defined	D25	User-defined
25	User-defined	D26	User-defined
26	User-defined	D27	User-defined
27	User-defined	D28	User-defined
28	User-defined	D29	User-defined
29	User-defined	D30	User-defined
30	User-defined	D31	User-defined
31	User-defined	GND	User-defined
32	User-defined	+5 V	User-defined

Appendixes

(These Appendixes are not a part of ANSI/IEEE Std 1014-1988, IEEE Standard for A Versatile Backplane Bus; VMEbus, but are included for information only.)

Appendix A
Glossary

A16. A type of module that provides or decodes an address on address lines A01 through A15.

A24. A type of module that provides or decodes an address on address lines A01 through A23.

A32. A type of module that provides or decodes an address on address lines A01 through A31.

arbitration. The process of assigning control of the DTB to a requester.

address-only cycle. A DTB cycle that consists of an address broadcast, but no data transfer. Slaves do not acknowledge address-only cycles and masters terminate the cycle without waiting for an acknowledgment.

arbiter. A functional module that accepts bus requests from requester modules and grants control of the DTB to one requester at a time.

arbitration bus. One of the four buses provided by the backplane. This bus allows an arbiter module and several requester modules to coordinate use of the DTB.

arbitration cycle. An arbitration cycle begins when the arbiter senses a bus request. The arbiter grants the bus to a requester, which signals that the DTB is busy. The requester terminates the cycle by taking away the bus busy signal, which causes the arbiter to sample the bus requests again.

backplane. A printed circuit board (pcb) with 96-pin connectors and signal paths that bus the connector pins. Some systems have a single pcb, called the J1 backplane. It provides the signal paths needed for basic operation. Other systems also have a second pcb, called a J2 backplane. It provides the additional 96-pin connectors and signal paths needed for wider data and address transfers.

Still others have a single pcb, called a J1/J2 backplane that provides the signal conductors and connectors of both the J1 and J2 backplanes.

backplane interface logic. Special logic that takes into account the characteristics of the backplane: its signal line impedance, propagation time, termination values, etc. The specification prescribes certain rules for the design of this logic based on the maximum length of the backplane and its maximum number of board slots.

block read cycle. A DTB cycle used to transfer a block of 1 to 256 bytes from a slave to a master. This transfer is done using a string of 1-, 2-, or 4-byte data transfers. Once the block transfer is started, the master does not release the DTB until all of the bytes have been transferred. It differs from a string of read cycles in that the master broadcasts only one address and address modifier (at the beginning of the cycle). Then the slave increments this address on each transfer so that the data for the next cycle is retrieved from the next higher location.

block write cycle. A DTB cycle used to transfer a block of 1 to 256 bytes from a master to a slave. The block write cycle is very similar to the block read cycle. It uses a string of 1-, 2-, or 4-byte data transfers and the master does not release the DTB until all of the bytes have been transferred. It differs from a string of write cycles in that the master broadcasts only one address and address modifier (at the beginning of the cycle). Then the slave increments this address on each transfer so that the next transfer is stored in the next higher location.

board. A printed circuit board (pcb), its collection of electronic components, and either one or two 96-pin connectors that can be plugged into the backplane connectors.

bus timer. A functional module that measures the time each data transfer takes on the DTB and terminates the DTB cycle if a transfer takes too long. Without this module, if the master tries to transfer data to or from a nonexistent slave location it could wait forever for a slave to respond. The bus timer prevents this by terminating the cycle.

D08(O). (1) A slave that sends and receives data 8 bits at a time over D00-D07, or

(2) An interrupt handler that receives 8 bit status/ID over D00-D07, or
(3) An interrupter that sends 8-bit status/ID over D00-D07

D08(EO). (1) A master that sends or receives data 8 bits at a time over either D00-D07 or D08-D15, or

(2) A slave that sends and receives data 8 bits at a time over either D00-D07 or D08-D15

D16. (1) A master that sends and receives data 16 bits at a time over D00-D15, or

(2) A slave that sends and receives data 16 bits at a time over D00-D15, or
(3) An interrupt handler that receives 16-bit status/ID over D00-D15, or
(4) An interrupter that sends 16-bit status/ID over D00-D15

D32. (1) A master that sends and receives data 32 bits at a time over D00-D31, or

(2) A slave that sends and receives data 32 bits at a time over D00-D31, or
(3) An interrupt handler that receives 32-bit status/ID over D00-D31, or
(4) An interrupter that sends 32-bit status/ID over D00-D31

daisy-chain. A special type of signal line that is used to propagate a signal level from board to board, starting with the first slot and ending with the last slot. There are four bus grant daisy-chains and one interrupt acknowledge daisy-chain on the backplane.

data transfer bus. One of the four buses provided by the backplane. The data transfer bus allows masters to direct the transfer of binary data between themselves and slaves (data transfer bus is often abbreviated DTB).

data-transfer-bus cycle. A sequence of level transitions on the signal lines of the DTB that result in the transfer of an address or an address and data between a master and a slave. There are 34 types of data transfer bus cycles.

DTB. A mnemonic for data transfer bus.

functional module. A collection of electronic circuitry that resides on one board and works together to accomplish a task.

IACK daisy-chain driver. A functional module that activates the interrupt acknowledge daisy-chain whenever an interrupt handler acknowledges an interrupt request. This daisy-chain ensures that only one interrupter will respond with its status/ID when more than one has generated an interrupt request on the same level.

interrupt acknowledge cycle. A DTB cycle, initiated by an interrupt handler, that reads a status/ID from an interrupter. An interrupt handler generates this cycle when it detects an interrupt request from an interrupter and it has control of the DTB.

interrupter. A functional module that generates an interrupt request on the priority interrupt bus and then provides status/ID information when the interrupt handler requests it.

interrupt handler. A functional module that detects interrupt requests generated by interrupters and responds to those requests by asking for status/ID information.

location monitor. A functional module that monitors data transfers over the DTB to detect accesses to the locations it has been assigned to watch. When an access occurs to one of these assigned locations, the location monitor generates an on-board signal.

master. A functional module that initiates DTB cycles to transfer data between itself and a slave module.

power monitor. A functional module that monitors the status of the primary power source to the system and signals when the power has strayed outside the limits required for reliable system operation. Since most systems are powered by an ac source, the power monitor is typically designed to detect drop-out or brown-out conditions on ac lines.

priority interrupt bus. One of the four buses provided by the backplane. The priority interrupt bus allows interrupter modules to send interrupt requests to interrupt handler modules, and interrupt handler modules to acknowledge these interrupt requests.

read cycle. A DTB cycle used to transfer 1-, 2-, 3-, or 4-bytes from a slave to a master. The cycle begins when the master broadcasts an address and an address modifier. Each slave captures this address and address modifier, and checks to see if it is to respond to the cycle. If so, it retrieves the data from its internal storage, places it on the data bus, and acknowledges the transfer. Then the master terminates the cycle.

read-modify-write cycle. A DTB cycle that is used to both read from, and write to, a slave's byte location(s) without permitting any other master to access that location during that cycle. This cycle is most useful in multiprocessing systems where certain memory locations are used to control access to certain systems resources, for example, semaphore locations.

requester. A functional module that resides on the same board as a master or interrupt handler and requests use of the DTB whenever its master or interrupt handler needs it.

serial clock driver. A functional module that provides a periodic timing sign l that synchronizes the operation of the IEEE 1132* serial bus. Timing specifications for the serial clock driver of the IEEE 1132 are given in Appendix C. Two backplane signal lines are reserved for use by a serial bus. However, the protocols of the serial bus are completely independent of the IEEE 1014, and the inclusion of a serial bus is not a required feature of the IEEE 1014.)

*At the time of publication of this standard the IEEE 1132 is under preparation. It is not an approved standard.

slave. A functional module that detects DTB cycles initiated by a master and, when those cycles specify its participation, transfers data between itself and the master.

slot. A position where a board can be inserted into a backplane. If the system has both a J1 and a J2 backplane (or a combination J1/J2 backplane) each slot provides a pair of 96-pin connectors. If the system has only a J1 backplane, then each slot provides a single 96-pin connector.

subrack. A rigid framework that provides mechanical support for boards inserted into the backplane, ensuring that the connectors mate properly and that adjacent boards do not contact each other. It also guides the cooling airflow through the system, and ensures that inserted boards do not disengage themselves from the backplane due to vibration or shock.

system clock driver. A functional module that provides a 16 MHz timing signal on the utility bus.

system controller board. A board that resides in slot 1 of the backplane and has a system clock driver, a DTB arbiter, an IACK daisy-chain driver, and a bus timer. Some also have a serial clock driver, a power monitor, or both.

UAT. A master that sends or receives data in an unaligned fashion.

utility bus. One of the four buses provided by the backplane. This bus includes signals that provide periodic timing and coordinate the power-up and power-down of sequence of the system.

write cycle. A DTB cycle used to transfer 1-, 2-, 3-, or 4-bytes from a master to a slave. The cycle begins when the master broadcasts an address and address modifier and places data on the DTB. Each slave captures this address and address modifier, and checks to see if it is to respond to the cycle. If so, it stores the data and then acknowledges the transfer. The master then terminates the cycle.

Appendix B

Signal Line Description

Table B1
Signal Identification

Signal Mnemonic	Signal Name and Description
A01-A15	**Address bus (bits 1-15).** Three-state driven address lines that are used to broadcast a short, standard, or extended address.
A16-A23	**Address bus (bits 16-23).** Three-state driven address lines that are used in conjunction with A01-A15 to broadcast a standard or an extended address.
A24-A31	**Address bus (bits 24-31).** Three-state driven address lines that are used in conjunction with A01-A23 to broadcast an extended address.
ACFAIL*	**AC failure.** An open-collector driven signal that indicates when the ac input to the power supply is no longer being provided or that the required ac input voltage levels are not being met.
AM0-AM5	**Address modifier (bits 0-5).** Three-state driven lines that are used to broadcast information such as address size, cycle type, or master identification, or a combination of these.
AS*	**Address Strobe.** A three-state driven signal that indicates when a valid address has been placed on the address bus.
BBSY*	**Bus busy.** An open-collector driven signal that is driven low by the requester that is associated with the current master, to indicate that its master is using the DTB. When the requester releases this line, the resultant rising edge causes the arbiter to sample the bus grant lines and grant the bus to the highest priority requester.
BCLR*	**Bus clear.** A totem-pole driven signal, generated by an arbiter to indicate when there is a higher priority request for the bus. This signal requests the current master to release the DTB.
BERR*	**Bus error.** An open-collector driven signal generated by a slave or bus timer. This signal indicates to the master that the data transfer was not completed.
BG0IN*-BG3IN*	**Bus grant (0-3) in.** Totem-pole driven signals generated by the arbiter. The *bus grant in* and the *bus grant out* signals form bus grant daisy-chains. The *bus grant in* signal indicates to the board receiving it that it has been granted use of the DTB.
BG0OUT*-BG3OUT*	**Bus Grant (0-3) out.** Totem-pole driven signals generated by requesters. The *bus grant out* signal indicates to the next board in the daisy-chain that it may use the DTB.

Table B1 (*Continued*)
Signal Identification

Signal Mnemonic	Signal Name and Description
BR0*-BR3*	**Bus request (0-3).** Open-collector driven signals generated by requesters. A low level on one of these lines indicates that some master needs to use the DTB.
D00-D31	**Data bus.** Three-state driven bidirectional lines used to transfer data between masters and slaves, and status/ID information from interrupters to interrupt handlers.
DS0*, DS1*	**Data strobe zero, one.** Three-state driven signals used in conjunction with LWORD* and A01 to indicate how many byte locations are being accessed (1, 2, 3, or 4). In addition, during a write cycle, the falling edge of the first data strobe indicates that valid data is available on the data bus. On a read cycle, the rising edge of the first data strobe indicates that data has been accepted from the data bus.
DTACK*	**Data transfer acknowledge.** An open-collector driven signal generated by a SLAVE. The falling edge of this signal indicates that valid data is available on the data bus during a read cycle, or that data has been accepted from the data bus during a write cycle. The rising edge indicates when the slave has released the data bus at the end of a read cycle.
GND	The dc voltage reference for the system.
IACK*	**Interrupt acknowledge.** An open-collector or three-state driven signal used by an interrupt handler to acknowledge an interrupt request. It is routed, by way of a backplane signal trace, to the IACKIN* pin of slot 1, where it is monitored by the IACK daisy-chain driver.
IACKIN*	**Interrupt acknowledge in.** A totem-pole driven signal. The IACKIN* and IACKOUT* signals form a daisy-chain. The IACKIN* signal indicates to the board receiving it that it is allowed to respond to the interrupt acknowledge cycle that is in progress.
IACKOUT*	**Interrupt acknowledge out.** A totem-pole driven ignal. The IACKIN* and IACKOUT* signals form a daisy-chain. The IACKOUT* signal is sent by a board to indicate to the next board in the daisy-chain that it is allowed to respond to the interrupt acknowledge cycle that is in progress.
IRQ1*-IRQ7*	**Interrupt request (1-7).** Open-collector driven signals, that are driven low by interrupters to request an interrupt. When several lines are monitored by a single interrupt handler the highest numbered line is given the highest priority.
LWORD*	**Longword.** A three-state driven signal used in conjunction with DS0*, DS1*, and A01 to select which byte location(s) within the 4-byte group are accessed during the data transfer.

Table B1 *(Continued)*
Signal Identification

Signal Mnemonic	Signal Name and Description
RESERVED	**Reserved.** A signal line reserved for future enhancements.
SERCLK	**Serial clock.** A totem-pole driven signal that is used to synchronize the data transmission on the VMSbus.
SERDAT*	**Serial data.** An open-collector driven signal that is used for VMSbus data transmission.
SYSCLK	**System clock.** A totem-pole driven signal that provides a constant 16 MHz clock signal that is independent of any other bus timing.
SYSFAIL*	**System fail.** An open-collector driven signal that indicates when a failure has occurred in the system. This signal can be generated by any board in the system.
SYSRESET*	**System reset.** An open-collector driven signal, which when low, causes the system to be reset.
WRITE*	**Write.** A three-state driven signal generated by the master to indicate whether the data transfer cycle is a read or a write. A high level indicates a read operation; a low level indicates a write operation.
+5 V STDBY	**+5 V dc standby.** This line supplies +5 Vdc to devices requiring battery backup.
+5 V	**+5 V dc power.** Used by system logic circuits.
+12 V	**+12 V dc Power.** Used by system logic circuits.
-12 V	**-12 V dc Power.** Used by system logic circuits.

Appendix C

Use of the SERCLK and SERDAT* Lines

Two signal lines on the backplane (SERCLK and SERDAT*) are designated for use by the VMSbus and provide a serial communication link between boards. The protocol used on the VMSbus is outside the scope of this standard. Since system controller board designers will want to include circuitry on their boards to drive SERCLK, this Appendix provides the necessary information.

SERCLK, like SYSCLK has no fixed timing relationship with any other IEEE 1014 signal (except SERDAT*, which carries data bits that are synchronized to SERCLK).

The drivers and receivers for SERCLK and SERDAT* are specified in Section 7.

Figure C1 and Table C1 show the required timing parameters for the SERCLK signal line. A SERCLK waveform with these timing values can be derived from a 32 MHz clock source. The timing values in Table C1 are for use when the SERCLK and SERDAT* lines are not extended beyond the backplane. If these signals are extended to carry intersystem information, each of the timing values given in Table C1 should be multiplied by a common scaling factor, greater than 1, to allow for the increased SERCLK and SERDAT* propagation times.

Recommendation C1. When designing the serial-clock-driver module, take into account the fact that the SERCLK line driver's propagation delays for the rising and falling edges will likely be different. This difference is emphasized when the SERCLK line is heavily loaded. When calculating the driver's propagation delays, use the delays specified on the manufacturer's data sheet for a 300 pF capacitive load. If the only propagation delays given are for a 30 pF load, add 10 ns to each of the propagation delays.

Suggestion C1. Design the serial-clock-driver so that it can be jumpered to work from various stages of a binary counter that is driven by a 32 MHz clock source. This allows the selection of 32 MHz, 16 MHz, 8 MHz, etc, as the base frequency for the serial-clock-driver and makes it easy to select a frequency appropriate for the length of the SERCLK and SERDAT* lines.

Observation C1. If a 32 MHz clock source is used to generate the SERCLK waveform, it can also be used to generate the 16 MHz SYSCLK signal.

Table C1
SERCLK Timing Values

Parameter Number	min	max
1	167	
2		194
3		51
4	25	
5	74	
6		100
7		51
8	25	
9	340	347

NOTE: All timing values are in nanoseconds

Suggestion C2. To allow multiple boards that include serial clock driver to be installed in the same backplane, design them with a jumper that disconnects the serial-clock-driver from the SERCLK line.

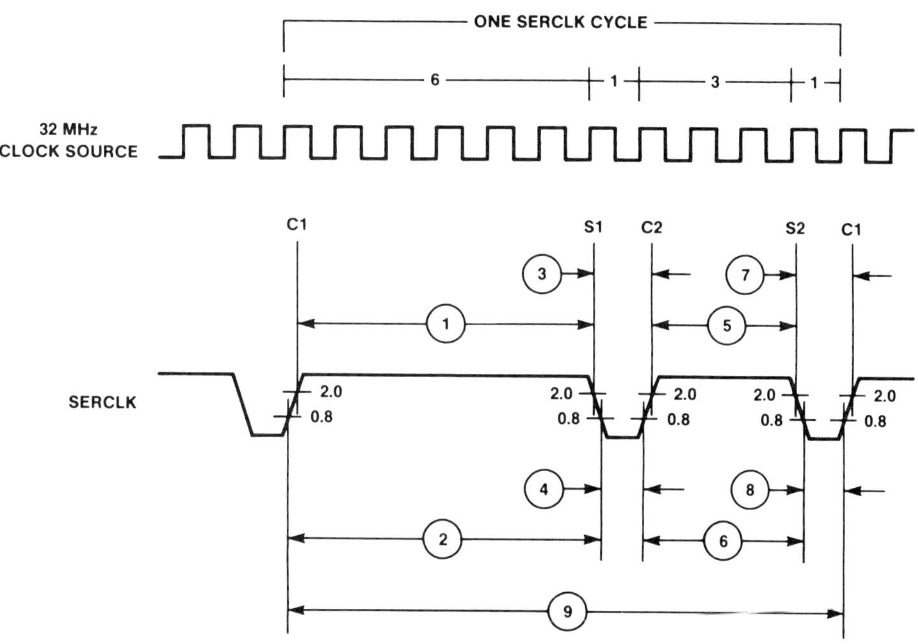

NOTE: See Table C1 for timing values.

Fig C1
SERCLK Timing Diagram

Appendix D

Metastability and Synchronization

D1. Introduction

This standard describes various functional modules that define how boards function. An examination of these modules shows that they contain quite a bit of state information; that is, that their operation depends on a current context and, thus, on past history. Fortunately for board designers, most state information is automatically maintained by processors and other large-scale components. However, some state information must still be handled explicitly by the board designer. Such state information is typically stored in devices known variously as latches, flip-flops, and registers. These terms are used somewhat interchangeably, but for the purposes of this Appendix a latch is the basic device, a flip-flop is a type of latch, and a register is a set of one or more flip-flops.

Devices that store states need to be signaled to

(1) Switch to the *off*, or the 0, state

(2) Switch to the *on*, or the 1, state

(3) Remember, or maintain, their current state

To signal three requirements, more than one input signal is needed: some state-storing devices have *set* and *reset* inputs; others have *clock* and *data* signals; still others have all four inputs. Regardless of which input signals a device has, there are certain specifications regarding how the inputs can be used. This Appendix explores these specifications, the reasons for them, and how they restrict the use of state-storing devices.

D2. A Simple Nand Latch

The simplest latch is a pair of Nand gates connected as shown in Fig D1, having two inputs and two outputs. The inputs are called SET* and RESET* and the outputs ON and OFF. Each of the two gates makes its output low only if both of its inputs are high; if either or both inputs are low, the gate makes its output high.

Suppose SET* is low and RESET* is high. Because SET* is low, the output ON of the upper gate will be high. This causes both inputs of the lower gate to be high, and its output OFF to be low.

Now suppose SET* goes high. Because OFF is low, the upper gate maintains ON high, and nothing else changes.

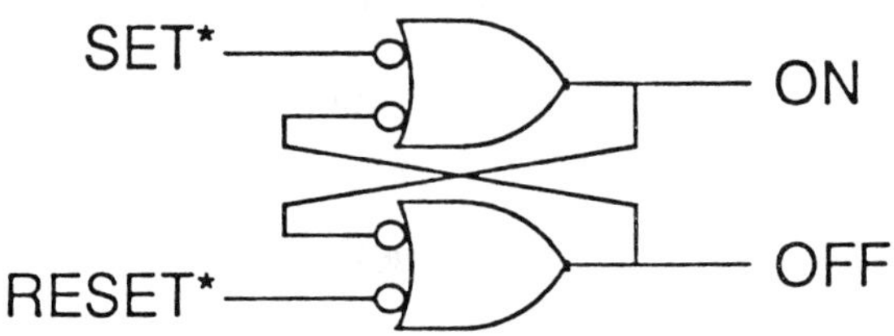

Fig D1
A Simple Nand Latch

Similarly, if RESET* goes low while SET* is high, OFF goes high and ON goes low. If RESET* then goes high, OFF stays high and ON stays low.

Thus, this latch fulfills the basic requirement for storing a state: when both of its inputs are high, it *remembers* which one was last low.

If both SET* and RESET* are low at the same time, both ON and OFF will be high. A stored state that is both ON and OFF is conceptually bothersome, but if we only use one of the outputs (for example, ON) in other logic, and if we change the name of OFF to something neutral, such as LATCHBACK, the conceptual problem goes away. As soon as SET* or RESET* changes to high, the associated gate makes its output low.

It is important to note that each Nand gate has a propagation time; that is, the time it takes for its output to change after its inputs have changed. Let's say that both of our gates take exactly the same time. We can now get a first glimpse of problems with state-storing devices by considering what happens if both the SET* and the RESET* inputs change from low to high simultaneously.

Because SET* and RESET* have been low, both ON and OFF are high. When SET* and RESET* go high both gates have both of their inputs high, and so they both make their respective outputs low. Now, since both gates have a low input they make ON and OFF high. If the gates are perfectly matched in propagation time, this keeps happening when both SET* and RESET* stay high. Obviously our Nand latch has another ability besides storing a state: it can also act as an oscillator!

Further, this is not the only way to get a Nand latch to act like an oscillator. Suppose that the latch is set so that ON is low, OFF is high, and both SET* and RESET* are high. Now suppose that a low pulse with a duration that is equal to the propagation time of the matched gates is then applied to the SET* input. In this case, a similar thing happens: a high-going pulse occurs on ON, then a low-going pulse occurs on OFF, etc.

Fortunately, it is not possible for an incoming pulse to have *exactly* the same width as a gate's propagation time, nor for two input signals to go high at *exactly* the same time, nor for two gates to have *exactly* the same propagation time. Therefore, a Nand latch never really oscillates indefinitely. Depending on how closely the gates are matched, how closely the input signaling approximates the ideal triggering condition, and how noisy the system is, a latch of this type may oscillate for some time, but eventually the oscillation will damp out and the latch will settle one way or the other.

D3. Edge Triggered Flip-Flops

Because of the problems of simple latches, designers have devised more reliable circuits to store state information. These circuits, called flip-flops, consist of one or more latch-like structures with interconnecting logic and feedback paths. instead of, or in addition to, inputs that set and clear the state, flip-flops have one or two *data inputs* that indicate what state to store, and a *clock input* that indicates when to store it. For example, a flip-flop might store the state of its data inputs when its clock switches from low to high.

It is important to remember that devices never switch from one guaranteed logic state to the other instantaneously. Rather, a driver has to drive its output's voltage through the linear, or undefined region in some measurable period of time. Without getting down to the transistor level, or even the logic gate level, there is a conceptual problem of how a flip-flop should behave if its clock and data inputs switch more or less simultaneously, that is, if its clock switches to high while its data input is in the linear region. From the flip-flop's point of view, this is the same as being presented with a value of *half* in a system where the only valid values are one and zero.

This conceptual problem has a physical reality. For any flip-flop, it is possible to calculate a setup time *Ts* and a hold time *Th*, such that if the state of the data signals stays high or low for a time *Ts* before the clock switches, and for a time *Th* after it switches, then the flip-flop will capture the state correctly and output it within a specified and reasonably short time thereafter. But if the data changes between the setup and hold times, the operation of the flip-flop is undefined.

Considerable effort and ingenuity have been spent designing flip-flops that have the shortest possible setup and hold times, and advances in integrated circuit technology have indeed made these times shorter and shorter. While it is possible to design flip-flops so that either *one* of the two times is zero or even negative, no circuit has yet been announced which eliminates *both* of them. The only problem with flip-flop improvements is that those same technological advances make higher system performance possible, which require yet shorter flip-flop resolution windows.

In addition to improving *setup-and-hold* times, circuit advances have made the consequences of not satisfying them less severe. While a latch with off-chip feedback paths can be pretty easily stimulated to act like an oscillator for several cycles, a modern flip-flop can be pretty much relied on to make no more than one extra voltage reversal if the window is missed, or to have its output remain in the undefined voltage region for only a relatively short time, or both.

Furthermore, the *effective* window in which a flip-flop will actually malfunction is typically 2-3 orders of magnitude shorter than the *setup-and-hold* window that the device manufacturer can guarantee. A high-speed flip-flop might have a *setup-and-hold* window of several nanoseconds; somewhere within that window there is a much shorter time during which the flip-flop will do strange things if the data is at an intermediate voltage. While this fact is interesting, it isn't very useful because there is no way to say where the effective window will fall within the *setup-and-hold* window.

So, while flip-flops are an improvement over latches with off-chip feedback paths, the end result is much the same. If the relationship among a statestoring device's input signals cannot be guaranteed, its output cannot be relied on for a much longer time than when this relationship is guaranteed. Only for rather small-scale logic circuits can the relationship between clock and data inputs be guaranteed for all the flip-flops in the system. As soon as the question of handling signals from outside the system arises, the question also arises of how flip-flops behave under all possible relationships of clock and data. That is to say, the problems of synchronization and metastability must be faced.

D4. Synchronous versus Asynchronous Design

Two schools of design methodology have arisen to cope with the problems of state-storing devices. Each has advantages and disadvantages, and each has its place in the design of electronic systems. Most electronic designs, while having one or the other dominant, employ a mixture of the two methodologies.

Synchronous designs employ a master clock signal that is used to clock all of their flip-flops. They synchronize inputs from the outside world by connecting each such signal to the data input of a flip-flop that is clocked by the master clock. The rate of the master clock is thus restricted by the flip-flops' resolution times when their *setup-and-hold* requirements are not met, rather than by how fast they can operate when the requirements are met.

Asynchronous designs, which tend to be less monolithic than synchronous ones, typically consist of a number of more or less autonomous blocks. Not including a master clock, these blocks might exchange signals at any time. Asynchronous designs handle inputs from the outside world by logically gating and synchronizing them to their internal signals, eliminating problems if an input switches at an inappropriate time. Two basic methods are used to do that. Preferably, the clock and data inputs of flip-flops are conditioned to meet the required *setup-and-hold* times of the flip-flop. When this is not possible, delay circuits are used to mask the flip-flop's outputs until they have resolved.

While the relative merits of synchronous and asynchronous design can be debated at great length by their respective proponents, an objective view reveals certain types of designs for which each is best. When a design task is well-defined and straightforward, asynchronous design is preferable because it does not involve the time penalty of input synchronization, and because each part of the circuit runs as fast as it can, rather than at a speed dictated by its slowest function.

When the complexity of a task increases, and particularly when it involves long sequences of action, a synchronous design is better, in part because it allows the designer to concentrate on the needed function rather than on the details of the devices used to accomplish the function. Synchronous designs also tend to be more adaptable to changing functional requirements, and to handling situations that were not foreseen in the initial stages of design.

But, in turn, the suitability of the synchronous design methodology for more complex circuits has an upper limit. In particular, as the physical size of a design increases, the time for a master clock to reach all of its components increases, and questions of skew between the clock and other signals become harder and harder to answer. Beyond a certain point of complexity, a design is best approached by decomposing it into functional blocks, each of which is implemented asynchronously or synchronously as its characteristics dictate.

For our purposes it is sufficient to note that both the asynchronous and synchronous design methodologies need to know how a flip-flop behaves when its *setup-and-hold* times cannot be met. For synchronous designs this information is an ingredient in determining the clock rate and the configuration of input synchronizers, while for asynchronous designs it is typically used to determine the characteristics of delay lines.

D5. Determining Flip-Flop Resolution Times

The problem of metastability in state-storing devices has been known for approximately 35 years, but only in the last few years have useful research results on this phenomenon become generally available. Laboratory results support theoretical results that indicate that flip-flop resolution times must be approached statistically. Reliance on statistical distributions might make some designers uncomfortable, but metastability is an inescapable fact that comes with use of flip-flops, regardless of whether they are used synchronously or asynchronously.

Depending on which inputs a flip-flop or latch provides, one of four methods can be used to measure its metastability characteristics:

(1) The device's data input is switched simultaneously with the sampling clock edge

(2) Both the set and reset inputs are switched off (for example, high) simultaneously

(3) The data input is set so that the device should change states, then a short pulse is applied to the sampling clock

(4) A short pulse is applied to a set or a reset input.

With any of the methods, the relative signal timing is adjusted very precisely until the device enters its metastable state. The duration of the metastable state is then measured as the timing is varied through the effective window in which metastability occurs.

From the resultant data, three constants, τ, T_0, and h, can be calculated for a device. These values can then be used to compute the mean time between failures (MTBF) for the device when it is used as a synchronizer and is given a time t' to resolve. A failure is defined as the device still being metastable t' ns after the clock edge. The formula is:

$$\text{MTBF}\ (t') = \frac{\epsilon^{\,t'/\tau}}{T_0\ (\text{clock rate})\ (\text{data switching rate})}, \text{ for } t' > h$$

where

(1) MTBF and T_0 are in seconds

(2) The clock and data switching rates are in hertz

(3) t' and τ are in the same time units

Since metastability can occur if either edge of the data signal coincides with the sampling clock edge, the data switching rate in the above formula is the average rate at which the signal switches in either direction, while the clock rate is the rate at which sampling edges occur. To use this formula for race conditions between set and clear inputs, simply substitute the average rate at which each line is released, for the clock and data rates. To use it for race conditions between the clock edge and the release of set or clear, substitute the average release rate for the data switching rate.

The formula is valid for random relationships between clock and data, where data transitions are distributed uniformly through the clock period, and for values of t' that are above a minimum value h. Table D1 shows lab results for τ, T_0, and h for commonly available devices. The subsequent columns of Table D1 show the MTBF of each device for $t' = 20$ ns, 30 ns, and 40 ns, at a clock rate of 25 MHz and a data switching frequency of 100 kHz (equivalent to 50 kHz signal frequency). The rightmost column shows the t' value needed to give an MTBF of 10^9 s (approximately 32 years) at the same switching frequencies.

Some general observations can be drawn from Table D1:

(1) The basic internal design of a flip-flop or latch is quite significant in determining the suitability of a device as a synchronizer. A Nand latch with off-chip feedback is not suitable at all.

(2) The technological family of a device is the other important factor in the performance of a device as a synchronizer. No 74LSxx device is suitable for use as a synchronizer.

(3) In general, if one device has shorter propagation, *setup-and-hold* times than another, it will also have a shorter metastable resolution time, but synchronizer performance improves more than linearly as the specified times decrease.

(4) The best devices in the table are the 74F74 and 74F374.

To use the information in Table D1, a designer can follow the following procedure for each case in which a flip-flop's setup and hold times cannot be guaranteed:

(1) Choose an MTBF figure. This is often the most difficult step; it involves trading off the performance impact of allowing a long time for resolution, against the reliability impact of a failure to resolve within the time allowed, and the overall reliability requirements of the design's application. In high-performance designs that don't have exceptional reliability needs, a value of 10^8 s (3 years) might be used as a starting point. If there are many synchronizers in a system, the MTBF of each synchronizer will have to be substantially higher than that for the system. When choosing an MTBF figure it might help to remember that the estimated age of the earth is about 2×10^{17} s. Requiring an MTBF above 10^{10} s may mean that you have an overly optimistic view of your product's life cycle.

(2) Select a device that has low values for τ and T_0, and still meets the specific needs of the design. Of the devices listed in Table D1, this pretty much suggests the choice of a 74F part.

(3) Verify whether data transitions are independent, random, or uniformly distributed with respect to the clock. If so, use the average data switching rate in the formula in the next step. If not, use the estimated data switching rate in the vicinity of the clock edge, that is, between the quoted setup and hold times.

Table D1
Metastability Lab Results

Device	# Tested /Mfger	Date Code	τ (ns)	T_0	h (ns)	(F_c = 25 MHz, F_d = 100 kHz) MTBF(s) for t' = 20 ns	30 ns	40 ns	t' (ns) for MTBF=10^9
7400 Latch	1/T	1973	3.2	0.2 us	29		0.024	0.54	110
74S00 Latch	1/T	1972	1.8	1 us	17			1800	64
74LS74[1]	3/T	1974	1.5	0.4 s	35			0.38	73
74S74[1]	59/F BEST	74-75	0.40	0.2 s	13	1×10^{10}	7×10^{20}	5×10^{31}	19
	WORST		0.89	2 ms	13	1.1	9×10^{4}	7×10^{9}	38
	5/T BEST	73-75	0.79	2 ms	15	20.0	6×10^{6}	2×10^{12}	34
	WORST		1.02	50 us	15	2.6	5×10^{4}	9×10^{8}	40
	5/N BEST	1974	1.14	30 us	15	0.6	4×10^{3}	2×10^{7}	44
	WORST		1.36	20 us	15	0.05	76	1×10^{5}	52
	5/S BEST	72-74	0.96	0.8 ms	16	0.6	2×10^{4}	6×10^{8}	40
	WORST		1.70	1 us	16	0.05	18	7×10^{3}	60
74S374	3/T AVG	1978	0.91	0.4 ms	15	3.5	2×10^{5}	1×10^{10}	38
74F74[2]	5/M BEST	1986	0.50	0.3 ms	8	3×10^{8}	2×10^{17}	7×10^{25}	21
	WORST		0.56	10 us	8	1×10^{8}	7×10^{15}	4×10^{23}	21
	5/F BEST	1986	0.33	0.2 s	8	4×10^{12}	6×10^{27}	8×10^{40}	16
	WORST		0.47	0.5 us	7	2×10^{10}	4×10^{19}	7×10^{28}	18
	5/S BEST	1986	0.31	0.4 s	7	1×10^{16}	1×10^{30}	1×10^{44}	15
	WORST		0.34	8 ms	7	2×10^{15}	1×10^{28}	6×10^{40}	15
74AS74[2]	5/T BEST	1986	0.49	0.1 ms	8	2×10^{9}	2×10^{18}	1×10^{27}	20
	WORST		0.52	40 us	8	5×10^{8}	1×10^{17}	3×10^{25}	20
74F175[2]	5/M BEST	1986	0.35	2 s	7	1×10^{12}	3×10^{24}	9×10^{36}	17
	WORST		0.72	60 ns	7	8×10^{6}	8×10^{12}	9×10^{18}	24
	5/F BEST	1986	0.36	2 ms	7	3×10^{14}	3×10^{26}	4×10^{38}	16
	WORST		0.43	0.7 ms	7	9×10^{10}	1×10^{21}	1×10^{31}	18
	5/S BEST	85-86	0.35	0.3 s	8	9×10^{12}	2×10^{25}	6×10^{37}	17
	WORST		0.46	0.5 ms	8	6×10^{9}	2×10^{19}	5×10^{28}	19
74F374	2/F AVG	1980	0.40	0.1 ms	6	2×10^{13}	2×10^{24}	1×10^{35}	16

(4) Given the clock and data (or set, or both, or reset, or a combination of these) rates for this case, calculate the minimum t' using the inverse formula:

$$t' = \tau \log_e [T_0 \text{ (MTBF) (clock rate) (data switching rate)}]$$

(5) If the flip-flop's output(s) pass through any intermediate gates whose

output can also be allowed to have anomalies, add the maximum propagation time of the gate(s) to t'.

(6) Also, if the latest anomalous signal is used as input to a flip-flop, add in the setup time of that flip-flop. If the latest anomalous signal is used in a gate that masks the anomaly, add in the gate's maximum mask time, and subtract its minimum unmask time. If anomalous signals are used in several ways, add in the largest of these factors.

(7) In a typical synchronous design, ensure that the master clock's period is greater than or equal to the largest value calculated in steps (1) through (6), for all the flip-flops in the design that can go metastable. In an asynchronous design, select or specify a delay line that ensures a clean signal where it is needed.

D6. Sample Circuits

There are three specific cases where a board designer must face the question of metastability and synchronization:

(1) Handling the BGxIN*/BGxOUT* arbitration daisy-chain on a requester

(2) Handling the IACKIN*/IACKOUT* interrupt acknowledge daisy-chain on an interrupter

(3) Handling the bus request lines on a multilevel arbiter

The architecture of a particular board may add other cases to these. For example, a processor board with dual-ported memory arbitrates between the on-board processor's access to the memory and access by other masters. The following paragraphs include sample circuits for the three cases D6(1), (2), and (3); the basic techniques can be easily adapted for other needs. Determining the specific values for clock periods and delay lines are left for the designer, as they depend on his particular reliability requirements and switching rates.

D6.1 Handling the Arbitration Daisy-Chain Asynchronously. Figure D2 shows an example of how a requester can handle the bus grant daisy-chain using asynchronous logic. Address decoding logic associated with the on-board master develops the high-active signal MASTER WANTS BUS. When this signal is high, the requester drives the BRx* line low. MASTER WANTS BUS has no particular timing relationship to the BGxIN* input. When BGxIN* goes low, the requester has to determine whether to drive BBSY* low and assume control of the bus, or to pass the low level on its BGxIN* down the daisy-chain by driving BGxOUT* low.

BGxIN* is received by inverter "A". Thus a falling edge on BGxIN* becomes a rising edge on BGxIN, which makes 74F74 flip-flop "B" sample the MASTER

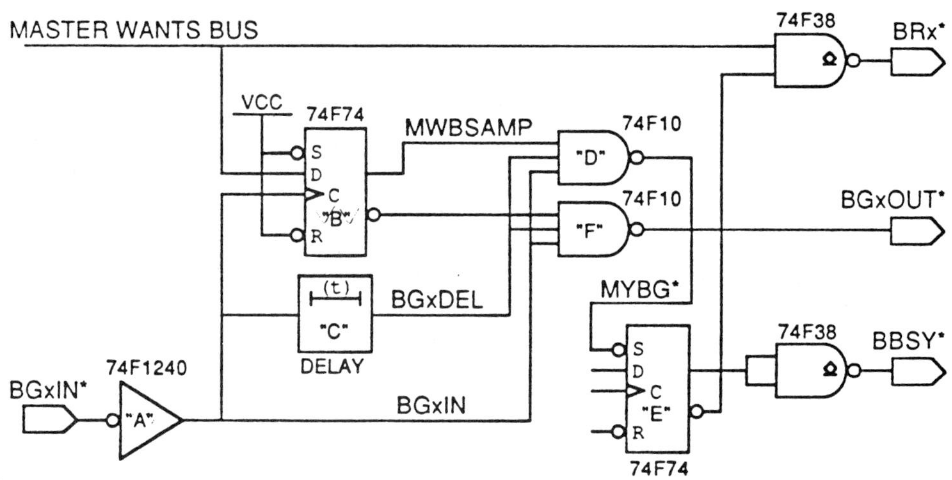

Fig D2
Handling the Arbitration Daisy-Chain Asynchronously

WANTS BUS signal. BGxIN also goes into delay line "C", the delay of which has been calculated for a selected MTBF as described in D5. By the time BGxDEL goes high, the output of flip-flop "B" DWBSAMP must be valid (at the selected MTBF). In particular, DWBSAMP will be high if MASTER WANTS BUS was high, in which case Nand gate "D" will drive MYBG* low, thus setting flip-flop "E" so that BBSY* is driven low, and BRx* is released high. If DWBSAMP is low when BGxDEL goes high, Nand gate "F" will drive BGxOUT* low. Note also that BGxIN is itself an input to both of the Nand gates "D" and "F", providing a rapid negation of BGxOUT* and MYBG* when BGxIN* goes high.

D6.2 Handling the Arbitration Daisy-Chain Synchronously. Figure D3 shows how a requester might be designed to handle the arbitration daisy-chain synchronously. The four inputs to 74F175 "A" are sampled on each rising edge of CLK. While BGxIN* is high and BGxIN is low, gates "A" and "B" allow a high on MASTER WANTS BUS to propagate and make BRB4BG* ("Bus Request Before Bus Grant") low. Once it has gone low, the feedback path to gate "B" will keep BRB4BG* low until DEVICE WANTS BUS goes low again. After BGxIN* goes low and BGxIN goes high, DEVICE WANTS BUS is blocked so that BRB4BG* cannot go low any longer while BGxIN remains high (although it will stay low if DEVICE WANTS BUS was high before BGxIN* went low). The last clock edge from which

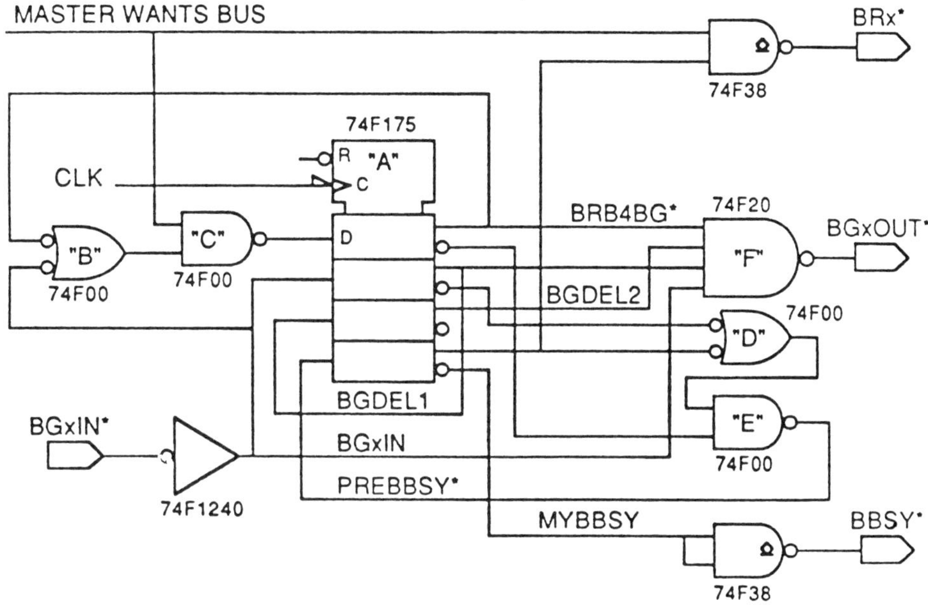

Fig D3
Handling the Arbitration Daisy-Chain Synchronously

BRB4BG* can go low is the one at which BGxIN is first sampled high, that is, the one from which BGDEL1 goes high.

After that clock edge, any of the signals BGDEL1 or BRB4BG*, or their complementary outputs, can go metastable. The period of CLK must be long enough to cover the resolution time of "A" for the selected MTBF, plus the propagation time of BGDEL1* through gates "D" and "E", plus the setup time for the bottom flip-flop in "A". If DEVICE WANTS BUS went high before BGxIN did, making BRB4BG high, then the signal PREBBSY* will be sampled low at the next clock edge, MYBBSY will go high from that edge, and BBSY* will be driven low. Otherwise, on that next clock edge PREBBSY* will be high; therefore BBSY* will not be driven low. Instead, the combination of BGDEL2 going high and BRB4BG* being high will qualify 74F20 "F", so that BGxOUT* will be driven low. Note that BGxIN is also an input to 74F20 "F", providing a rapid egation of BGxOUT* when BGxIN* is negated. Note also that BGxIN is not included in gate "E" — to do so would make MYBBSY subject to metastability when BGxIN* goes high.

The MTBF of this circuit can be calculated from the period of CLK, the values of τ and T_0 for the 74F175, and the estimated switching rates of BGxIN* and DEVICE WANTS BUS.

D6.3 Handling the Interrupt Acknowledge Daisy-Chain Asynchronously. Figure D4 is an example of how an interrupter might handle the interrupt acknowledge daisy-chain in an asynchronous manner. The logic associated with an on-board interrupt source drives the signal MYIRQ high to request an interrupt on one of IRQ1*-IRQ7*. When an interrupt acknowledge cycle is detected, the interrupter has to determine whether to respond to the cycle or not. If this board is requesting an interrupt at the level being acknowledged, it responds to the interrupt acknowledge cycle by driving its status/ID onto the data lines, and then asserting DTACK*. Otherwise, it passes the low level on its IACKIN* down the daisy-chain by driving IACKOUT* low. The choice between these two alternatives is made by 74F85 "A", and is reflected in the signal MYLEVEL.

AS* is received and inverted by 74F1240 "B", to make AS, the input to the 2-tap delay line "C". t1 nanoseconds after AS goes high, the rising edge on the output of the first stage of "C" samples MYLEVEL into 74F74 "D". If the rising

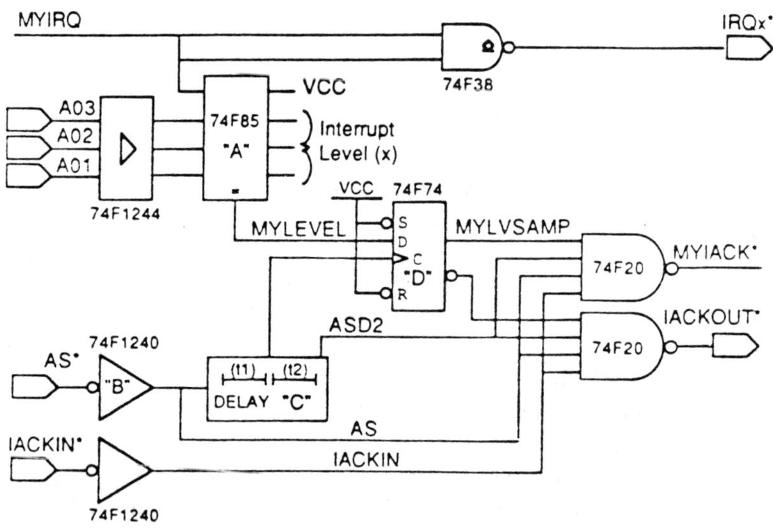

Fig D4
Handling the Interrupt Daisy-Chain Asynchronously

edge samples MYLEVEL high, making MYLVSAMP go high, the upper 74F20 is qualified and MYIACK* is driven low; otherwise, the lower 74F20 is qualified and IACKOUT* is driven low. t1 is calculated so that the contribution of the A01-A03 lines to MYLEVEL meets the setup time for "D". Since MYIRQ has no particular timing relationship to AS*, there is no way to guarantee overall setup time for "D". That is, "D" may go metastable if MYIRQ goes high and AS* goes low in just the right (wrong) relationship. This problem is solved by the second stage of delay line "C". As described in D5, the delay t2 between the two outputs of "C", must be long enough to cover the resolution time of "D" at the selected MTBF, plus the skew of the 74F20's. When the second stage output ASD2 of the delay line "C" goes high, MYLVSAMP and its complement will be valid. At that time the two 74F20's will be ready to respond to a low on IACKIN*, by either driving MYIACK* low and initiating this board's response to the interrupt acknowledge cycle, or by driving IACKOUT* low, passing the interrupt acknowledge down the daisy chain to the next interrupter board. Note that AS is also an input to the 74F20's, providing rapid negation of IACKOUT* (or MYIACK*) when AS* goes high. Note also that if there are several interrupters such as this in a system, they will all resolve their decisions in parallel, so that the actual IACK daisy-chain propagation will proceed at combinatorial logic speed.

D6.4 An Asynchronous Arbiter. Figure D4 is an example of an asynchronous arbiter. The four BRx* lines, the BBSY* line and the SYSRESET* line are received by 74F1244's "A" and "B", their outputs being called BBR0* through BBR3*, BBBSY*, and BSRES* respectively. BBR0* through BBR3* are ORed by 74F20 "C" to generate the high-active signal BR, which is ANDed with BBSY* and BSRES* to generate ARBGO out of 74F11 "D". Note that ARBGO will remain low while SYSRESET* is asserted on the bus. A high on ARBGO means that one or more of BR0*-BR3* are low and that both BBSY* and BSRES* are high. This is the signal for the arbiter to arbitrate for the bus, driving one of BG0IN*-BG3IN* low at slot 1 of the backplane. The rising edge on ARBGO samples BBR0*-BBR3* into 74F175 "E", which may go metastable if one or more of BBR3*-BBR0* are changing from high to low at the same time that ARBGO goes high.

ARBGO is also the input to delay line "F". While the high level on ARBGO is working its way through the delay line, the combinatorial block "grant logic" is selecting among the outputs of E to determine the next grant (grant logic might use a priority algorithm, a round-robin algorithm, or a mixture of both). The delay of "F" should be calculated to cover the metastable resolution time of "E" at the selected MTBF, plus the total propagation of the "priority logic" block, as described in D5. Thus, by the time ARBGODEL goes high, the outputs WIN0-WIN3, one of which is high, will be stable. The selected 74F00 gate then drives one of BG0IN*-BG3IN* low.

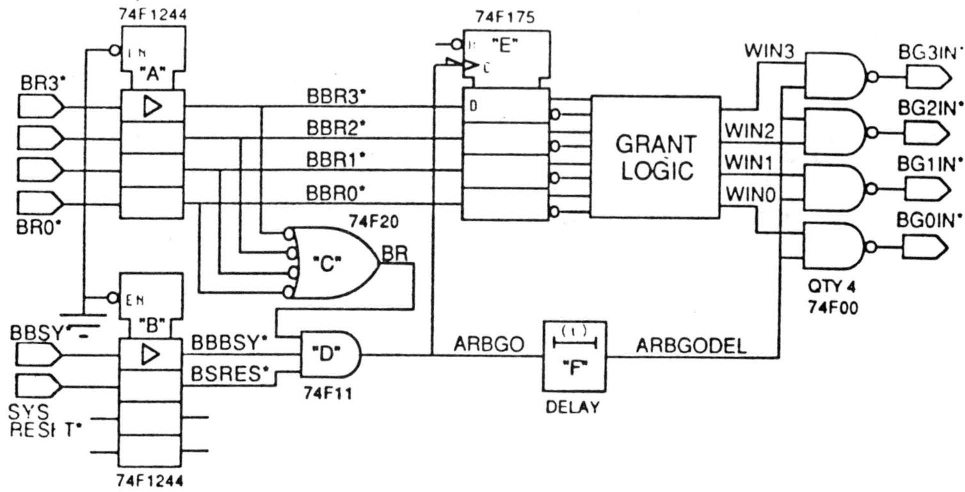

Fig D5
An Asynchronous Arbiter

Note that, unlike the preceding daisy-chain examples, neither BBSY* nor ARBGO is brought into the BGxIN* drivers to provide a rapid negation when the winning requester drives BBSY* low. The circuit is designed negate BGxIN* after the delay of "F" for two reasons:

(1) There is no reason to negate BGxIN* quickly, because a requester is required to maintain BBSY* low for a minimum of 90 ns, which is a relatively long time.

(2) Assuming that "F" is a single-stage hybridactive-RLC delay line (not a multitap or other compound device), it will act as a filter for any noise that may be coupled onto BBSY* in the backplane, up to a duration of approximately half its delay.

D7. Additional Information

While every effort was extended to make the information in this Appendix accurate, it was impossible to make it exhaustive. The following material should be read to gain more insight into the phenomenon of metastability:

[D1] LUBKIN, S. Asynchronous Signals in Digital Computers. *Mathematical Tables and other Aids to Computation*, Oct 1952, pp 238-241.

[D2] CHANEY, T. J. AND MOLNAR, C. E. Anomalous Behavior of Synchronizer and Arbiter Circuits. *IEEE Transactions on Computers*, vol 5C-22, Apr 1973, pp 421-422.

[D3] CHANEY, T. J. Measured Flip-Flop Responses to Marginal Triggering. *IEEE Transactions on Computers*, vol C-32, no 12, Dec 1983, pp 1207-1209.

[D4] CHANEY, T. J. A Comprehensive Bibliography on Synchronizers and Arbiters. *Technical Memorandum no 306B*, Computer Systems Laboratory, Washington University, St. Louis, MO. Oct 1985 (updated Mar 1986; lists and describes over 80 papers and articles).

Appendix E

Permissible Capability Subsets

E1. Introduction

This Appendix summarizes the subset capabilities that the various functional modules are permitted to support. In addition, the interoperability of the capability subsets are tabulated. To aid in the tabulation, the permissible subsets are assigned mnemonics, which are defined in the tables.

E2. Permissible Subsets of DTB Modules

Data-transfer-bus capabilities are defined for three of the four types of DTB functional modules: master, slave, and location monitor. These capabilities pertain to the module's ability to generate, respond to, or monitor cycles that access byte locations in various address ranges, or perform specific types of data transfers. However, not all of the described capabilities are optional. As specified in Section 2, some modules are required to provide some of them, while other modules are not. This section summarizes the permissible subsets of data-transfer-bus capabilities.

E2.1 Permissible Subsets of Addressing Capabilities. Section 2 defines addressing capabilities in regards to the size of the address, and to the module's ability to execute address-only cycles.

E2.1.1 Address Size. A master is designated A32, A24, or A16, or a combination of these according to whether it can generate bus cycles with addresses of these widths. A slave is similarly designated according to whether it can respond to cycles of this address width.

These three independent address spaces are identified by address-modifier codes that are driven on the address-modifier lines at the beginning of each cycle. The AM codes further divide the address space to supervisor versus user, and program versus data space. Further, the functional distinction between block-transfer and single-transfer cycles is also carried on the AM lines. A block of AM codes is also reserved for user definition.

The specification requires all slaves to decode the address-modifier lines, and not respond to a cycle if they do not reside in the requested address space, or cannot perform the requested operation. In addition, the specification allows a slave to respond in more than one address space. This facility is often used by memory boards to respond in all of the supervisor, user, program, and data spaces. The specification requires that A32 masters also have A24 and A16 capability, and that A24 masters also have A16 capability.

E2.1.2 Address-Only Cycles. A master is designated ADO if it can generate an address-only cycle, that is, a cycle that transfers no data. In such a cycle, the master presents an address modifier code, an address, and an address strobe, but does not assert any data strobe. It holds the addressing information valid and maintains the address strobe asserted for a specified minimum time, and then withdraws them.

When related to a slave, the ADO capability describes its ability to correctly acknowledge a cycle that follows a cycle that has been terminated without ever asserting a data strobe. While making it optional for masters, all slaves are required to include the ADO capability.

Table E1 defines the mnemonics that describe the permissible subsets of addressing capabilities for masters, slaves, and location monitors.

Table E2 shows how the permissible subsets of the addressing capabilities interoperate. It should be pointed out that the design of the board will determine whether the described interoperability can be configured statically, for example, with the aid of jumpers, or dynamically, for example, by way of control register bits.

Table E1
Permissible Subsets of Addressing Capabilities

When the Following Mnemonic is Applied to a Board . . .	It Includes the Following Addressing Capabilities:			
	A16	A24	A32	ADO
Master Subsets				
MA16	X			
MADO16	X			X
MA24	X	X		
MADO24	X	X		X
MA32	X	X	X	
MADO32	X	X	X	X
Slave Subsets				
SADO16	X			X
SADO24	X	X		X
SADO32	X	X	X	X
Location Monitor Subsets				
LMA16	X			
LMA24	X	X		
LMA32	X	X	X	

Table E2
Interoperability Among the Permissible Addressing Subsets

Can a Board of the Type . . .	Respond to or Monitor a Master of the Type . . .					
	MA16	MA24	MA32	MADO16	MADO24	MADO32
Slave subset						
SADO16	Yes	Yes	Yes	Yes	Yes	Yes
SADO24	Yes	Yes	Yes	Yes	Yes	Yes
SADO32	Yes	Yes	Yes	Yes	Yes	Yes
Location Monitor Subset						
LMA16	Yes	Yes	Yes	Yes	Yes	Yes
LMA24	Yes	Yes	Yes	Yes	Yes	Yes
LMA32	Yes	Yes	Yes	Yes	Yes	Yes

E2.2 Permissible Subsets of Data-Transfer Capabilities. Section 2 defines data-transfer capabilities in regards to the size of the data, to the ability to execute unaligned transfer cycles (UAT), block transfer cycles (BLT), and read-modify-write cycles (RMW).

E2.2.1 Data Size. A master is designated D32, D16, or D08(EO), or a combination of these, according to whether it can initiate cycles for 32 bits of data, 16 bits of data, and 8 bits of data.

A slave is designated D32, D16, D08(EO), or D08(O), or a combination of these, according to whether it can respond to cycles for 32 bits of data, 16 bits of data, 8 bits of data on both even and odd addresses, or 8 bits of data on odd addresses only.

The specification requires that D32 masters, and slaves, also include the D16 and D08(EO) capabilities, and that D16 masters, and slaves also include the D08(EO) capability. A D08(EO) master can access both even-addressed and odd-addressed bytes, but only one byte at a time.

E2.2.2 Unaligned Transfer Capability. The size designations described in E2.2.1 apply to "aligned" data transfers, that is, transfers in which a 16-bit datum is addressed at an even address, and in which a 32-bit datum is addressed at an address that's a multiple of 4. D32 masters are further designated UAT if they can generate cycles which involve:

(1) The lowest-addressed 3 bytes of a 32-bit datum,
(2) The highest-addressed 3 bytes, and
(3) The middle 2 bytes

The distinction among these data transfers is signaled by the master on the lines DS1*, DS0*, LWORD*, and A01. While making it optional for masters, the specification requires all D32 slaves to include the UAT capability. In addition, the specification requires all other kinds of slaves to fully decode these four lines. If a slave is selected by the AM and address lines for a transfer size that it cannot handle, it can either respond by signaling a bus error, or ignore the transfer, which leads to the same net result when the bus timer module times out and makes a bus error.

E2.2.3 Block Transfers Capability. A master is designated BLT if it can generate a cycle that includes more than one data transfer, to/from successively ascending addresses. A master signals a block transfer on the address modifier lines, and then keeps address strobe asserted across several data transfers. A slave is designated BLT if it can respond to a block transfer cycle.

There are no "BLT-only boards": all BLT masters, BLT slaves, and BLT location monitors are required to also support single-transfer cycles.

E2.2.4 Read-Modify-Write Capability. A master is designated RMW if it can generate an indivisible read-modify-write cycle, and a slave is designated RMW if it can respond to one. Such a cycle consists of one read cycle followed by one write cycle at the same address, with the address strobe remaining asserted through both transfers.

Indivisibility across a more extensive or generalized set of transfers must be handled by designing masters to not release control of the DTB (that is, to hold Bus Busy low) until such a set is completed.

Table E3 defines the mnemonics that describe the permissible subsets of data transfer capabilities of masters.

Table E4 defines the mnemonics that describe the permissible subsets of data transfer capabilities of slaves.

Table E5 defines the mnemonics that describe the permissible subsets of data transfer capabilities of location monitors.

Table E6 shows how the permissible subsets of data transfer capabilities interoperate.

Table E3
Master: Permissible Subsets of Data Transfer Capabilities

When the Following Mnemonic is Applied to a Board . . .	It Means That its Master has the Following Data-Transfer Capabilities:					
	D08(EO)	D16	D32	UAT	BLT	RMW
MD8	X					
MBLT8	X				X	
MRMW8	X					X
MALL8	X				X	X
MD16	X	X				
MBLT16	X	X			X	
MRMW16	X	X				X
MALL16	X	X			X	X
MD32	X	X	X			
MBLT32	X	X	X		X	
MRMW32	X	X	X			X
MALL32	X	X	X		X	X
MD32+UAT	X	X	X	X		
MRMW32+UAT	X	X	X	X		X

Table E4
Slave: Permissible Subsets of Data Transfer Capabilities

When the Following Mnemonic is Applied to a Board . . .	It Means That its Slave has the Following Capabilities:						
	D08(O)	D08(EO)	D16	D32	UAT	BLT	RMW
SD8(O)	X						
SRMW8(O)	X						X
SD8		X					
SBLT8		X				X	
SRMW8		X					X
SALL8		X				X	X
SD16		X	X				
SBLT16		X	X			X	
SRMW16		X	X				X
SALL16		X	X			X	X
SD32		X	X	X	X		
SBLT32		X	X	X		X	
SRMW32		X	X	X	X		X
SALL32		X	X	X		X	X

Table E5
Location Monitor: Permissible Subsets of Data Transfer Detection Capabilities

When the Following Mnemonic is Applied to a Board . . .	It Means That its Location Monitor has the Following Capabilities:					
	D08(EO)	D16	D32	UAT	BLT	RMW
LMBLT32	X	X	X		X	
LMRMW32	X	X	X	X		X
LMALL32+UAT	X	X	X		X	X

Table E6
Interoperability Among the Permissible Data Transfer Subsets

A Master of the Type . . .	Can Transfer Data to a Slave Type . . .	By Executing a Single Transfer Cycle That Accesses These Byte Locations:									
		0	1	2	3	0-1	1-2	2-3	0-2	1-3	0-3
MD8	SD8(O)		X		X						
or	SD8	X	X	X	X						
MBLT8	SD16	X	X	X	X						
	SD32	X	X	X	X						
MD16	SD8(O)		X		X						
or	SD8	X	X	X	X						
MBLT16	SD16	X	X	X	X	X		X			
	SD32	X	X	X	X	X		X			
MD32	SD8(O)		X		X						
or	SD8	X	X	X	X						
MBLT32	SD16	X	X	X	X	X		X			
	SD32	X	X	X	X	X		X			X
MD32+UATS	D8(O)		X		X						
	SD8	X	X	X	X						
	SD16	X	X	X	X	X		X			
	SD32	X	X	X	X	X	X	X	X	X	X

NOTES: (1) Only slaves that have BLT capability can respond to block transfer cycles. However, as shown in this table, masters of the type MBLTxx can transfer data to slaves of the type SDxx by executing single transfer cycles. Similarly, masters of the type MDxx can transfer data to slaves of the type MBLTxx by executing single transfer cycles.

(2) Read-modify-write cycles can only be responded by slaves that have RMW capability.

(3) In this table, the boxes that contain an X represent data transfers to which the addressed slave responds by driving DTACK* low. Conversely, the empty boxes describe data transfers to which the addressed slave is not allowed to respond by driving DTACK* low. These cycles are terminated by either the addressed slave or by the bus timer by driving BERR* low.

E3. Interoperability Among Arbitration Bus Modules

The arbitration bus defines two functional modules: the arbiter and the requester. Section 3 describes three capabilities that are associated with these modules. The three capabilities defined for the arbiter are single (SGL), priority (PRI), and round-robin-select (RRS). The three capabilities defined for the requester are release on request (ROR), release when done (RWD), and FAIR.

E3.1 Capabilities of the Arbiter. Section 3 introduces the concept of a central arbiter, which receives requests for control of the bus from requesters, and grants control to them. Since the question of "fairness" versus priority is moot and irreconcilable, various applications needing one or the other or something in between, the algorithm by which an arbiter grants the bus is loosely specified. The specification gives the example of a strict priority arbiter (PRI) and a round-robin one (RRS). However, the overall signaling protocol for requesting, granting, and assuming control of the bus is fixed. There are no compatibility issues involved in regards to requesting the bus from the two types of arbiters.

The third type, the SGL arbiter, uses the same signaling protocol, but only recognizes and grants requests for control of the bus on request level 3.

E3.2 Capabilities of the Requester. The method that a requester uses to release control of the DTB is loosely specified by giving two examples:

(1) A requester that monitors bus requests from other requesters and releases the bus only when there is such a request (ROR), and

(2) A requester that does not do so, but simply releases the bus when it is "done" using it (RWD)

Greater "fairness" in bus use (than that afforded the arbiter rotating grants

Table E7
Interoperability Among Arbiters and Requesters

Can An Arbiter of the Type . . .	Arbitrate a Request From a Requester of the Type:		
	ROR	RWD	FAIR
SGL	Yes (1)	Yes (1)	Yes (1)
PRI	Yes	Yes	Yes
RRS	Yes	Yes	Yes

NOTE: The SGL arbiter only monitors BR3* and grants the bus by driving BG3IN*.

among the four request/grant levels) is implemented with the FAIR requester. It requires more strict discipline as to when the requester can re-request the DTB after releasing it.

Table E7 shows how the various requesters interoperate with the various arbiters.

E4. Interoperability Among Priority Interrupt Bus Modules

The priority interrupt bus defines two functional modules: the interrupter and the interrupt handler. Section 4 describes the capabilities that are associated with these modules. The capabilities defined for the interrupt handler pertain to the size of the status/ID it requests. The capabilities defined for the interrupter pertain to the size of the status/ID it can provide, and to the protocol for releasing the interrupt request line.

E4.1 Size of Status/ID. The distinction among D32, D16, and D08 is also reflected in the size of the status/ID that is passed in the course of an interrupt acknowledge cycle. An interrupt handler can request any of the three sizes, and an interrupter might respond with any size, but the relationship between the two is not the same as in other bus cycles. An interrupter is only allowed to respond with a status/ID that is of the size requested by the interrupt handler, or smaller. If it responds with a smaller size, the bus terminating resistors guarantee that the more significant data lines read by the interrupt handler are in a defined state, that is, High or 1. If an interrupter encounters an interrupt acknowledge cycle that requests a smaller vector width than it is designed to provide, it is not allowed to respond to the cycle, but rather is required to pass the cycle down the interrupt-acknowledge daisy-chain. If there are no further active interrupters down the chain, the net result will be a bus error when the bus-timer module times out.

Table E8 shows how the interrupter and interrupt handlers with various status/ID transfer capabilities interoperate.

E4.2 Release of Interrupt Requests. Interrupters are designated ROAK if they release their interrupt request during the interrupt acknowledge cycle, or RORA if they release their request when an on-board register is accessed in the course of the interrupt service routine. The only issue pertaining to interoperability is that the service routine that handles an RORA interrupter must access the register and clear the request before it re-enables interrupts on that level.

Table E8
Interoperability of Interrupters and Interrupt Handlers

Can it Service Interrupts From An Interrupter of the Type . . .	If an Interrupt Handler Requests a Status/ID as:		
	D08	D16	D32
D08 only?	Yes	Yes	Yes
D16 only?	No	Yes	Yes
D08 and D16?	Yes	Yes	Yes
D32 only?	No	No	Yes
D32 and D16 and D08?	Yes	Yes	Yes

Index

PAGE

PAGE

PAGE

PAGE

PAGE

PAGE

PAGE

PAGE

PAGE

PAGE

PAGE